PERGAMON GENERAL PSYCHOLOGY SERIES

Editors: Arnold P. Goldstein, *Syracuse University*
Leonard Krasner, *SUNY*, *Stony Brook*

Methods and Evaluation in Clinical and Counseling Psychology

PGPS-40

Methods and Evaluation in Clinical and Counseling Psychology

THEODORE C. KAHN
JAMES T. CAMERON

Southern Colorado State College
Pueblo, Colorado

MARTIN B. GIFFEN

The University of Texas Health Science Center
San Antonio, Texas

PERGAMON PRESS INC.

New York · Toronto · Oxford · Sydney · Braunschweig

PERGAMON PRESS INC.
Maxwell House, Fairview Park, Elmsford, N.Y. 10523

PERGAMON OF CANADA LTD.
207 Queen's Quay West, Toronto 117, Ontario

PERGAMON PRESS LTD.
Headington Hill Hall, Oxford

PERGAMON PRESS (AUST.) PTY. LTD.
Rushcutters Bay, Sydney, N.S.W.

PERGAMON GmbH
D - 3300 Braunschweig, Burgplatz 1

Library of Congress Cataloging in Publication Data

Kahn, Theodore Charles.
Methods and evaluation in clinical and counseling psychology.

(Pergamon general psychology series - 40)
A revision and expansion of an earlier work by Theodore C. Kahn and Martin B. Giffen, published in 1960 under title: Psychological techniques in diagnosis and evaluation.
Bibliography: p.
1. Clinical psychology. I. Cameron, James T., joint author. II. Giffen, Martin B., joint author. III. Title. [DNLM: 1. Counseling. 2. Psychological tests. 3. Psychotherapy. WM145 K13p 1975]

RC467.K3 1974 616.8'9'075 74-2002
ISBN 0-08-017862-6
ISBN 0-08-017863-4 pbk.

Printed in the United States of America

This book is dedicated to our children:
Brent, Suzanne, Kathryn, Steven, Susan,
Donald, Cheryl, and Marsha

The Authors

Theodore C. Kahn (Ph.D., Southern California and Sc.D., University of Mainz, Germany), internationally known psychologist and educator, is Professor and Head of the Department of Behavioral Science, Southern Colorado State College. He has served as senior counselor at the University of California, psychological consultant to the Los Angeles City School System, chief clinical psychologist for a number of large diagnostic neuropsychiatric hospitals and community mental health clinics, and has held teaching positions at the University of Southern California, the University of Maryland, and Wittenberg University. Dr. Kahn has won numerous national awards for research and teaching, including Outstanding Educator in America. He has done pioneer work in audio-visual-tactile rhythm therapy and introduced hominology, a new way to view and study the whole man. Dr. Kahn is the author of several books and numerous professional articles as well as the designer of a number of psychological tests used in the United States and abroad. He is the Founder and first President of the International Society of the Study of Symbols and Honorary President of the Japanese Society for the Study of KTSA.

James T. Cameron (Ph.D., University of Colorado) is Associate Professor of Psychology at Southern Colorado State College and Director of the Crisis Telephone Training Program. His other professional interests include private practice, direction of a sensitivity training program, and consultation and evaluation of educational and mental health programs.

Martin B. Giffen (M.D., The University of Pittsburgh School of Medicine) is Professor of Psychiatry and Coordinator of the Residency Programs of The University of Texas Health Science Center at San Antonio (Department of Psychiatry, The Medical School) and Director of Psychiatric Inpatient Services of the Bexar County Hospital, San Antonio, Texas. His primary interests are in the delivery of health care, forensic psychiatry, the professional training of psychiatrists, psychologists, and medical students, and development of concepts of acute and crisis triage facilities. Dr. Giffen is a member of several professional societies and his published works concern the use of hospital facilities and theory of forensic psychiatry.

Contents

Preface

This book represents the collaboration of a professor of psychiatry at The Medical School, The University of Texas Health Science Center, San Antonio, Texas; a counseling psychologist, who is a counselor and an associate professor of psychology at Southern Colorado State College; and the Chairman of the Department of Behavioral Science at Southern Colorado State College, who has had many years of practical experience in the field of clinical psychology.

In effect, the book represents a greatly expanded edition of an early work, *Psychological Techniques in Diagnosis and Evaluation* (Pergamon Press, 1960) by Kahn and Giffen. The authors have rewritten the earlier materials and brought them up-to-date. There are many new chapters in addition to reviews and discussions on psychotherapy, counseling, innovative methods, and other features not found in the earlier edition. Dr. James T. Cameron has managed the production of this new book and as a coauthor has added to it considerable material reflecting his experience as a modern therapist and educator.

The authors attempted to bring to the reader the many-sided problems that contemporary psychology faces. At the same time, the contributions that psychology can make in many areas of human concern have been described in some detail. We tried to answer as fully and clearly as possible the question: What do modern practicing psychologists do, and how do they do it? We wanted to make this answer intelligible to our colleagues in the other professions that deal with human welfare—social workers, correctional workers, and those who are employed in the various specialties of medicine, law, the ministry, and education. The book was also designed to be used as a textbook for courses in clinical and counseling psychology. It was the intention of the authors to make available to the reader the essential information that could explain the kinds of methods, skills, techniques, and services that clinical and counseling psychologists can render.

A serious effort was made to present both sides of controversial issues and to give a balanced view throughout the book of all those topics that are subject to differences of opinion. An attempt was also made to present those methods, tests, and therapeutic techniques that are representative of the contemporary scene in psychology. However, if one of the authors had a special expertise or a unique experience within the field of clinical psychology we did not hesitate to include information on the topic if we felt that it might be of interest to the reader.

We also kept in mind that the reader might be interested in the future role of psychology as a profession. Prediction is a hazardous matter; however, a number of topics were selected in Appendix A that the authors believed represent trends in the future development of psychology as a science and profession.

It is hoped that the reader, whether colleague or student of psychology, will find the contents of these pages interesting and stimulating. Furthermore, we hope that the book will give him an overview of that challenging and sometimes puzzling profession—psychology as it is practiced today.

We wish to acknowledge with special gratitude the loyal support and invaluable editorial contributions of Shirley Kahn, Jean Cameron, and Margaret Giffen.

Theodore C. Kahn, Ph.D., Sc.D.

CHAPTER 1

Introduction

The recognition of clinical psychology as a bona fide member of the psychological profession has less than 100 years of historical precedence. It is a mere infant historically when compared with the older, more established physical sciences. Even within the profession of psychology, the clinician is considered a "late bloomer." In view of this, the growth of the profession has been astonishing. Today, clinical psychologists constitute approximately 29 percent of all psychologists and, when combined with the allied counseling field, this figure is increased to almost 40 percent[319].

Not only has the introduction of clinical psychology altered the complexion of the psychology profession, but its internal composition has constantly been subjected to experimentation, exploration, and an ever-changing image. It is remarkable that this comparatively young profession has attracted such a large number of members in less than a century while still reflecting an unsettled and ever-evolving identity. A perusal of historical antecedents and current movements may be helpful in bringing this complex and sometimes conflict-ridden profession into perspective.

THE MEDICAL MODEL

It is impossible to discuss the history of clinical psychology as an isolated movement. Other professions, especially medicine, have influenced the clinical identity of psychology. Even the name clinical—which comes from the Greek word *klinnikos*, meaning "of the bed"—is adapted from medical terminology.

Medicine had the responsibility to treat the mentally ill and to provide services for the maladjusted. Thus, clinical psychology initially was modeled on the medical profession and psychologists concentrated their efforts on the assessment and treatment of mental and physically related pathologies. This alliance with the medical profession has provided the clinician with a useful function but it has also led to some problems, which will be discussed later. Other historical trends have affected the professional development of the clinical psychologist. His commitment to psychological research has guided much of his training and professional behavior. A growing emphasis has been placed on the integration of research and treatment and this has given the practice of clinical psychology its identity.

Many different people have made significant contributions to the early movement in clinical psychology. The humanitarian efforts of such people as Philippe Pinel (who started the humanistic reform in mental institutions) in France during the 19th century, the crusades of Dorothea Dix (American crusader for humane treatment of the mentally ill), and later the work of Clifford Beers (founder of the National Committee for Mental Hygiene and author of the book *A Mind That Found Itself* [35]) brought about major changes in the physical conditions of mental asylums and in the treatment of the mentally ill. Methods of diagnosis and treatment were also being developed during this period. Emil Kraepelin established a systematic method of classifying pathology by symptoms. His work had a major influence on the early establishment of a diagnostic model for pathology. Treatment, which was long neglected, was also being considered. Jean Martin Charcot demonstrated how physical symptoms in hysteria could be alleviated with the use of hypnosis. The impetus of his early discoveries greatly influenced the work of Sigmund Freud and others.

It was Freud more than any other individual who established the first comprehensive system of psychological techniques for treatment. Freud's impact was phenomenal and his contributions affected almost every facet of psychology. Most important to the field of clinical psychology were Freud's theories, hypotheses, and explanations of human behavior, particularly in the area of maladjustment. This, coupled with his treatment method (which he termed psychoanalysis), supplied the basic model for the many methods of therapy and the numerous theories of abnormal behavior that followed. His work also provided the stimulus for ensuing volumes of research that have greatly enhanced the understanding of psychology.

Adherence to the medical model has given the clinician a useful and recognized position in the field of mental health. However, for some psychologists it has also led to some conflicts in professional role identification. Even more basic to this problem than the medical model was the psychologist's role in providing a variety of services to those who suffered from pathology. Historically, the clinician perceived himself as a provider of services to those who were ill; it was this position that narrowed his vision to other aspects of clinical psychology in which he participates today.

THE SCIENTIFIC MODEL

Other historical trends have affected the clinical model. The commitment of psychologists to legitimize the field of psychology as a science has led to an emphasis on research and methodology, which has provided structure for much of the academic training and professional experience. The acceptance of the scientific method within psychology dates from the early work of Wilhelm Wundt, who established the first psychological laboratory in Leipzig, Germany, in 1879. The rigors of the laboratory allowed Wundt to apply objective measures and to utilize strict controls for his experiments. Possibly more important was the fact that the program established by Wundt was utilized in the training of a number of young psychologists who later became prominent and gave direction to the new science of psychology.

Paralleling the work of Wundt was an equally ingenious laboratory approach developed by Ivan Pavlov in measuring the connection between a stimulus and a response. In his early work with dogs in the laboratories, Pavlov [284] was able to create what he termed a "psychic secretion" by pairing the tone of a tuning fork with meat powder blown into the animal's mouth, causing salivation. The pairing was repeated a number of times until the tone by itself could produce the response (salivation). Thus, Pavlov demonstrated by the use of objective experimental methods that behavior could be modified. It is from this basic premise that one therapeutic approach in the area of behavior modification was developed.

One of the students trained at Leipzig was Lightner Witmer. At the University of Pennsylvania in 1896, this American psychologist adapted his laboratory training and techniques to a clinical setting designed for the assessment and treatment of emotional disorders in children. Witmer is given credit for applying the term "clinical" in psychology and for demonstrating that the rigors of the laboratory can be utilized in a practitioner's setting.

William James was another product of the Wundt laboratories. He became the most influential American psychologist and his work carried on Wundt's tradition of research and methodology. An even stronger advocate of objective experimentation was John Watson, who rejected the early ideas of introspection and, instead, stressed prediction and control of behavior through rigorous objective methodology. He started the behavioristic movement in the United States, which later fell into disrepute but still has a number of adherents. Continuing psychological inquiry into the area of learning were such researchers as E. L. Thorndike, who proposed specific laws of learning, and B. F. Skinner, who has become the major proponent of operant conditioning. The currently popular behavior modification therapy can trace its roots to the basic premises of these learning theorists.

MEASUREMENT OF INDIVIDUAL DIFFERENCES

The recognition and measurement of individual differences has also made a unique and major contribution to the role of the clinical psychologist.

Possibly from the first written notation of individual differences (reflected in the disputed calculations of the distance to Venus by two astronomers, Kennybrook and Maskelyne, in 1796) to the work of Charles Darwin in the early 19th century, man has become increasingly aware of individual differences and the need to measure and understand them. Darwin's work stressed individuality and how differences made some animals more adaptable than others. He emphasized the scientific approach, which appealed to the infant science of psychology. However, more important to the development of psychology was the work of Darwin's cousin, Sir Francis Galton, who directly applied psychological techniques to the study of individual differences in human behavior. Galton's interest centered in the area of heredity and its effect on individual differences. He carried out a number of studies on lineages of successful, prominent families and also families who were marginal in their adjustment. He recognized the need and provided the impetus for the development of a quantitative method to validate his research. The statistical techniques of correlation were developed by Karl Pearson from a grant supported by Galton. Galton also designed a number of tests to measure the various facets of individual differences, including intelligence. Unfortunately, he was influenced by the laboratories of Germany and many of his tests consisted of sensory motor items that have little relationship to the kinds of psychological tests in use today.

No one made a greater contribution to the study of individual differences and measurement of intelligence than Alfred Binet. His early work as director of the Laboratory of Physiological Psychology at the Sorbonne laid the foundation for his eventual involvement in the development of a measure of intelligence. This opportunity presented itself when he and Theodore Simon were commissioned by the Ministry of Education to develop a test that could distinguish normal children from those who were retarded. Binet and Simon did not follow the early example of Galton but, instead, measured a variety of mental functions such as attention span, reporting sequence of digits, identifying vocabulary words, comprehension, etc. Thus, a series of tests was developed (1905, 1908, 1911) that would revolutionize psychological testing. The measures had a number of unique characteristics: questions were arranged in a hierarchy of difficulty, levels were established for different ages (thus leading to the concept of mental age), a quantitative scoring system was applied, and specific instructions for administration were built into the test. Translations of the Binet Scales were common. The two that had the greatest effect on the psychological testing movement in the United States were H. H. Goddard's translations of 1908 and 1910 and L. M. Terman's revision in 1916. Terman's revision made major changes in the Binet Scales. The length of the test was increased with the addition of a number of new scales. Original tests were aligned to age levels according to new norms, and the concept of the intelligence quotient developed by William Stern was added to mental age. Terman's revision, called the Stanford-Binet, became the standard for intelligence testing and today still maintains an important role.

In the early part of the 20th century, testing centered on assessment of intelligence in children. However, the involvement of the United States in World War I placed a new demand on the testing field. Prior to this, tests were usually given on an individual basis, but with the war came the need for mass testing of over two million adults. The American Psychological Association was called on to produce measures that would meet this need. Primarily through the efforts of Robert M. Yerkes, President of the Association, a committee composed of W. V. Bingham, H. H. Goddard, T. H. Haines, L. M. Terman, F. L. Wells, and G. M. Whipple was formed to complete this task. Criteria for tests were established; analyses of test items and standardization procedures were carried out under the direction of E. L. Thorndike at Princeton. This effort resulted in the design of the Army version of Alpha and Beta Group Intelligence Tests. Much credit for this development must also be given to Arthur S. Otis, a student of Terman, who designed a group test that was used as a model for the Army Alpha. There seems little doubt that the involvement of psychologists in this monumental task established psychology, and particularly clinical psychology, as an applied profession and the role of testing as an integral part of that profession. At the same time, psychologists began to be recognized for their unique skills and there was a growing demand for their services in many fields.

After World War I, ability testing was greatly expanded, particularly in institutional settings where group tests could be applied. Personality assessment also received increased attention. Several publications in personality assessment followed Robert Woodworth's early work on the Personal Data Sheet developed at the close of World War I. Some of the contributors in personality assessment at this time were L. W. Pressey, D. A. Laird, Gordon Allport, L. L. Thurstone, and Edward Strong, who developed a vocational interest inventory. One of the most successful yet most controversial personality measures was designed by J. C. McKinley and S. R. Hathaway in the late 1930s. The Minnesota Multiphasic Personality Inventory (MMPI) was developed as a method for the prediction and diagnosis of psychological pathology. The construction of the test incorporated many of the better statistical characteristics of a standard test, such as using control and experimental groups for validation, having a large number of questions to aid statistical analysis, and reporting the test scores in standard test form. No single test has been more thoroughly scrutinized by research and this has led to numerous innovations hinging on the use of this method of testing. Some psychologists feel that the MMPI is the single best measure for the prediction of psychological pathology [17]. There is little doubt that the data yielded by the MMPI increased the demands for psychological services. Other clinicians believe that this test has been used far too extensively. They feel that it has been overrated as a clinical instrument by those who admire its statistical structure but fail to recognize that it can be anxiety provoking to some clients. A popular reaction that may have received its impetus from this type of testing has been the publication of a number of anti-psychological test paperbacks—such as *The Brain Watchers* [154]—which attack most of the psychological tests in common use.

While American psychologists stressed the more objective tests, their European counterparts tended to favor the association techniques of Carl

Jung and others. From the association method of Jung, Hermann Rorschach, a Swiss psychiatrist, developed a projective technique utilizing amorphous, symmetrical inkblots. The advantage of such a technique is that it allows the client taking the test to express his own uniqueness as he perceives and organizes the amorphous stimuli. This approach was quite different from the more objective assessment methods utilized by American psychologists. It was not until the early 1930s, when David M. Levy and Samuel J. Beck introduced the Rorschach Test to American psychologists, that the projective technique was accepted by practitioners in the United States. Another factor that helped the acceptance of personality assessments in general and projective tests in particular was the influx of European psychologists and psychiatrists into the United States during the 1930s. This movement not only increased support for acceptance of personality measures but also heightened interest in the practice of psychotherapy.

The most notable projective technique that followed the Rorschach was the Thematic Apperception Test (TAT) developed by C. D. Morgan and H. A. Murray at Harvard (1935). Unlike the Rorschach, TAT cards contain photographs and drawings taken from magazines and art sources. The pictures are identifiable but quite ambiguous, so that a person's responses to the stimuli are unique. Other methods utilizing projection have since been developed. These newer methods include tasks such as finishing incomplete sentences, responding to stimulus words, drawing persons, manipulating and responding to culturally structured symbolic objects, and handling a variety of stimuli having different colors, shapes, and designs. By the 1940s, personality evaluation using both objective and projective approaches had become as important to the clinical psychologist's professional activities as the assessment of intellectual qualities.

The recognition and the subsequent assessment of individual differences has made a unique contribution to the role of clinical psychologists. This movement more than any other has provided the "tools of the trade" for the clinician and has become recognized as a major area of expertise.

TREATMENT

As mentioned earlier, some clinical psychologists were not satisfied with their role in diagnosis and assessment. The Second World War marked the next major turning point in the evolution of the clinical psychologist's professional role. World War II greatly expanded the demand for psychological services. Not only was there an increased need for diagnostic services, but also a vast demand developed for trained therapists to work with returning veterans. Psychiatrists could not cope with the flood of veterans who needed psychological assistance and evaluation. Therefore, the Veterans Administration and the United States Public Health Service gave a number of universities extensive financial support for training clinical psychologists. The subsequent employment of psychologists in these government-sponsored programs in veteran and public health facilities helped to extend the role of the clinician from diagnosis and assessment to include treatment. The clientele of the clinician now encompassed the adult population in addition to children.

Equally important at this time was the presentation of a new approach to therapy by Carl Rogers. In his book *Counseling and Psychotherapy*, published in 1942[306], and other subsequent publications—notably *Client-Centered Therapy*, published in 1951[307]—he presented an alternative to the analytic method of therapy. Rogers' approach restructured the relationship between client and therapist so that much responsibility for improvement of behavior was placed on the client. This non-directive or client-centered method, developed by Rogers, provided a comparatively short-term approach to therapy that was free from many of the factors that had brought criticism to the analytic model. The method was developed outside of the traditional medical model and, therefore, represented a contribution that was unique to the profession of clinical psychology. Of equal importance was the development by Rogers of methods to quantitatively evaluate the effect of therapy. The ability to measure the therapeutic processes and consequent results had high appeal to clinical psychologists. Client-centered therapy allowed the clinician to provide services that incorporated to a maximum extent the utilization of a scientific approach.

The period after World War II saw the field of clinical psychology expand at an ever-increasing rate, particularly in the diagnosis and treatment of adults. This new emphasis led to a broadening of employment potential of psychologists, including their entering into private practice. It was at this point that it became necessary to evaluate training and experience of psychologists more closely in order to protect the public from those practicing without sufficient qualifications. The Boulder Conference of 1949 established minimum academic requirements for clinical psychologists and recognized their dual role as scientist-practitioners. During this period, there was also pressure brought to bear on state legislative bodies to establish licensing practices. In 1953 the American Psychological Association also attempted some self-regulation by adopting a code of Ethical Standards of Psychologists. Other conferences followed the Boulder meetings (Stanford, 1957; Miami, 1959; Chicago, 1965). The theme of these conferences continued to emphasize the training and functions of the clinical psychologist.

CONTEMPORARY TRENDS

Current movements in the field reflect several distinct problems: some clinicians are challenging the traditional scientist-practitioner model, thus causing some graduate schools to modify or eliminate their clinical programs. This has also led to the creation of some new, autonomous schools whose curricula stress the applied training of practitioners and deemphasize the research orientation. Fellow psychologists are, at times, at odds with clinical psychologists, since they perceive the clinician as interested primarily in private practice and not particularly committed to the profession of psychology as a scientist. Thus, the question of role identification continues to be a point of difficulty for the clinical psychologist [133].

Alternatives to the Medical Model

The learning theorists of several decades ago serve as the pioneers of a development that offers contemporary psychologists some alternative approaches to both personality diagnosis and personality change. A new vocabulary has been developed to enable psychologists to avoid placing human behavior within an illness-health continuum. Thus, atypical behavior is no longer confined to a model that was built around the idea of abnormal or pathological. This new vocabulary has been evolved from the learning theory psychology of such researchers as E. C. Tolman. He and his associates, B. F. Ritchie and D. Kalish, tried to confirm the concept of a cognitive map as part of the perceptive equipment of experimental animals. They did this by demonstrating that animals have a disposition to run maze pathways after training because they acquire a map-like, directional sensitivity toward the goal if the motivation to achieve the goal is sufficiently strong.

Motivation required an explanation and a hypothesis. A reinforcement doctrine to explain motivational drive was the subject of considerable discussion by several British philosophers, including Herbert Spencer and Alexander Bain. Additionally, an American psychologist, James M. Baldwin, who at the turn of the century founded the *Psychological*

Review, proposed the revolutionary idea that the basis of Darwin's natural selection was a pleasantness-unpleasantness motivational continuum.

In 1911, Edward L. Thorndike gave the reinforcement hypothesis an additional boost by postulating a *Law of Effect*. Much of the rationale of the scientific model currently popular among psychologists hinges on the credibility of this law. The law maintains that of several responses made to the same situation those that are accompanied or closely followed by satisfaction to the animal will be more firmly connected with the situation, so that if there is a recurrence of the situation the responses will likely recur also.

On the other hand, those responses that are accompanied by or closely followed by discomfort to the animal will have their connection with the situation weakened, so that if there is a recurrence of the situation they will be less likely to recur. The greater the satisfaction or discomfort the greater the strengthening or weakening of the bond between the situation and the response. Thorndike gave objective, observable definitions to "satisfactions" and "discomfort."

A more detailed stimulus-response reinforcement theory was evolved by Clark L. Hull, who attempted to utilize the strict logic of the empirical philosophers in formulating postulates, definitions, and theorems pertaining to animal learning. Using numerous symbols and notations, Hull described three stages, consisting of the input—the *independent variable*, the second stage—or the *intervening variable*, and the third stage, which is the output—the *dependent variable.*

At first, the concept appears to resemble the Stimulus-Organism-Response idea but actually there is much more involved. Hull's independent variable consists of reinforced trials made by an animal. The intervening variable is the habit strength between the stimulus and the response created during the learning situation. Habit strength can be reinforced when such needs as hunger or thirst exist. The satisfying of these needs leads to *homeostasis* or to an equilibrium with an accompanying reduction in drive. Hull's law of reinforcement does not depend on the animal's response or behavior but only on the closeness of the relationship between drive-reduction and the stimulus-response.

This view of reinforcement led to the idea of operant conditioning on which much of modern behavioral modification theory hinges. Operant behavior is also described as instrumental in that it is *emitted* by the organism because it occurs spontaneously instead of being initiated by some external stimulus. It is instrumental in that the response serves to obtain a change in the organism's relationship with the environment. The well-known example is the Skinner-box, which is a small soundproof chamber that contains a lever and a food receptacle. A food pellet drops into a food tray when the animal presses a small lever. Generalizing this concept to the extent where it may apply to the modification of human behavior, we might say that when a person makes a response chosen by the experimenter (or therapist) as correct, the response is immediately followed by a reward, which is termed a reinforcement. Punishment, such as a small electric shock, may be administered if it is desired that the response be extinguished or "negatively reinforced." Psychologists who work in this area have been called operant conditioners or modification therapists.

Hull's complicated theory construction represented a sharp contrast to E. R. Guthrie's conception of learning in which he reduces both operant and classical conditioning to two fundamental assumptions: (1) if a stimulus accompanies a response, the stimulus, when it recurs, will be followed by a recurrence of the response; (2) when a stimulus accompanies *two* or *more* successive responses, when the stimulus recurs, it will tend to be followed by a recurrence of the *last* response only. Whereas psychologists respect Guthrie's efforts, it is generally believed that his reduction of all learning behavior to two concepts represents too simplified an assumption of a much more complex phenomenon.

Wolpe and Eysenck introjected methods, concepts, and techniques into the practice of psychotherapy that were based on learning theory and, therefore, represented a significant departure from the traditional medical model used by many clinical psychologists at this time.

Wolpe, who was increasingly dissatisfied with the results obtained through traditional psychotherapy, decided to ascertain whether or not the behaviorist approach, which had proven successful in changing the behavior of laboratory animals, could modify neurotic behavior in humans. Working with cats, Wolpe was able to create "neurotic" fear by introducing mild electric shocks while exposing the animals to such stimuli as toy mice, rubber balls, and flashing lights. He was able to reverse the process by giving them gratification, thus extinguishing the fear response and restoring the cats to apparent normalcy. He termed this process "desensitization," a term that is also applied to the gradual development of immunity to irritating allergens among sufferers of hayfever by means of introducing mild quantities of the offending substance intermuscularly.

In order to induce a state of relaxation in his patients, Wolpe adapted a modified version of E. Jacobson's relaxation therapy, since he reasoned that a person cannot be relaxed and anxious at the same time. Jacobson's method consisted of teaching the patient to relax one muscle at a time until the entire body was devoid of muscle tensions. This state of relaxation served to be an ideal physiological state for desensitization in which anxiety-provoking stimuli are extinguished and anxiety responses are weakened. Wolpe claimed that desensitization was quicker and significantly more effective than traditional psychotherapy based on the medical model. But, as is true of much research involving human beings, the results of initial successes could not always be repeated.

In an attempt to compare different kinds of treatment, Gordon Paul (at the University of Illinois) divided persons suffering from stage fright into four groups. One group received desensitization-relaxation therapy, another was given conventional psychotherapy, while another group was placed into a situation in which the client and therapist met without any attempt at therapy; a fourth group was left to its own devices without any interaction with any therapist. Ratings made before and after treatment showed that patients given behavioral therapy showed the greatest average reduction of anxiety. Some psychologists, however, were skeptical, pointing out that the experimenters all believed in the Wolpe approach and that this could tend to bias the evaluation of the results.

Gordon Paul and Donald Shannon were among the first to utilize behavioral therapy with a group. Five subjects were used in this experiment, and it was found that the group application was as effective as individual treatment. As in the case of the individual, the therapy consists of unlearning certain responses that create anxiety. The key concept in behavioral modification therapies is that undesirable response patterns are learned and may become unlearned or extinct with a subsequent remission of the unwanted symptom. Such symptoms could include anxiety, phobias, depression, and compulsive habit patterns.

A second order of symptomatic behavior amenable to modification through conditioning includes sociopathic activity in which antisocial performance is tied to a lack of social responsibility. In this case, the socially undesirable behavior pattern has become associated with emotions that are pleasurable to the client, giving him a sense of personal worth, status, comfort, sexual arousal, or tension reduction. In such cases, the therapist must break the association between the conditioned stimulus—such as, for example, causing someone else discomfort—and the pleasant sensation of personal power over the victimized individual. This may be accomplished by linking the sense of personal power with an unpleasant experience. Creating this type of distressing conditioned response is referred to as aversion therapy. It has been used with some success in the treatment of alcoholism, sexual deviation, and among persons suffering from persistent character and behavior disorders.

Operant Conditioning Used with Psychotics

B. F. Skinner, who experimented with cats, pigeons, and other animals, is credited with much of the pioneer work that later was expanded and applied to human beings. After the notion of instrumental conditioning caught on, a number of therapists, such as Colin Blakemore of the Maudsley Hospital, tried this approach with psychotic adults and disturbed children. Behavioral modification therapists used their method with hard-core schizophrenics who had all been given up as incurable. The modification therapist must be credited with at least some notable successes (which are well-documented) by having taught such "hopeless" psychotics to relinquish behavior that identified them as insane.

The theoretical implications of behavioral modification therapy must not be overlooked. It reverses the theoretical concept that thought precedes and produces action. Behavioral therapy suggests that the modification of behavior can actually change the client's thought processes and his mental set. There is a likelihood that thought and action are a circular process, each serving to reinforce the other. At any one point, the bond between these two may be strengthened or weakened by operant conditioning, leading to the desired trait alteration and subsequent behavioral modification.

Behavioral therapy implies that the therapist need not be an all-pervasive mother or father symbolic figure whose role compensates for something that has been missing in the client's earlier life. Wolpe's original postulates imply that the ingredients in successful behavioral therapy consist of a conditioned stimulus combined with relaxation or behavioral modification. The question has been raised whether learning machines could replace the traditional role of the psychotherapist. Peter Lang of the University of Wisconsin had already demonstrated that behavioral therapy can be programmed and that, at least under a number of experimental situations created by the researchers, the desensitization to anxiety-provoking stimuli can be carried out. As anyone can see, the implications of this to future methods of psychotherapy are profound. "Treatment machines" represent one of the challenges of the next several decades. When these are combined with modern bio-feedback mechanisms, an entirely new approach to the rehabilitation of persons with undesirable habit patterns may become an exciting possibility.

There are two additional trends in psychotherapy that are being given increasing attention within the contemporary scene. One of these involved therapeutic bio-feedback techniques that are described in some detail later in this book. The other could be considered to be an almost direct opposite to this concept. In 1963 Viktor E. Frankl, who had spent many years in a German concentration camp during the Hitler era, wrote a book in which he developed the idea of Logotherapy. In it he observed that "Man's search for meaning is a primary force in his life and not a 'secondary rationalization' of instinctual drives." Frankl holds the chair at the University of Vienna once held by Freud, and he has his own clinic as well as being in wide demand as a lecturer in the United States and in many other countries. Referring to behaviorists who "contend that meanings and values are nothing but defense mechanisms (either of the pleasure or pain types), reaction formations and sublimations," he claims that he would not be willing to live merely for the sake of his defense mechanisms—or the pleasure principle—nor would he be ready to die merely for the sake of his "reaction formations." Professor Frankl's theories are given added weight by the fact that he evolved them in what undoubtedly was one of the most severe "laboratory conditions" with which human nature has had to contend in its entire history.

A New Frontier in Psychiatry

Utilizing the importance of goals, but in a different way than did Frankl, C. David Jones, M.D. (instructor at the University of Chicago Medical School and director of a private psychiatric clinic) has repudiated the very concept of mental illness and has visualized instead a condition of nonconformity to social norms. In this way the so-called "ill" person may be perfectly sane while the society in which he resides is faulty and deficient. Jones maintains that self-understanding is impossible without the utilization of specific techniques that clarify not only one's own behavior but also the social and cultural level of the milieu in which the individual lives. As he sees and explains this new therapy in his recent book, *Hominology—Psychiatry's Newest Frontier* [193], the process is essentially an educational one in which both the therapist and the client together explore the client's potentialities for forming new relationships as alternatives to present ones. The unique aspects of Jones' views are that the client's nonconformity to social norms often cannot and *should not* be reconditioned or modified. Instead, in some cases, mental balance is achieved by the client only if he can constructively challenge society instead of being subjected to modification therapy himself. At other times, a tolerance to the society that rejects him can be achieved by the client only when he has developed insight into the reason for the rejection. He is then capable of adjusting his atypical behavior to existing norms without resorting to hedonistic response patterns. The implications of this thesis for minority and atypical culture groups may cause this new approach to become, in the future, an acceptable alternative to present popular modification therapies. Jones and his co-workers not only claim success for this new method but feel it permits their clients to maintain their human dignity. They consider this to be a prerequisite for the future emotional growth of both the individual and his society.

The Non-Medical Model and the Role of Psychological Tests

Many of the modification therapists have repudiated the use of psychological testing as a residual of the medical concept in psychology. In most universities with strong experimental orientations, psychological testing is presented as a passing fad almost analogous to phrenology of a century ago. A number of textbooks in psychology have reflected this view. Undoubtedly, some of the impetus to this rejection of psychological testing—especially projective testing—stems from the present desire by many psychologists to rid themselves of every possible vestige of the medical model in psychology.

In the book *Readings in Psychology Today* (Del Mar, Calif.: CRM Books, 1969), graphology is given a much higher rating than the standard psychological testing, which is described in a chapter entitled, "Psychological Testing—A Smoke Screen Against Logic." As is customary with such critics of psychological testing, evidence is presented very forcefully that indicates how different "experts" on such tests as the Rorschach disagree with each other when they are given the same protocol to examine. What these writers fail to mention in their critical reviews is the impressive validation that also exists and that is available to students if they will examine copies of *Psychological Abstracts* for the past several years.

As in all types of reactions to human behavior, psychological testing is subject to fashions. Ideas rejected in one decade often are "rediscovered" several decades later, usually with some modifications and improvements. The argument against psychological testing seems, on the surface, to be valid. It is claimed that there can be no substitute for observation and not only observation but constant reevaluation of behavioral dynamics through continued observation. Thus, an initial impression about the client's condition can change many times—always with the goal of self-correction. This appears to be not only more accurate but actually "more fair" to the client than test description. In itself the point is well-made.

However, there are factors that seem to make such a conclusion an oversimplification. As is true of test evaluation, anyone who has ever attended a psychiatric staffing can testify to the fact that different professional observers quite often come to different diagnostic conclusions and even differ radically, at times, regarding the meaning and interpretation of what they have all observed in terms of the client's behavior. In other words, the implication that test evaluators will differ in their conclusions while behavioral observers will agree is a fallacy that is not given sufficient emphasis. The simple fact is that no matter what method a person utilizes in attempting to judge the behavior of another human being, the conclusions are subject to controversy, disagreement, and error, as well as to personal prejudice and expected mental set. There is no escape from this dilemma, either with psychological testing or by the use of any alternative method such as constant clinical observation.

Testing suffers from being an artificial situation. But it gains in being a standardized procedure, capable of yielding comparisons with collected data and not solely dependent on the subjective judgment of a limited number of observers even if they use check lists to give their observation a semblance of objectivity. Both methods of evaluation have their disadvantages and both have their usefulness. There is no reason why they should not be combined. A number of modification therapists have already reached this conclusion. However, their emphasis has been on newer types of tests, especially those that have a projective-objective formulation. For example, W. Greenlief (cited in the *International Journal of Symbology*, Monograph No. 1, December 1972) indicated that in a study of behavioral modification in a state mental hospital, using emotionally disturbed teenagers 12–18 years of age, he obtained a significant correlation between the results of the Kahn Test of Symbol Arrangement (KTSA) and success in operant conditioning procedures.

It is likely that other tests will be designed or discovered that fit into the schema of the non-medical model in psychology. In the meantime no treatise of contemporary psychology can afford to ignore the impact of tests such as the Rorschach, the Thematic Apperception Test, the Minnesota Multiphasic Personality Inventory, since a nationwide survey reported in *Professional Psychology* [242] revealed that these and other tests are used extensively in clinics and treatment centers throughout the United States. Just as there can be a reevaluation by constant observations, retesting at frequent intervals can likewise up-date behavioral changes. Alternative test forms could forestall the criticism that the client may become "test-wise." Whereas some psychologists are rendering a useful service by alerting the psychology student to test abuses, to interpretations that are not professionally or ethically sound, and to unwarranted assumptions based on utilizing the results of only one or two tests, a psychological test battery adequately administered and professionally interpreted appears to be a continuing phenomenon on the American psychological scene. In some areas, such as in vocational and educational guidance, more rather than fewer tests are being used, to help in saving interview time and in assisting in personnel classification. It seems, then, that there is a dichotomy in contemporary psychology, causing a division that is not unlike similar divisions of thoughts and trends presently appearing in many of the other social and behavioral sciences.

THE FUTURE OF CLINICAL PSYCHOLOGY

As the field of clinical psychology evolves, there appear to be emerging several programs oriented toward preventive mental health and rehabilitation. Decentralization of mental health centers will take place as the need to reach all segments of communities becomes paramount and the demands for treatment from economically depressed areas increase. Such a program will require the use of paraprofessionals who have the specific skills required for special community work. This will necessitate the clinical psychologist becoming not only a practitioner but an instructor, a consultant, and, in many cases, an administrator as well. These new demands will, in turn, require new programs and new approaches to mental health problems. There is little doubt that innovations in therapeutic procedures will evolve and some of the more traditional mental health practices may no longer be appropriate. Current examples of new programs already being tried are sensitivity training (which might be considered a preventive method in mental health) and the various types of group psychotherapy and behavior modification (which utilize short-term treatment sessions that can be carried out by paraprofessionals under the direction of a trained clinician). (A more detailed discussion of new and traditional methods of therapy will be found in Chapters 9 and 10.) More sophisticated and better designed research will be needed to test these new programs and to evaluate their contributions to society. Demands will also be placed on the research skills of the clinician to provide more efficient methods of diagnosis and assessment of emotionally maladjusted persons. It is quite possible that this may be developed outside of the guidelines of traditional historical models that marked the early efforts in the field of mental health.

However, innovation should not be at the expense of what has previously been found useful unless there is conclusive evidence that the new substitutes are superior. Presently some university psychology departments fail to expose their students to the methods and theory of psychological testing because they consider such methods to be inadequate. Training is confined to observation and interviewing.

Even with controls such as checklists and repetition, the interpretation of observations and interviews is a form of "projective evaluation" without the benefits of standardization and statistical validation. The shortcomings of testing should always be kept in mind but this is insufficient reason for discarding all psychological tests. Instead, it should be an impetus for constant improvement in test construction, validation and interpretation.

Interviewing and observation date from prehistoric times and, to some extent, are even used by animals. Standardized tests were developed to avoid errors in judgment that are apt to creep into evaluation based solely on these methods. Instead of shunning testing, the professional investigator of human behavior should utilize a variety of sources of information including properly standardized and validated psychological tests.

The academic training of psychology and counseling students should be broad enough to include new methods of assessment as well as psychological testing so that later, in their professional practice, they will have a choice of techniques at their disposal.

SUMMARY

Clinical psychology will play an important role in the expanding field of mental health. It will be the involvement of the members of the profession that will decide what will be accepted and what identity the clinician will have both in the profession of clinical psychology and in the field of mental health. The historical precedent of the profession, though brief, supplemented by contemporary development, will provide a basis for the continuing growth of the profession and the role of the clinical psychologist in the future.

CHAPTER 2

The Construction and Use of Psychological Tests

When a clinical psychologist selects a test battery for a client, his choice of tests depends on his professional orientation, which provides him with a theoretical basis for understanding his client's behavioral characteristics. Several complex factors such as the psychologist's academic training, type of professional experience, and personal biases influence his selection of specific tests.

IMPRESSIONISTIC-PROJECTIVE APPROACHES

In general, there are two main classifications of psychometric techniques: (1) impressionistic-projective tests, which are sensitive to nonverbal cues; and (2) actuarial tests, which are paper-and-pencil techniques that are primarily verbally oriented. Clinical psychologists who focus on obtaining a wide variety of insights regarding the client's behavior are apt to favor impressionistic approaches. These psychologists believe that in order for the test interpretation to yield the most useful information, the client who takes the test must be given the opportunity to contribute uniquely and spontaneously to the interpretive data. Thus, the individual performance typical of the person taking a test extends the dimensions of the clinical evaluation and permits the client a maximum amount of freedom in self-expression during the test.

An important aspect of impressionistic techniques is that the client is usually not fully aware of the significance of his responses. Thus, he is not apt to be as emotionally blocked, defensive, or successfully evasive as if he were giving answers to direct questions requiring a "yes," "no," or "don't know" response. It has been found that some clients resist or resent a test situation in which written verbal communication is the only method of client-test interaction. Impressionistic techniques are usually individually administered, permitting the clinician to modify his impression of the test responses by observing the client's behavior during the testing.

Tests representing the impressionistic approaches (e.g., the Rorschach) usually require the client to project aspects of his personality onto ambiguous test stimuli. This aspect of the impressionistic approach has been the subject of much criticism by psychologists who prefer other methods of psychological testing since they feel that they cannot measure such projections accurately. Obviously, interpretation of such tests requires skill and experience in order to avoid unwarranted conclusions. Fortunately, the American Psychological Association has established formal guidelines for standardization and validation of all types of psychological tests, including projectives. Nevertheless, clinical experience plays a greater role in the interpretation of impressionistic test responses than it does when the actuarial approach is used.

ACTUARIAL APPROACHES

The psychologist who favors the actuarial approach must adhere rigidly to the administration, scoring, and written interpretive procedures described in the test manual. An actuarial-type test may be administered individually, but it lends itself most easily to group administration—thus saving much time and expense. Considerably more emphasis is placed on formal scores and test patterns than in most impressionistic tests. This adds an element of neutrality of interpretation which, in some cases, may be an important consideration. Psychologists who use actuarial-type tests claim that these techniques do not deny the uniqueness of the individual but lend themselves more efficiently to empirical verification and statistical control. They also feel that actuarial test scores are more manageable in terms of being amenable to machine scoring and computer analysis.

Psychologists who prefer impressionistic methods of client evaluation point out that actuarial approaches may be favored by psychologists who are relatively untrained or inexperienced in the use of impressionistic techniques, whereas those who utilize actuarial methods feel that the impressionistic methods depend too much on the intuition and subjective judgment of the evaluator.

The test users preferring actuarial methods are sometimes referred to as "hard-nosed," whereas those who are inclined to use impressionistic techniques are called "soft-nosed." Some authors believe that the difference between these two kinds of psychologists is not simply one of choice of technique but represents a much deeper cleavage, reflecting philosophical outlooks or "criteria of reality." One author, Kahn[201], writes:

> In psychology, so-called soft-nosed scientists have devoted much effort to clinical evaluation. They use projective techniques such as the Rorschach Inkblot test and find that these methods help them in arriving at diagnostic evaluation of mental patients. On the other hand, a representative of the "hard-nosed" group describes the Rorschach as "all speculation and surmise." Hard-nosed psychologists prefer statistical techniques from which objective data can be abstracted. Analogous situations exist in other behavioral sciences. Scientists who fail to recognize that their differences in outlook involve different criteria of reality cannot expect to resolve their disagreements[201].

It should be obvious that each of the two methods—the impressionistic and the actuarial—has its advantages and disadvantages. The clinical psychologist who understands that his choice of tests may stem from his conceptual framework of reality probably would be inclined to include both types of tests in his customary psychological battery in order to make allowance for his bias.

Finally, it must be mentioned that there are several psychological techniques that have been specifically designed to incorporate the advantages of both the impressionistic and actuarial tests. These use *projective* stimuli materials in an *objective* manner; they are capable of eliciting an actuarial score or a psychograph that permits statistical analysis while maintaining the flexibility inherent in the impressionistic approach. Some psychologists view the development of such objective-projective techniques as representing a desirable future trend. Among the tests and test modifications of this category are certain offshoots of the Rorschach and Thematic Apperception Test, and the Kahn Test of Symbol Arrangement.

STANDARDIZATION

In order to standardize a technique, all conditions that affect a client's performance and ultimately the test results must be controlled. When a test is selected by the clinical psychologist, he must ascertain that the manual supplied by the publisher contains explicit directions for the administration of the test. He must be certain that the manual reports adequate normative data from which scores can be calculated and that the scores are independent of the subjective judgment of the examiner. He must be sure that the normative sample reflects a representative cross section and a normal distribution of the population with which the test will be used.

Every new test must be administered to a representative number of individuals who form a distinct group or category (such as normals, neurotics, delinquents) before it can be said that normative data exist for the group. The psychologist must constantly bear in mind that standardization for one group does not automatically mean standardization for another group. A test standardized on eight-year-old children cannot be appropriately used with nine-year olds unless the justification for doing this has been statistically established. A test standardized on schizophrenics with an urban background may not be valid for use with schizophrenics who have a rural background. Additionally, normative data must be periodically updated to insure that changes in the norm group do not make the test invalid. There is considerable discussion in current psychological literature concerning the shortcomings of intelligence tests in this respect.

Since norms are based on the actual test performance of the group of persons used in the standardization, the clinical psychologist can evaluate his client's performance by comparing it with the sample, and can interpret his client's test scores meaningfully as they fall on some point along the normative distribution. Thus, administration, scoring, and, in many cases, interpretation of the results are removed as far as practical from the subjective judgment of the test administrator. However, it should be noted that, since norm groups are selected from a larger population and statistics only give probability, some subjective judgment in the interpretation can never be totally avoided.

VALIDITY

If a test correctly measures the quality that it has been designed to measure, it is said that the test has validity. A technique without some form of validity cannot be considered professionally sound or adequate. Validity may be established by various methods, but the validity preferred by psychologists is based on empirical evidence.

No one type of validity can be applied to all tests. Therefore, it is necessary to select the method most appropriate for the type of test being validated. The qualified clinical psychologist is familiar with the various types of validities that are pertinent to the psychological tests he uses.

Face Validity

This is usually not acceptable since it represents only a subjective evaluation—that is, a guess by the test constructor. Unfortunately, there are a number of unqualified persons who use "psychological tests" that have no more than face validity. The use of such unproven tests may cause considerable emotional damage in some cases.

Content Validity

This approach to validity usually requires a systematic examination of the test items so that the adequacy of their sampling may be ascertained. While content validity has wide use in measures of educational achievement, its value in clinical psychological testing is extremely limited. Since test content is not empirically established, this method of obtaining validity is often ambiguous. For example, a mechanical aptitude test employing a series of mechanical puzzles may have content validity. The validity is derived from the fact that mechanical problems are used to determine mechanical ability. However, if the test were to be given to a large number of subjects, it is possible that it might prove to measure general intelligence rather than mechanical ability.

Criterion-Related Validity

The validity methods presented have been based on the inspection of test items rather than on a statistical evaluation of the items. Criterion-related validity utilizes external criteria selected to represent those qualities that the test purports to measure. This type of validation is desirable since a comparison between external criteria and the test can be experimentally evaluated through statistical analysis. Such an analysis permits the psychologist to measure the relationship between the items and the data, and to judge (with an established level of confidence) whether the results obtained were due to the actual relationship between the test and the external criteria or to chance. Levels of confidence accepted by psychologists are 0.05 (5 chances out of 100) and 0.01 (1 chance out of 100) that chance alone could explain the results obtained. The most common statistical procedure in establishing validity is *correla-*

tion. This allows the examiner to measure the relationship between the test and the characteristics that the test is attempting to measure—the external criteria.

Two methods most often used in establishing criterion-related validity are commonly termed "predictive" and "concurrent" approaches. The predictive technique compares the test results with a performance (criterion) that will take place in the future. This requires a passage of time between the administration of the test and the actual criterion performance. The predictive approach is frequently utilized in establishing validity for aptitude measures and, to a lesser extent, in intelligence testing. Concurrent validity is employed when the use of predictive methods is not practical or when the purpose of the test is to assess existing personality characteristics. Criteria used in this type of validity usually consist of a comparison of the experimental test with an established test or expert's ratings or with diagnoses already available. This approach is a relatively simple, quick method of establishing validity and is one that is most acceptable for validating personality measures.

Construct Validity

Construct validity incorporates all other validation procedures and attempts to validate the theoretical construct or trait of the test. To establish construct validity, the psychologist must be satisfied that the test construct or theory has been thoroughly tested. In order to evaluate test construct, information regarding validity studies, factor analysis of test items, research utilizing the test, and other data supporting the test construct is required.

RELIABILITY

Validity is one of several requirements in evaluating the acceptability of a test. Reliability, which measures the stability of the test, must also be established. A test is reliable if it is internally consistent and if it yields a similar result when the test is administered to the same individual at different times. Obviously, if one gives the same test to the same person on different days and obtains a wide discrepancy in results, the reliability of the test is questionable. When two dissimilar test scores are obtained from a test administered to the same person after a time lapse, the test interpreter would not know which of the two scores is the accurate measure. As with validation, there are several methods of establishing the degree of internal consistency of a test.

The Test-Retest Method

This is most appropriate for establishing the reliability of projective techniques. The test-retest method requires the client to retake the same test after a predetermined time interval. The most obvious disadvantage of this method of establishing reliability is that the statistical results can be influenced by changes in the test situation (temporal error). The person may have changed in some respect during the time interval or the effect of practice may result in the client becoming "test-wise." However, it is impossible to recreate the exact environment of the original testing.

Equivalent-Form Test

This form of reliability requires the administration of two alternate forms of a test that theoretically should produce similar results. The test items of the alternate forms must be dissimilar, so that knowledge gained from one is not transferable to the other. On the other hand, the two forms must elicit the same skills, traits, or aptitudes. Although equivalent-form test reliability circumvents some of the objections of the test-retest method, it offers new difficulties since the test constructor cannot design two measures that are completely identical.

The Split-Half Method

This method of establishing reliability requires that scores on the odd-numbered questions be compared with scores on the even-numbered questions or that the last half of a test be compared with the first half. While temporal error is controlled, the split-half method has basic weaknesses. It has been established that reliability is affected by the number of relevent test items and, since this approach utilizes only one half of the items, the chance of error is increased. Also an identity of the paired items is also assumed. This method is not applicable to projective techniques, but has some advantages when used with educational or proficiency tests of the paper-and-pencil variety.

USABILITY

Technically, the usability of a psychological technique is of less importance than validity and reliability; however, it may be the deciding factor when a psychologist selects a test. Usability takes into account clarity of directions, readability of test items, and length of time needed for administration and scoring of the test results. Scoring procedures consist of standard score format, percentile rank, or, preferably, a combination of these two. If hand-scored forms are utilized, the psychologist must check the efficiency of the scoring keys and must consider the availability of computer-scoring services that process tests for minimal fees. The cost of the test materials can be a significant factor if large numbers of tests are needed.

As has already been mentioned, tests approved by the American Psychological Association are accompanied by a booklet or manual giving a description of the standardization procedures, validity, and other pertinent information. A good manual will also describe previous studies, list the shortcomings as well as the advantages of the technique, and suggest areas for future research. It must give clear instructions for test administration to insure that all subjects are given the test in the same manner. The scoring method must be explained so that it can be readily understood and followed. In the final evaluation, the psychologist is dependent on the test manual for sufficient normative data to make his test interpretations meaningful.

CONTROL OF PSYCHOLOGICAL TESTS

The responsibility for test security and control is shared by the test manufacturer and the test user. Specific guidelines are set down for the psychologist in "Ethical Standards for Psychologists," [11] particularly in Principles 13, 14, and 15.*

> Principle 13. Test Security. Psychological tests and other assessment devices, the value of which depends in part on the naiveté of the subject, are not reproduced or described in popular publications in ways that might invalidate the techniques. Access to such devices is limited to persons with professional interests who will safeguard their use.
>
> a. Sample items made up to resemble those of tests being discussed may be reproduced in popular articles and elsewhere, but scorable tests and actual test items are not reproduced except in professional publications.
>
> b. The psychologist is responsible for the control of psychological tests and other devices and procedures used for instruction when their value might be damaged by revealing to the general public their specific contents or underlying principles.
>
> Principle 14. Test Interpretation. Test scores, like test materials, are released only to persons who are qualified to interpret and use them properly.
>
> a. Materials for reporting test scores to parents, or which are designed for self-appraisal purposes in schools, social agencies, or industry are closely supervised by qualified psychologists or counselors with provisions for referring and counseling individuals when needed.

b. Test results or other assessment data used for evaluation or classification are communicated to employers, relatives, or other appropriate persons in such a manner as to guard against misinterpretation or misuse. In the usual case, an interpretation of the test result rather than the score is communicated.
c. When test results are communicated directly to parents and students, they are accompanied by adequate interpretive aids or advice.

Principle 15. Test Publication. Psychological tests are offered for commercial publication only to publishers who present their tests in a professional way and distribute them only to qualified users.

a. A test manual, technical handbook, or other suitable report on the test is provided which describes the method of constructing and standardizing the test, and summarizes the validation research.
b. The populations for which the test has been developed and the purposes for which it is recommended are stated in the manual. Limitations upon the test's dependability, and aspects of its validity on which research is lacking or incomplete, are clearly stated. In particular, the manual contains a warning regarding interpretations likely to be made which have not yet been substantiated by research.
c. The catalog and manual indicate the training or professional qualifications required for sound interpretation of the test.
d. The test manual and supporting documents take into account the principles enunciated in the *Technical Recommendations for Psychological Tests and Diagnostic Techniques.*
e. Test advertisements are factual and descriptive rather than emotional and persuasive.

Standards for Educational and Psychological Tests and Manuals [12] was published by the American Psychological Association to provide guidelines for test manufacturers. Sale and distribution are functions of the manufacturer and, theoretically, it is his responsibility to check that his customers have the proper credentials for purchasing psychological tests. Realistically, this control is less than adequate and often it becomes the responsibility of the psychologist to recognize his own limitations in training and test expertise.

TESTS IN USE

The number and kinds of psychological tests in print are a constant source of confusion if not amazement to the average person who attempts to review those available. This is not surprising in view of the fact that in *The Seventh Mental Measurements Yearbook* [63] there were 5426 tests and techniques listed. Each one was designed to elicit information regarding some aspect of human behavior, aptitude, or knowledge. Adding confusion is the fact that the reviews that follow the description of these tests sometimes are contradictory, naive, and outdated. Some reviews of tests are more than 15 years old although there has been much published research with the tests in the intervening years. Some of the reviewers in this standard reference book have had little experience with the tests they were reviewing. Personal bias in the test reviews is inevitable since most psychologists have strong feelings about certain types of tests. The best source of information regarding any psychological test or technique may be the test author's manual, supplemented by other publications of the test's capabilities and potentialities.

Psychological tests fall into six separate categories: achievement, aptitude, intelligence, vocational interest inventories, personality tests, and those designed to elicit the presence and location of diseases of the central and peripheral nervous system. We will comment on each of these types of tests; however, our main concern will be intelligence tests, the personality assessment techniques, and tests designed to identify diseases of the brain and nervous system.

Achievement Tests

Achievement tests are usually designed to measure a specific learned skill. They are used as an evaluative technique in measuring how well the client has performed a task and they are usually administered upon the completion of a specific learning experience. Because of their wide use in educational settings, achievement tests are the most used of all standardized measures.

Aptitude Tests

Many people are confused by the word "aptitude." They equate ability, intelligence, and sometimes interest with "aptitudes." "Aptitude" implies *potential* capacity to learn or perform. The idea of potential is important because the crux of aptitude is that it denotes an ability that has not yet been manifested. A person may have a high musical aptitude without ever having played a musical note. High musical aptitude means that if a person were trained in music, he would learn more quickly than the average person and, after the training, he would perform well. Only after training was successfully completed would ability in music be manifested. Ability is what a person can do; aptitude is his potential to do this. Aptitude tests are used in a variety of settings where prediction of performance is needed. However, performance on aptitude tests, like most other measurable human characteristics, is influenced by the effects of past learning.

Intelligence Tests

Intelligence tests are a form of aptitude tests that measure a broad area of skills and are applicable to a variety of test settings. As is true of personality measurements, intelligence tests may be divided into two large categories: paper-and-pencil and individually administered. Of the two, individually administered tests are usually more satisfactory in a clinical setting since the performance of each client can be observed. As with personality evaluation, this is important since motivation, anxiety, or hostility toward the testing situation can significantly influence test results. Individually administered intelligence tests are usually constructed so that the client is able to demonstrate a variety of skills and reactions. For example, some clients react more favorably to three-dimensional stimuli than to two-dimensional ones such as printed materials.

Paper-and-pencil tests have the advantage of permitting group administration, which makes it possible to test many persons at the same time and simplifies the problem of validation and standardization. However, paper-and-pencil intelligence tests offer neither as accurate nor as broad a picture of a client's mental capacity as individually administered tests. Paper-and-pencil tests may be satisfactory for screening purposes where large groups must be tested in a limited time. If there is need for a clinical evaluation—such as in the case of suspected retardation, malingering, or cultural differences—the individual test becomes mandatory. As we have already seen, the same reasoning may be applied to tests utilized for personality evaluation.

Vocational Interest Inventories

Interest inventories have become popular because of the increasing complexity in the field of employment. It is impossible for a young person to be able to gain wide experience in the job market or to be exposed to the large number of vocations that may be available to him. The knowledge that he may have concerning a specific vocation may be superficial or distorted. Even without any clear idea of his present vocational interests, a client can respond to such questions as:

Do you like to work with people?
Do you like to help people who are in trouble?
Would you prefer to work with tools rather than manage an office?
Do you prefer participation in outdoor sports to reading a book or writing a story?

Such questions are typical of the items in interest inventories. The scoring system of these inventories brings together interest clusters that have a meaningful relationship to vocational areas. These areas usually include: arts, interpersonal relationships, science, engineering, sales and persuasive interests, agricultural, clerical, social service and mechanical interests. In addition, there are different score patterns for auto mechanics and graduate mechanical engineers, although both of these occupations require high mechanical interests. Some inventories, such as the *Strong Vocational Interest Blank* [346] and the *Kuder Occupational Interest Survey* [223] relate a person's vocational interest to a specific occupation and, in the case of the *Kuder Occupational Interest Survey*, to a college major as well.

Personality Tests

Of all the qualities we have described, personality is the most difficult to test and evaluate. Authors of paper-and-pencil or actuarial-type personality tests admit difficulty in designing instruments that avoid being superficial. Personality is an elusive, tenuous, and many-faceted concept that does not readily lend itself to analysis by multiple-choice-type questions. As in testing intelligence, paper-and-pencil tests may be justified for the initial screening of clients; however, they should not be a substitute for individually administered techniques. These latter tests require more time to administer and evaluate but they are correspondingly more useful in eliciting multidimensional personality characteristics when administered by a trained clinical psychologist. Since the interpretations of these tend to be subjective, they should be combined with actuarial-type methods into a personality test battery.

Tests of the Central and Peripheral Nervous System

Psychological tests can be of considerable value when used in conjunction with a neurological examination to identify the presence and extent of damage to the peripheral or central nervous system. The experiences of the authors have verified the claim that, at times, psychological test signs of organic brain disease may be the first indication of the presence of such conditions. A possible explanation of this is that subtle behavioral reactions to incipient neurological pathology provide characteristic prodromal signs on some psychological tests. Additionally, psychological tests can help locate the site of a lesion and estimate possible behavioral limitations.

It is in the area of neurological assessment that there is presently an opportunity to expand the utilization of the psychologist's clinical skills. Many neurologists and neurosurgeons are becoming aware of the value of utilizing psychological testing in cases of brain lesions and diseases of the central and peripheral nervous system. However, many graduate schools fail to train their clinical psychology students to utilize such skills. Those psychologists often narrowly confine themselves to one method or system of evaluation instead of utilizing a diversity of available techniques that would increase the validity of their diagnosis and would give their evaluations a much greater scope.

SUMMARY

This chapter describes how psychological tests are used and under what circumstances their use is appropriate. Clinical psychologists utilize both the actuarial and impressionistic tests in their attempt to understand human behavior. The selection of the tests given to a client is usually left to the discretion of the examiner since he is most familiar with the client's needs. No matter what test is utilized, the psychologist must insure that proper validity, reliability, and other essential test characteristics are present.

CHAPTER 3

Intelligence Tests

Is the use of intelligence tests in school and for employment screening justified? Many people feel that intelligence tests may be "unfair" assessments of intelligence, pointing out that those widely used were primarily standardized and validated on urban, middle-class whites and therefore discriminate against persons with rural backgrounds as well as those of ethnic and racial minorities.

Is intelligence an inherited quality or one that is primarily determined by cultural exposure, performance, motivation, and learning opportunity? Occasionally, a researcher will announce that his studies show that a given ethnic or racial group is "intellectually inferior" [177, 192]. Since the answers to these questions are controversial, the applied meaning of intelligence is also controversial.

A definition of intelligence found in a dictionary is "the ability to comprehend facts." One might ask, however, what kind of facts? A boy who has a limited vocabulary may have an extensive knowledge of the rules of basketball and football. It is important to realize that motivation and familiarity are elements that play a role in a knowledge of facts. Another definition of intelligence sometimes used is that it is a measure of the capacity to adapt. But the question that must be asked is: adapt to what? Using one's immediate environment as a criterion for adaptability is not sound since environments vary in their complexity and adaptive demands. This definition may well lead one to the conclusion that the world's most intelligent people are the Eskimos, followed, perhaps, by the indigenous inhabitants of the central Australian wastelands who (until recently, when their ecologies were upset by intruders) were able to eke out an existence where "civilized man" would find it difficult to survive. Certainly the aborigines of the world's arctic and desert regions could adapt more easily to New York, Moscow, London, or Tokyo than the inhabitants of any of our modern cities could adapt to the harsh tundras and barren wildernesses of the earth. Yet who would score higher on the intelligence tests supposedly designed to measure capacity for adaptation?

Many behavioral scientists maintain that a reasonable definition of intelligence would be: intelligence is that quality that is measured by an intelligence test. If "intelligence" is defined as that combination of qualities that an intelligence test measures, how can we support such a definition in view of the fact that these tests differ in content matter and in scoring procedures? Is it possible for an individual to be superior on one intelligence test, average on another, and below average on a third? A client may score high on a test that is heavily weighted with verbal tasks and perform poorly on one in which manipulation and psychomotor skills are emphasized. Some tests give separate verbal and performance scores but others do not make such distinctions. It is, therefore, important that anyone who uses the results of intelligence tests knows the nature and content of the test and is familiar with such aspects as standardization procedures, validity, and reliability. With all their shortcomings, intelligence tests may still be one of the most practical techniques available to the psychologist for measuring certain types of human abilities.

SPECIFIC TESTS IN COMMON USE

Wechsler Scales

From his work as chief psychologist at Bellevue Hospital in New York City, David Wechsler recognized the need for an individually administered intelligence test that would hold the interest of an adult client and would provide a variety of clinical cues and actuarial findings. As a result of this, he designed the original Wechsler Bellevue Scales in 1939. Three Wechsler Scales have followed the original instrument. The Wechsler Adult Intelligence Scale (WAIS)[386] published in 1955 is primarily a revision of the initial Wechsler Bellevue. In the WAIS, each subtest was extended to improve the range of difficulty of the items and subsequently enhance reliability. Also, restandardization was carried out on a more representative population. The Wechsler Intelligence Scale for Children

(WISC)[385] and the Wechsler Intelligence Scale for Children—Revised* (WISC-R) are a downward extension of the Wechsler Bellevue, paralleling the adult scale in construction. The WISC is designed for children between the ages of five through 15 years and the WISC-R for ages six through 16. In 1967, the Wechsler Preschool and Primary Scale of Intelligence (WPPSI)[388] was introduced for children ages four-years through six-years-six-months. While this test has many of the characteristics of the WAIS and WISC, and shares test items with the WISC, it is more than an extension of the WISC because the measure provides new subtests not found in the other Wechsler Scales. Surveys taken of tests most used in psychology reflect that the current Wechsler Scales continue to share the popularity of their predecessor[242].

The Wechsler Adult Intelligence Scale

The WAIS consists of 11 subtests divided into verbal and performance groups. Each subtest is arranged with simple to increasingly difficult items. A more specific examination of the subtests reflects the abilities measured by the Wechsler Scales.

A. *Verbal Subtests*

1. Information: This scale is a measurement of the general knowledge that the client has acquired through experience or education. Questions such as "How many weeks are there in a year?" and "What is ethnology?" reflect the diversity and level of knowledge probed by this subtest.
2. Comprehension: It has been stated that this is a measurement of logical thinking or common sense. Wechsler points out that the scale reflects experience of a practical nature. Examples that show the logical or common sense theme are: "Why should we stay away from bad company?" "Why are child labor laws needed?"
3. Arithmetic: Mathematical reasoning, concentration, and alertness are purportedly measured by this subtest. Problems presented are typical of elementary-school-level mathematics including addition, subtraction, multiplication, percentages, etc. The quality of responses is affected by education and certain types of vocational experiences.
4. Similarities: This subtest requires the client to find a characteristic common to several objects. It seems to measure the ability to think abstractly.

*See Appendix D.

5. Digit Span: Wechsler utilizes two approaches for repeating digits. The first requires repeating digits as presented by the examiner. For example, the examiner states, "2-5-7-9" and the client should reply, "2-5-7-9." In the second part, the client repeats digits in reverse. The examiner states, "2-5-7-9" and the client should reply, "9-7-5-2." According to Wechsler, digit span is the poorest indicator of general intelligence, but it is probably included in the test because of its clinical value.

6. Vocabulary: It should be noted that this subtest is culture-loaded. In identifying emotional blocking or loss of recall due to brain pathology, it has been found to be the best overall single predictor on the Wechsler among the norm group used in standardization. The ability of the client to define a word is judged as well as the quality of the definition. The range of vocabulary is from such common words as "breakfast" to more difficult words such as "audacious."

B. *Performance Subtests*

1. Digit Symbol: Wechsler patterned this subtest after code substitution, which requires the association of symbols with numerals. The client must copy symbols in the blank provided beneath the associated numerals. The test also measures eye-hand coordination and immediate visual recall. Speed as well as accuracy is rewarded.

2. Picture Completion: The primary characteristic of this subtest is that an important detail in a picture has been omitted which the client must identify as missing. It is a measure of the ability of the client to make visual discriminations and to conceptualize whole objects.

3. Block Design: Colored blocks with red, white, and red and white sides are used to make various designs. Four blocks are used for simple designs and nine blocks are used at the more difficult level. This subtest, which has a variety of clinical indicators, is a measure of visual perception and psychomotor organization. Both performance and speed are weighed in scoring.

4. Picture Arrangement: A series of pictures that tells a story is presented in a disarranged order and the client is required to put them into a logical sequence. Wechsler points out that this scale is an attempt to apply general intelligence to a social situation and to measure the ability of a client to conceptualize a total entity. Even though cartoon characters are used in many of the stories to deemphasize the social and cultural impact, the test has cultural loading. Accuracy as well as speed in sequencing is rewarded.

5. Object Assembly: The client is given a number of cardboard pieces that he must fit together to make a common object, such as a hand or animal. Time limits are established and bonus points are given for speed of performance.

Upon completion of the administration, raw scores from each subtest are converted to a standard score form. When these standard scores are combined, they yield three separate scores called deviation intelligence scores: the Verbal IQ (VIQ), the Performance IQ (PIQ), and the Full Scale IQ (FSIQ). The deviation IQ form employed by Wechsler utilizes a mean of 100 and a standard deviation of 15. Standard scores are also available for individual subtests but it is recommended that they not be interpreted as separate deviation IQ scores.

The adoption of a standard score method for calculating the intelligence provides a more equitable way of taking into account age variability in the adult population. An example of this allowance for the so-called "mental deterioration" that occurs with increasing age is that in order to obtain the same Full Scale IQ, a client age 18 must earn a higher total raw score than one age 65.

When one compares the WAIS with the Stanford-Binet Intelligence Scale [364], the other popular individually administered intelligence measure, there seem to be some advantages favoring the Wechsler Scales. The recognition of age variability and its inclusion in the calculation of intelligence improves the accuracy of the evaluation. Some other characteristics in favor of the WAIS are reporting multiple IQ scores, organiza-

Fig. 3.1 Administration of one of the Wechsler Adult Intelligence Scale Subtests.

tion of materials, subtests that are more interesting to an adult population, and clinical assessments that can be derived from a number of the subtests. Since there is a high correlation between Wechsler and Stanford-Binet scores, it seems that the Wechsler test may be preferred in many cases.

Wechsler Intelligence Scales for Children

The WISC and WISC-R are intelligence measures for children ages five through 15 years and six through 16 years. The tests yield the same pattern of IQ scores as the WAIS and use the same mean and standard deviation. Subtests are similar with the exception that alternate tests are provided in both verbal and performance groupings. Verbal tests include: (1) Information, (2) Comprehension, (3) Arithmetic, (4) Similarities, and (5) Vocabulary, with Digit Span used as an alternate for verbal tests. Performance tests include: (1) Picture Completion, (2) Picture Arrangement, (3) Block Design, (4) Object Assembly, (5) Coding (Digit Symbol), and a set of mazes as an alternate for performance tests. The alternates provide flexibility in cases of administrative error or physical handicaps. The similarities between the WISC, WISC-R, and the WAIS are obvious and descriptions of subtests need not be repeated. Research seems to suggest that the WISC and WISC-R correlate highly with other measures of intelligence[233] and they are recognized as relatively accurate measures among appropriate culture groups. For further information concerning the 1974 revision of the WISC (the WISC-R) see Appendix D.

Fig. 3.2 Administration of one of the Wechsler Intelligence Scale for Children Subtests.

Wechsler Preschool and Primary Scale of Intelligence

The WPPSI is the newest of the Wechsler Scales and is still considered by some to be in an experimental stage. It tests children between the ages of four through six-years-six-months and is composed of ten scorable subtests with one alternate. Eight of the 11 subtests are downward extensions of the WISC, while three are new to the Wechsler Scales. Wechsler notes that these new subtests are closely tied to the age measured and may have valuable diagnostic characteristics [388]. Two of the new additions are the "Animal House," which is a type of coding test, and the "Geometric Design," which measures perceptual and visual motor organization. The third, which he calls "Sentences," is used as an alternate to the verbal subtests. This is a short-term or rote memory recall task and replaces Digit Span found on the WISC and WAIS. The WPPSI yields the same pattern of standard scores as the WISC and WAIS. However, the administration of the WPPSI differs in that the verbal and performance tests are given alternately to maintain interest among young subjects.

The usefulness of the third Wechsler Scale will be judged as it is used. Current data, although limited, suggest that the WPPSI is well-standardized and shows good positive correlation when compared with other established tests [388].

Fig. 3.3 Administration of one of the Wechsler Pre-School and Primary Subtests. (Courtesy of The Psychological Corporation.)

The Stanford-Binet Intelligence Scale

The Stanford-Binet Intelligence Scale has long been recognized as the standard for the measurement of intelligence. It has functioned as "the model" for other intellectual measures and has become the main validation criterion for newer IQ tests.

The Stanford-Binet is important in the history of psychological testing. From the first Binet Scales of 1905, 1908, and 1911 to the present Terman and Merrill edition of 1960, the volume and wealth of data collected are immense. In fact, the retention of these accumulated data was a major factor in the construction of the 1960 revision.

Stanford-Binet—1960 *Revision*

The 1960 version of the Stanford-Binet is a combination of the 1937 edition of forms L and M. The best items from each form were selected, thereby preserving the numerous studies and research data collected prior to this revision. By combining forms L and M, out-of-date items were discarded and those retained were then checked for level of difficulty without having to reestablish validity and reliability on totally new tasks. While the content materials did not change except for some updating of pictures, etc., several technical improvements were introduced.

The most important modification in the 1960 edition was the adoption of the Standard Score method (called deviation IQ score) for computation of the IQ. This replaced the old ratio formula ($MA/CA \times 100$), which had been used since its introduction by Terman in 1916. The ratio IQ did not provide a good linear comparison at the various age levels since the standard deviation among age levels varied as much as eight points. The current form has established a mean of 100 and a standard deviation of 16 points for all levels, which provides a linear comparison among the various mental ages. Computation of the deviation IQ was simplified by the development of conversion tables by Pinneau [293], which are included in the 1960 manual.

Another change was the extension of the mental age from 16 through 18 years. Several studies have shown that mental age continued to develop beyond age 16 [33, 55]. While this extension has improved the test for use with adolescents, the Stanford-Binet still appears to be inadequate for the measurement of Average to Superior Adult.

The 1960 revision is made up of 20 separate levels ranging from year II through Superior Adult III. The early years (II–V) are divided into two measurements per year whereas VI–XIV consist of one measure per year.

There are four adult tests ranging from Average Adult through Superior Adult III. At each level there are six subtests and one alternate, with the exception of Average Adult level which has eight subtests and one alternate. Some of the subtests are repeated at advanced levels utilizing a higher number of correct responses to establish credit.

Summary of the Administration of the Stanford-Binet

The examiner first establishes a basal age by finding the highest level at which the client can pass all subtests. With normal children, the examiner usually begins the test one year below their chronological age or he may administer the vocabulary sections (picture or verbal, depending on age) to find a criterion for a starting base. Level XIV is the common starting point for use of the Stanford-Binet with normal adults. When a base is established, the client progresses through the test until he fails all subtests at a particular age level. This is usually referred to as the ceiling or maximum level. When a ceiling is reached, testing is terminated. The following are examples of items utilized at various age levels:

<u>2 years, 3 months:</u> Show the paper doll and say, "Show me the dolly's hair." Same for mouth, ears, and hands.

<u>3 years, 5 months:</u> Give the child a pencil, pointing to the circle in the booklet, say, "Make one just like this."

<u>4 years, 3 months:</u> Point to incomplete drawing in the record booklet and say, "What is this?" Whether the child recognizes it or not, say, "It's a man, isn't it? See he has only one leg. You finish him. Make all the rest of him."

<u>5 years, 10 months:</u> Child repeats without error, "Jane wants to build a big castle in her playhouse."

<u>7 years, 6 months:</u> Child copies a diamond.

<u>10 years:</u> Child correctly defines 11 words given him by examiner.

<u>12 years, 6 months:</u> Child repeats five digits reversed.

<u>13 years, 10 months:</u> Child places disarranged words in proper sequence. "For the Started An We Country Early at Hour."

The Stanford-Binet is still one of the most popular individual tests for the measurement of intelligence, although its usage has decreased somewhat since the introduction of the Wechsler Scales[242]. The Stanford-Binet appears to be a valid and reliable measure of certain intellectual factors, particularly those that are related to scholastic ability. The test is verbally loaded (especially at the upper levels) and therefore the results

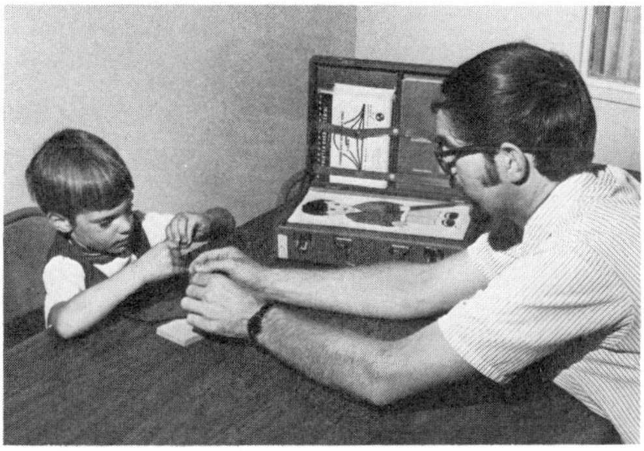

Fig. 3.4 Administration of one of the Stanford-Binet Subtests.

obtained from clients with verbal handicaps may be questionable. The Stanford-Binet's lack of suitability for use with Average to Superior Adults stems from the fact that in some cases adequate ceilings cannot be measured. It should also be kept in mind that the test items themselves hold relatively little interest for adults and therefore may create negative motivational and performance reactions.

GROUP INTELLIGENCE TESTS

When it is necessary for the psychologist to test a large number of clients in a short period of time and when observing the client is not important, he can choose one of the many group techniques available. In *The Seventh Mental Measurements Yearbook* [63] over 700 group intelligence tests are listed in addition to literally hundreds of tests measuring special abilities. Generally, these tests are used in industrial settings, military induction centers, employment services, educational institutions, and other agencies that process large numbers of subjects.

One advantage of group tests is that they can be given to many people at one time, which is a saving of both time and money. The number tested is limited only by the amount of room to seat the clients and the number of proctors to supervise them. Another advantage of group measurement is inherent in the construction of these tests. Since group tests are usually of paper-and-pencil-type with multiple-choice responses, the tests are comparatively simple to administer, score, and interpret. This maximizes standardization of these tests and permits their use by an examiner with limited training since much interpretive information can be taken directly from the test manual.

There are obvious disadvantages to the group form of intelligence test. Since there is little opportunity to observe individual performance, the psychologist is unable to identify factors such as motivation, test anxiety, and the individual's manner of approach to problem-solving. Group intelligence tests are usually speed tests—the greater number answered correctly within a given time, the higher the score. There are many individuals who do not perform well under such time-stress conditions. Such persons may do significantly better in an atmosphere where the examiner has established rapport, as is customary when individually administered intelligence tests are given. Some clients require reassurance during the testing process and will perform poorly if they are not encouraged. The observational notes made by the examiner during the administration of individual intelligence tests often yield valuable clues to understanding the personality of the client. Observing behavior during testing enables the psychologist to determine the validity of the score obtained. Finally, most of the group tests depend heavily on verbal skills that are directly related to academic learning experiences. This tends to magnify the results of cultural differences and school-related learning disabilities.

Table 3.1 lists the group tests most often used by those specializing in psychological testing[17, 305]. Three of the more popular tests mentioned in Table 3.1 are described below.

Table 3.1 Representative group intelligence tests.

Battery	Grade Levels	Publisher
Analysis of Learning Potential (ALP)	K-12, College	Harcourt Brace Jovanovich, Inc.
California Test of Mental Maturity, 1963 Revision (CTMM)	K-12	California Test Bureau
Cooperative School and College Ability Tests (SCAT)	4-16	Educational Testing Service
Henmon-Nelson Tests of Mental Ability, Revised Edition	3-17	Houghton Mifflin
Kuhlmann-Anderson Intelligence Tests, Seventh Edition	K-12	Personnel Press, Inc.
Lorge-Thorndike Intelligence Test	K-13	Houghton Mifflin
Otis-Lennon Mental Ability Test	K-12	Harcourt Brace Jovanovich, Inc.
Pintner General Ability Tests—Revised	K-12	Harcourt Brace Jovanovich, Inc.
SRA Tests of Educational Ability, 1962 Edition (TEA)	4-6,6-9, 9-12,4-12	Science Research Association

California Test of Mental Maturity [354]

This test was constructed to parallel the Stanford-Binet. It is composed of a verbal and nonverbal section. The levels of the test parallel school grades kindergarten through 12; however, level 12 should not be used with adults.

Otis-Lennon Mental Ability Test [279]

Both verbal and nonverbal tasks are combined on this test, which is heavily loaded to evaluate school-related abilities. The test authors state that this is a test designed to measure aspects of the American culture that stress reasoning abilities. It can be used from the second half of kindergarten through 12th grade.

Lorge-Thorndike Intelligence Test [237]

This test also provides both a verbal and nonverbal battery. Appropriate grade levels measured range from kindergarten through first year of college, depending on the form used.

CULTURE-MINIMIZED INTELLIGENCE TESTS

Since intelligence tests are greatly influenced by cultural and educational opportunity, one might ask what alternatives there are to such tests. Is there a "fair" way to evaluate intelligence? There are a number of tests available that have been called "nonverbal," "culture-free," and "culture-fair." The authors doubt whether such tests are really what they imply. A better description of such tests is that they are, at most, *relatively* culture-fair or, better, "culture-minimized." One can hardly be entirely "culture-free" and still measure intelligence since one aspect of intelligence is the capacity to adjust to culture. Furthermore, it is primarily through cultural symbols that humans are able to communicate with each other. Therefore, without using some form of cultural medium, an assessment of intelligence would not be possible.

A number of ingenious methods have been devised to attempt to circumvent the crucial role that culture plays in the more popular intelligence measures now in use. The following tests have been selected because each one represents a different approach to the challenge of measuring intelligence with a minimum amount of cultural and educational contamination.

Goodenough-Harris Drawing Test [150]

In this test the client is asked to draw a picture of a man and a woman. Intelligence is judged by the subject's conceptual thinking and not by his artistic ability. Seventy-three items (such as body parts, clothing, and perspective) are scored. This test was widely used for a number of years; however, more recent studies reveal that a moderately strong cultural bias enters into the test evaluation. Also, artistic ability cannot entirely be excluded and clients with such ability scored spuriously high on the test. A recent source on the use of tests shows a definite decline in the popularity of the Goodenough-Harris Drawing Test [242].

The Culture Fair Intelligence Test [79]

This paper-and-pencil test designed by R. B. Cattell can be given at age four through Superior Adult. Intelligence is tested by such tasks as selecting an item that correctly completes a series of designs; identifying the item that fits into drawn geometric patterns; and meeting prescribed conditions such as placing dots into circles, triangles, and rectangles. The test has been used in Europe, North and South America, and in several African and Asian countries. Satisfactory results were obtained among cultures that were more or less equally sophisticated but the original norms were not well sustained among cultures that differed considerably from those in the United States. The test is strongly biased in favor of nonverbal aptitudes such as spatial relations and mechanical skills.

The Leiter International Performance Scale [232]

Elementary and high school students, representing a variety of ethnic backgrounds, served as initial norm groups for the development of this scale. Research was continued in the United States, as well as in several African and Asian countries. The Leiter Scale requires minimal instructions to administer. A number of frames that have designs or pictures drawn on them are presented to the client along with a series of cards. The client is required to make an association between the pictures on the frame and the proper card. For example, the frame may show five circles of various sizes. The test subject is given five cards, each one showing a square that corresponds in size to one of the circles on the frame. The test task consists of matching the sizes of the designs on the frame with those shown on the cards.

Matching problems involve such concepts as colors, designs, spatial relations, classification of animals, series completions, and other tasks requiring recognition and judgment. The tests are individually administered and the tasks are arranged from age two to 18 years. Among the objections to the test raised by some psychologists is that the test is expensive and cumbersome. There is a repetitive element in the test that tends to make it monotonous, and this can result in loss of motivation.

Kahn Intelligence Test (KIT) [199]

The identical materials of the Kahn Test of Symbol Arrangement [197] described on page 149 are used with this test—16 plastic objects and a felt strip. The box that contains the test materials is also utilized in some of the tasks. The test tasks, which become progressively more difficult, are designed to be used from infant to superior adult. A method is provided to enable the examiner to make a quick estimate of a client's range of abilities. This is followed by a more detailed exploration of the subject's capacities.

Some sample KIT tasks are as follows:

2–3 years: Examiner: "I'm going to hide this doggie and then see if you can find it." In full view of child the examiner rolls the white dog in the strip, places strip in box, puts the anchor, cross, and parrot on top of box, saying: "Now find the doggie—show me where I hid it."
6 years: The examiner hands the child the large transparent heart and the small red one, saying: "Name three ways in which these two hearts are different." Performance required: Child states size, color, and thickness. Plus score is given if three qualities are mentioned. Transparency is acceptable as one of the differentiating qualities.
11 years: Examiner places objects on the strip in this order: red star, white dog, red heart, cross, red star; he exposes them for five seconds, mixes them up, and asks child to replace them exactly as they were.

Examples of the Use of the KIT with Blind Children

3–4 years: Examiner gives child the two red stars and the red heart, saying: "Find the one that is different and give it to me. Keep the two that are the same."
10–11 years: Examiner hands child the following objects, two at a time, asking each time which one is the heaviest: the large dog and the large heart, the butterfly and a small dog.

Example of the Use of KIT when Test Subject and Examiner Cannot Communicate Verbally

> 2–3 years: The examiner takes one red star and the small black dog and hands child the white dog and the other red star. The examiner places his red star on the dog, removes it, and repeats this several times, he finally leaves his red star on the dog, pointing at the same time to the object that the child has in his hands and then back to his own objects. Plus is scored if the child imitates the examiner's model by placing the star on the dog as the examiner did.

Recognition, recall, judgment, comprehension, association, psychomotor skill, and conceptualization are utilized in gaining an impression of intellectual capacity. The manual contains instructions for the administration of the KIT using sign language. Research with the test has been reported from countries such as Lebanon, India, Argentina, Japan, as well as the United States. Carse [72] writes:

> Since the KIT manual reports adequate reliability, and with the correlations obtained in this study, the indications are that the KIT does yield an adequate measure of intelligence. Perhaps the greatest factor in favor of the KIT was the greater ease of administration that both examiners noted .... Greater interest was maintained when the KIT was given. This could be accounted for either by the nature of the items—the KIT allows the child to manipulate more objects or the few verbal responses that are required. Observations by the examiners indicate that it was the fewer verbal responses of the KIT which allows for a faster and a more enjoyable testing experience. [It is] an excellent supplementary test for school counselors and psychologists to use when they suspect that the group intelligence tests are discriminating against culturally different children in their schools.

As is true of all culture-minimized tests, the KIT could benefit from additional research to further support the favorable results already reported in the literature [96, 221].

Arthur Point Scale of Performance Tests [22]

Form I of this test has been in use since 1925. A revised Form II is now available; like its predecessor, it attempts to establish mental levels based on manipulative rather than verbal skills. It is designed for use with ages five through 15 years. It offers a means of measuring the abilities of deaf children, those suffering from reading disabilities, those with delayed or defective speech, and those who do not speak the same language as the examiner. Form II has five parts:

1. A test requiring the manipulation of cubes.
2. A form-board requiring the client to place cut-outs into the correct openings.

3. Arthur Stencil Design Test, in which the client is required to reproduce designs from a combination of cards and cut-out stencils in several colors.
4. Porteus Maze Test.
5. Healy Picture Completion Test.

Progressive Matrices [303]

This technique is a multiform nonverbal test developed by Raven as a measure of the Spearman G factor, which is a general factor theory of intelligence. The British test is composed of a set of matrices with a section omitted from each matrix. The client must select the missing part from a group of alternatives. Sixty matrices are usually administered with 12 matrices composing each of five levels. Currently there are three forms available. Sets A through E, published in 1938, measure 3-year olds through adults. A colored set for young children and retarded adults has also been developed. A new form, published in 1965, extended the upward range of the original series to Superior Adult.

The technique of Progressive Matrices has been gaining popularity in the United States because it is not as educationally bound nor does it reflect the heavy verbal loading of the more traditional tests; however, it has serious limitations that should be considered before it is used. To date, adequate norms based on a United States population are not available. The norms now in use are of British subjects collected during World War II. Some generalization may be possible, but norms should always be established on the population upon which a test is used. The manual does not clearly state specific directions for administration and provides little information concerning reliability and validity.

The Full Range Picture Vocabulary Test [14], **the Quick Test** [15], **the Columbia Mental Maturity Scale** [62], **and the Peabody Picture Vocabulary Test** [104]

The Full Range Picture Vocabulary Test and the more popular Quick Test were designed by Ammons for use with clients with physical or verbal impairment. The Quick Test is a short version of the same idea used in The Full Range Picture Vocabulary Test. Four cartoon-like drawings appear on each card. The examiner is provided with an answer sheet printed with the words to be used with each picture. The test consists of asking the client to make a correct association between a word and a picture. For example, a picture showing a police car could be coupled with the word, "protection." A picture of a happy group of dancers might be identified by the word, "hilarity." Both the Columbia Mental Maturity Scale and the Peabody Picture Vocabulary Test utilize stimulus words, which are given orally. The test subject is required to identify the word that best suits the theme of the picture.

These four tests are culture-minimized only in a limited way. By depending on words and pictures, the cultural factor is relatively high. Whereas the age range covered by such tests is wider, the spectrum of skills measured is very narrow. These techniques are of considerable help when testing persons suffering from cerebral palsy and other types of physical and verbal impairments. By obtaining the required norms, these tests can be relatively quickly adapted to any given culture. Standardization is uncomplicated and test administration is easy and fast.

Estimating Intelligence from the Rorschach Test [317]

In addition to personality assessment, the Rorschach Test has been used to measure intelligence. Some types of intelligence are better reflected by use of stimuli materials such as the Rorschach offers. This is particularly true of what one might term "creative intelligence," which is bypassed by the average intelligence test. The capacity to organize stimuli, to use imagination, and to express creative energies represents a big void in present-day intelligence testing.

An analysis of Table 3.2 shows that in some respects the extremes of intelligence seem to meet. Both Very Superior people and mental

Table 3.2 Intelligence derived from the Rorschach.*

Level of Intelligence	Number Whole Card Responses	Number Human Move-ment Responses	Number Pure Color Responses	Percent Good Form Responses	Percent Animal Responses	Percent Original Responses
Very superior	10+	5+	4–7	90–100	10–20	30–50
Superior	7–10	5	1.5–3.5	80–100	20–35	0–20
Average to high	4–7	2–4	1.5–2.5	70–80	30–55	0–20
Low average	3–4	0–2	1.5–0.6	60–70	50–70	0–20†
Moron	1–3	0	4.7	45–60	60–80	30–40†
Imbecile	0–2	0	5.5–8.5	0–45	80–100	40–70†

*Adapted from the Rorschach Test as applied to a feeble-minded group [34].
†Original responses with poor form.

defectives have a relatively large number of pure color (color without form) responses and, likewise, a high percentage of original (non-popular) responses. An important difference between these two groups can be found by inspecting the percentage of good form responses. The original concepts of mental defectives almost always have poor form, whereas those of the superior subject are usually of good form. Furthermore, the number of pure color responses found among superior Rorschach records represent only a small percentage of the total number of responses, whereas among mental defectives they may represent over half of the total responses. The striking difference between records of clients with low or high intelligence is seen in the number of human movement responses. The capacity to see human movement seems to be related not only to good emotional health (except in the case of certain types of paranoids), but also seems to reflect the effective use of creative imagination.

In the following signs of mental deficiency, it is noteworthy that one of the ten characteristics cited is an absence of human movement. The signs delineated by Klopfer[217] are:

1. Poor form of the concepts perceived.
2. Defining the blot areas instead of saying what they look like.
3. Many pure color responses. Responses where form is not a factor in the perception.
4. No human movement responses.
5. Frequent occurrence of poor whole card responses given on the basis of some details on the cards.
6. Few good whole card responses.
7. Lack of systematic approach in conceptualization. That is, not proceeding from small to large or from large to small details on the cards.
8. Little content variety.
9. High animal percentage.
10. Emphasis on unusual detail.

The Future of Culture-Minimizing Tests

In view of the increasing awareness of the limitations of the heavily culture-weighted intelligence measures, it is important to realize that culture-minimized intelligence techniques offer an alternative to such tests on the one hand and to subjective appraisals based solely on interviews or case histories on the other. With good reason, minority and ethnic groups voice objections to intelligence assessments that rely on cultural experiences to which their members have had only minimal exposure.

If psychological evaluation of intelligence survives the present antagonism that seems increasingly evident, culture-minimized tests represent the trend of the future. What seems to be needed now is not so much a rash of new culture-minimized intelligence tests, but rather a more careful standardization and validation of those tests already available.

INTERPRETING MENTAL DEFICIENCY

The arbitrary labels attached to those who are categorized as mentally retarded are many times misleading and difficult to interpret. Table 3.3 presents the five-level classification system of the American Association on Mental Deficiency based on intelligence test scores. In the past, great importance was placed on the testing of the retarded and major decisions based on test results were made concerning their care, custody, and control. It has been shown in this chapter that intelligence tests are fallible and may not always yield an accurate and meaningful score. The content of the test materials and the many factors of administration, standardization, evaluation as well as the effect of culture, add to the possibility of error in test scores as well as misuse of results. Nevertheless, when used carefully, intelligence tests are helpful. Intelligence tests are utilized in

Table 3.3 Five-level classification system of the American Association on Mental Deficiency based on intelligence test scores.

			Corresponding Range in IQ Scores for National Sample on Whom Test was Administered	
Descriptive Terminology	Levels of Impairment	Standard Deviation Ranges	Stanford-Binet (SD = 16)	Wechsler Scales (SD = 15)
Borderline	−1	−1.01–−2.00	68–83	70–84
Mild	−2	−2.01–−3.00	52–67	55–69
Moderate	−3	−3.01–−4.00	36–51	40–54
Severe	−4	−4.01–−5.00	20–35	25–39
Profound	−5	Below −5.00	Below 20	Below 25

specialized centers and other institutions for the mentally retarded. In current practice they are primarily used to establish a baseline for placing the retarded in an appropriate training program. With the vast improvement in facilities and the sophistication of new training programs [99], many people who were considered untrainable have become productive citizens.

The following description is a general guide to the capacities and limitations of the retarded:

Mild. As adults have mental age of seven to twelve years

1. Capacities:
   a. Can perform routine factory or farm work.
   b. Can learn to read and write.
   c. Can evolve into self-supporting citizens under favorable environment.
2. Limitations:
   a. Do not usually progress past five to six years of schooling.
   b. Often incapable of recognizing their moral and legal obligations and therefore apt to become delinquents, prostitutes, and petty thieves when not properly guided.
   c. Their physical maturity in the absence of corresponding mental maturity predisposes them to unregulated and sometimes antisocial behavior. For example, in the United States, the frequency of illegitimate motherhood is highest among mildly retarded girls.

Severe to Moderate. As adults have mental age of three to seven years

1. Capacities:
   a. Can learn to talk.
   b. Can do simple work under supervision, such as mopping floors, rough painting, digging, and simple farm chores.
   c. If tractable and closely supervised, may possibly be self-supporting.
2. Limitations:
   a. Usually do not understand the value of money.
   b. Usually should not be permitted to live outside of institutions or away from very close supervision of the families.
   c. May be dangerous to self or others when emotionally upset or sexually aroused.

Profound. As adults have mental age of two years

1. Capacities:
   a. May learn to eat food without aid.
   b. May make themselves understood by grunts or even a few simple words.
   c. May learn to partially dress themselves.
2. Limitations:
   a. Must be institutionalized to avoid common dangers in life.
   b. Often have poor physical stamina and subject to early demise.
   c. Usually unable to contribute constructively in any task and require constant supervision.

SUMMARY

The measurement of intelligence is a complex and, many times, a controversial subject. There is no one single intelligence test that is accepted as a "true" measure of the intellect. The psychologist must select the test that best meets his client's needs.

CHAPTER 4

Evaluation and Testing of Children

Parents, teachers, and juvenile authorities are becoming increasingly aware of the assistance the psychologist can render in the understanding of children. The problem child who causes disturbances in school is frequently referred for psychological evaluation. Even more cogent is a thorough investigation of the "child with a problem" as distinguished from the problem child. The former may not exhibit any symptoms that draw the teacher's attention. His behavior may be exemplary and, of all the children in the class, he may be the last to cause trouble. The lack of signs of outward disturbance is no guarantee of the absence of inner turbulence. Experienced teachers realize that the child who is "too quiet" or behaves too well may be in need of closer psychological scrutiny than one whose boisterous behavior disrupts the classroom.

The successful child psychologist must be flexible, spontaneous, and able to show something of himself with which the child can identify. Rigid adults who represent to the child only the promontories of authority will fail in spite of forced smiles, kind words, and a profound knowledge of theory. It is obvious from this that not everyone otherwise qualified is temperamentally suited to examine children psychologically. We have found that interest in child psychology is not a sufficient criterion to guarantee success in testing children.

Persons who have children themselves are often more understanding of the parental side of children's problems than those who do not. Of course, there are exceptions, but psychologists who are also parents tend to refrain from placing all the blame for a child's problems automatically on the father and mother. Two extremes must be avoided: casting parents as villains in a drama in which the child is the ever-defenseless, blameless victim of environmental circumstances and viewing the child as a mere bundle of disturbing sights and sounds that can best be controlled by the use of the restrictive techniques of archaic penal systems. A child is an immature human being in the process of attempting to adjust to a complicated civilization. Empathy, sensitivity, a good awareness of reality, a sense of humor, and a genuine appreciation of the difficult task of parenthood are qualities that the psychologist who wishes to work with children should possess.

Those who work psychologically with children must also know how psychological instruments can be utilized with a youthful population and how test responses differ, not only between child and adult but also among children of various age groups and cultural backgrounds. A plausible case can be made for "blind analysis" of test responses. Here, the atmosphere of the laboratory can be maintained and results can be analyzed by a psychologist who is free from the contaminating influence of having seen or interviewed the client personally. However, when children are involved, blind analysis cannot be justified since the observation of the child during testing by the experienced clinician constitutes an important factor in the assessment of the child's test responses. Psychometrists have been able to record such test concomitants as fear, hesitation, and resistance, which must be considered by the psychologist when he integrates the test results into a final diagnostic impression.

There is no substitute for observation and it should begin the moment the child enters the room for the first time. Does he enter willingly or is he forced? Does he look around as he enters? Does he hesitate or go directly to the chair that the psychologist offers? Does he look at the psychologist? Does he appear curious, frightened, or suspicious? Does he speak softly, slowly, rapidly, or distinctly? Does he choose his words carefully or do they burst forth without restraint? Does the clothing he wears reflect care on the part of his parents? Is he disheveled, dirty, and unkempt looking or is he "too neatly" dressed, perhaps implying an obsessive preoccupation with cleanliness and external appearance. When he takes his chair, can he sit quietly or does he appear to be in constant motion? Does he exhibit any nervous mannerisms? Does he listen attentively? What is his approach to the test situation? How does he handle the materials?

Questions regarding a child's adjustment usually involve an evaluation of his intelligence. The tests most commonly used for this purpose are reviewed in Chapter 3. When a child's tested IQ clearly demonstrates that he is not utilizing his potential, the psychologist is confronted with the task of probing further for possible explanations.

DRAWING TECHNIQUES

Almost every child likes to draw—and this is usually true even of disturbed children. For this reason, art of one type or another usually has a place in the test battery designed for use with children. Age is no barrier in the use of drawing or painting techniques. Few children under two years of age are form-conscious; for this reason, they will draw what they feel instead of what they see. Maladjustment among very young children—two-and-a-half years or less—is manifested by confinement to one color when many colors are readily available. On the other hand, it is possible that a child may become so involved with the task of drawing that he sticks to one color, and this must be interpreted differently. Another consideration is the use of space. Normally, young children will use over half a page, making wide, roving strokes. The inhibited or anxious child will confine his work to narrow limits, using only a small portion of the paper. Such children may draw small circular objects in one of the corners. Others may make a few dots or one or two little lines. Hyperactive children of this age draw wildly over the paper, sometimes going beyond its edges. They may dig deeply into the paper, tearing it with the pressure of their pencil, or they may crumble the crayon as they draw. Their movements are rapid and they finish the task quickly.

As children grow older, the form of the drawing plays an important part. The psychologist must judge how well the child performed the task, how adequate was the visual representation and how coordinated was his psychomotor execution. Children may be asked to draw "whatever comes to your mind—draw anything you would like." The pertinency and maturity of the choice the child makes for the subject of his drawing is a valuable diagnostic aid. Subsequently, the same child may be asked to draw his own family and the psychologist should observe closely which family member is drawn first or last, who is given the central position, and if anyone is left out. Such drawings help the psychologist evaluate the child's feelings about his parents and siblings and understand the child's position in the family constellation. Judging drawings requires experience and, because this is subjective, care must be taken in this evaluation not to jump to conclusions without support from other types of testing.

THE RORSCHACH TEST[317] AND EMOTIONAL GROWTH

The Rorschach is being increasingly used at both extremes of the human span of life. This test has proved valuable in the evaluation of maturity both with children and the aged. Increasingly, psychologists are using it in a variety of gerontological studies[32]. The use of the Rorschach with children is described in publications such as *Child Rorschach Responses: Developmental Trends from Two to Ten Years*, by members of the Gesell Institute of Child Development[13]. This test is useful in establishing the emotional maturity level of a child and ascertaining how it differs from the intellectual level as determined by intelligence tests. For example, Dr. Kahn, one of the authors of this book, tested a child nine years of age who was intellectually equipped to skip to the fifth grade. The Rorschach reinforced our observations that this child's emotional development was barely at the level of a third-grade child. This inconsistency in mental and emotional maturity prompted us to recommend that he be placed in the fourth grade rather than move to the fifth as we believed the child would have had difficulty with interpersonal relationships at school with children who greatly outstripped him in emotional development.

Psychologists working with children have found that Rorschach response patterns at the two-year level consist of the child's impressions rather than an attempt at accurate discernment. Concepts such as "pretty flower" may be repeated several times as a response to color, regardless of the blot shape. At two-and-a-half, the response is similar to that of the two-year old, except that there is more variety of content. At three years, responses are less stereotyped and of better form. At four years, the average child gives approximately 15 responses. Human movement and animal movement responses are nearly doubled from the three-year level. At five years, the child shows considerable generalizing ability and color responses are fewer than at any succeeding age until ten. At five-and-a-half, the equilibrium sometimes associated with five-year olds tends to break up and this is manifested by an emphasis on small detail and an increase in inanimate movement responses. Sometimes, overt discomfort caused by the blots is expressed in initial exclamations.

Perception at six is increasingly accurate and the form of the blots is used in about 80 percent of the responses. This trend continues until seven years when a definite inwardizing of experience occurs, manifested by more movement and less color than at younger ages. At eight, the responses are much clearer and the child expresses more uncertainty and qualifications. At nine, detail for the first time exceeds whole responses. At ten, concepts implying movement often outweigh color responses.

An interesting study of Rorschach responses of adolescents was conducted at the Institute of Child Welfare, University of California, which showed how developmental trends during the adolescent's growth are reflected on this test. Sex differences were noted in the study and it was found that adolescent girls averaged a higher number of responses and, with striking consistency, made greater use of all the color variables than did boys of the same age[255].

THE KAHN TEST OF SYMBOL ARRANGEMENT (KTSA)[197]

Because it utilizes colorful three-dimensional materials and the tasks are easily understood by children, the KTSA is being increasingly used by school psychologists and by clinical psychologists who specialize in child evaluation. In 1957, a paper presented to the American Psychological Association by Kahn and Fink gave the results of a comparison of normal with emotionally disturbed children utilizing the KTSA[204]. The investigators found that these groups could be distinguished by their symbol patterns. A ratio between the child's mental age and the numerical element (i.e., the number score) of the symbol pattern yielded an index of the extent of the disturbance. A variety of studies with children were performed by different investigators since that time, and each study added additional information[379]. Some studies emphasized the need for further research. An earlier standardization of the test with children is reported in the KTSA Manual[198] and shows developmental trends from ages six to 14 years. The average numerical element of the symbol pattern increases gradually during these years from an average low of 57 to a high of 92. The average numerical element on the symbol patterns of a group of disturbed children remained at 58 regardless of their ages in the study described in the manual. "D" (naming) was the most common response used by the disturbed children. This is in contrast with other "X," "Y," and "Z" responses (abstractions) elicited from the groups of children who were not emotionally disturbed.

The manual also describes a method of determining the expected numerical elements for different ages: the child's mental age or chronological age (if mental age is not available) is multiplied by six. Thus, we would expect a seven-year-old child to obtain a numerical element of 42 and a ten-year-old child to obtain one of 60. If the child obtains a much lower score on the test, it is a sign suggestive of emotional or organic disturbance. A score that is very high, far exceeding expectation, may indicate the use of "protective coloration" by the child. He may be utilizing a kind of cultural role-playing that gives others the impression that he is brighter or more sophisticated than he actually is. This pseudosophistication has often led parents and teachers to assume that the results of the intelligence test were wrong. The KTSA has been used to identify such children who sometimes are able to make an excellent impression on adults so that their lack of real capacity is obscured.

Another value of the KTSA lies in the chance it affords the psychologist to watch the child at work. The repetitive nature of the tasks gives the examiner an opportunity to see whether the child approaches a new situation with initial enthusiasm followed by a loss of interest with resulting deterioration in performance, or whether he maintains good performance throughout. Improvement in the performance of tasks as the child proceeds is related to favorable outcome of therapy and general adjustment. Poor performance in the first arrangement is most common among children having emotional problems. If poor performance is caused by brain damage, there will be no improvement in performance. Even if the child fails to give good reasons for his first and second arrangements, improvement in his future adjustment is predicted if he demonstrates good organizational ability on the test and offers an acceptable reason for having made the final arrangement of objects on the strip. The child's estimate of his ability to replace the objects exactly as he had them before, his associations in the sorting task, and the amount of slanting or orderliness in placing the objects on the strip all play a role in the final evaluation.

APPERCEPTION TESTS

Children who are most severely inhibited are often the ones who project most readily. Apperception tests, which give the child a chance to tell a story, offer an effective method for eliciting information regarding the nature of the child's conflicts and insecurities. Murray's Thematic Apperception Test [272] was designed primarily for adults and older adolescents but is used in child guidance clinics because some children over seven years of age do not identify with pictures of animals in human stances or in ludicrous positions. Other psychologists feel that children can best identify with animals; therefore, they justify the use of pictures such as those in the Children's Apperception Test, which was designed for use with children from three to ten years of age [37].

Apperception tests designed for use with children have experienced increasing popularity. The Michigan Picture Test [170] was designed for use with children from eight to 14 years of age. It consists of 16 pictures: four to be used with boys, four with girls, and eight with boys and girls.

The plates contain figures of children and are structured to elicit reactions toward home and school as well as conflicts regarding adolescence, parents, peers, and sexual drives.

The Symonds' Picture Story Test[360] designed for use with adolescents 12–18 years old depicts young adults in situations that Symonds believed elicit clues regarding the manner in which the client handles hostility, eroticism, moral standards, status drives, guilt, depression, and sublimation.

One of the most effective apperception tests, The Make-A-Picture Story Test (MAPS), developed by Shneidman in 1949[330, 331], permits the client to structure his own thema. Because the test permits manipulation and selection of figures and backgrounds, dynamics may be revealed even if the client blocks verbally. The Shneidman technique consists of 67 cardboard figures—animal and human. There are 22 scenes, representing a large variety of backgrounds, for use with a slotted stage that holds the materials the client selects. The method enables the client to create a psychodrama in which he plays all the roles. The figures include male and female adults, children, persons of various racial groups, legendary and fictitious characters, as well as silhouettes and figures with blank faces. The background scenes include a schoolroom, nursery, bedroom, living room, bathroom, attic, cellar, shanty house, bridge, raft, street, cemetery, forest, cave, doorway, landscapes, and scenes from story books. The test instructions require the client to tell a story about the situation he has created, explain the scene, the selection of characters, and give the outcome of the story. Insight is gained into the client's emotional difficulties and his efforts to handle these. The fact that this technique requires the client to play several roles permits verbalizations that serve to reduce tensions. Therefore, the test has a therapeutic as well as a diagnostic function.

WORLD-BUILDING TECHNIQUES

Other tests exist that permit the child to play and act out a variety of needs and to display his creative imagination. These utilize small life-like objects such as animals, people, houses, and trees. The child is permitted to handle these objects freely and to use them in building a world as he conceives it. Several varieties of toy-world-building techniques are available. The World Test, designed by Buhler and Kelly[61], presents realistic miniature reproductions of a variety of things normally seen by children; they are encouraged to play with these toys in any way they desire. In scoring the test, the examiner notes the type of people, animals, or objects used in the play and analyzes the activity with the aid of a scoring sheet that describes signs of aggressive, empty, or distorted worlds. The Lowenfeld Mosaic Test [240] enables the child to use colors and shapes spontaneously and has some of the advantages of free-association drawings.

The play methods designed for testing the child in the psychologist's office represent a compromise between no play opportunity and the ideal situation of unhampered play with real toys in a room designed for this purpose. Practically all modern, well-equipped, child guidance clinics have one or more rooms in which the psychologist may observe the child's activities through a one-way viewing screen. These rooms are usually stocked with a variety of toys, including large-sized playhorses upon which a child can climb, building blocks, tools, drawing materials, dolls, stuffed animals, and puppets. In the selection of toys and equipment, the age and sex of the child is taken into account in addition to the specific diagnostic and therapeutic problems involved in the case. Some rooms can be prepared for special situations and the toys can then be carefully selected to enable the child to project specific needs or anxieties that the psychologist and his staff wish to study. Thus, a child may find only female puppets in the room or only dolls and baby clothes.

If the child is a member of a play group, sociometric techniques developed by Moreno [266] and others may be used. This method measures attraction and repulsion between individuals in a group and permits the data to be drawn graphically in the form of sociograms that can be examined and studied at a later date. A knowledge of the sociometric status of a child adds another dimension from which the personality of the child may be viewed. Additionally, reports of the child's behavior in the classroom, his academic progress, description of his home adjustment, relationships with other children, his physical health, and the pattern of his growth are all portions of the total fabric that must be studied in its entirety.

Since children are apt to be changeable and unpredictable, the psychologist can obtain a clearer picture if he sees the child several times and under varying circumstances. This is particularly important in cases where the child has a short attention span. For these reasons, it is desirable that not all of the testing be given on a single day. Both parents should be interviewed, if possible, and a case history of their own adjustment should be provided by the social worker.

CHILDREN'S QUESTIONNAIRE

Dr. Kahn has developed 20 questions that have been used in a number of child guidance clinics with children in the five to nine years age group to help discover conflict areas. The questions are:

1. Imagine that you are a magician and could make any changes in the world that you wanted. Tell me whom you would change and how you would change the world.
2. Suppose you could turn people into animals. Tell me what people you would turn into animals and what kind of animals they would be.
3. Name some things that are right to do, things that good people do.
4. Name some things that are wrong to do, things that bad people do.
5. What are you going to be when you grow up?
6. If you were the richest person in the world, name some of the things that you would do with your money. Tell me some of the things you would buy.
7. What kind of things make you feel angry? Happy? Sad?
8. If you had a whole day to do what you wanted, name some of the things you would do.
9. Tell me some of the things you would like to get for Christmas or for your birthday.
10. Who do you like best in your family? Mother? Father? Sister? Brother? Can you tell me why you like this person best?
11. Are you mostly happy? Unhappy?
12. Tell me some things that make you feel afraid. What things scare you? What are you afraid of?
13. Do you think that children in other families are luckier than you? If so, why are they luckier?
14. Could you give me your own idea of why your parents took you to see me?
15. Tell me what is the best thing that ever happened to you. What is the worst thing that ever happened to you?
16. Do you have any secrets that you wouldn't tell anyone? Do you worry about these secret thoughts?
17. What kind of games do you like to play? Would you rather play alone or play with other children?
18. What kind of children do you like to play with most? Boys or girls? Children who are older than you? Children who are younger than you? Children who are your own age? Children who play rough games or children who play quiet games?

19. If you were shipwrecked on a deserted island and could only have one other person with you—whom would you choose? If you could have two persons, three persons, four persons, etc., whom would you choose?

20. I am a psychologist and my job is to help people by trying to understand how they feel. Most of us have some problems and worries, and that is true of people my age as well as of children. I know that you don't really know me very well yet, but let me be your friend. Is there anything that bothers you that you would like to talk about?

Questions such as these supplement, but cannot replace, a thorough and objective description of the environmental pressures and conditions that the child faces. Likewise, an evaluation based on routinely selected psychological tests is insufficient. The psychologist must be aware of the child's social and cultural background as well as his socioeconomic level in order to utilize interview techniques to full advantage. A knowledge of the child's home life is a prerequisite in determining which test materials or test methods are most likely to be successful. A knowledge of his school adjustment helps the psychologist prepare for testing the child's intelligence.

Many times in the course of his evaluation of children, the psychologist will be thrown upon his own resources and will have to create his own methods of best reaching the child with whom he is working. He may have to joke with the child to see how he reacts toward the attempt to be funny. He may have to feign ignorance of a simple question to see whether the child helps him to answer it and to note what the child's reaction is toward an adult who does not appear to know simple answers. In all these probings and play-acting, care must be taken that the psychologist does not lose the child's respect and that the child considers the visit seriously.

For a psychologist to act at times naive, at other times wise, be responsive to needs that may be antisocial in their expression, be an adult, and yet retain enough of childhood for the child to be able to make an identification, requires versatility and flexibility. This together with good testing techniques and an understanding of the emotional and physical growth of children are essential for success in the field of child psychology. The use of well-selected psychological batteries correctly applied and carefully interpreted are of considerable help in the difficult and highly responsible job that falls upon the adult who attempts to understand the current function and the future adjustment of a child.

SUMMARY

Understanding and relating to children requires flexibility and experience. Additionally, clinical psychologists who evaluate children with emotional problems must know how psychological tests can be utilized with a youthful population. This chapter describes a variety of tests and techniques available to the clinical psychologists who work with children. A sample of the type of questions that may be asked to elicit significant information is included.

CHAPTER 5

Normals, Behavioral Disorders, and Differential Diagnosis

The clinical psychologist is often faced with the problem of deciding which of several diagnostic possibilities could most appropriately be applied to describe and communicate the behavioral characteristics of a client. The psychologist's task is further complicated by the fact that his diagnostic impression must be sufficiently discrete to exclude or minimize conflicting possibilities. If there are conflicting impressions, it is his responsibility to account for them systematically and logically and to define their dimensions and their possible consequences. He must justify his use of combined categories such as neurosis-with-behavior-disorder or schizo-affective-psychosis and explain why there is overlapping. In cases where test results contradict each other, he must account for what he finds and suggest a tentative conclusion. It is easy to report the presence of a little of everything and thus evade the challenge of diagnosis.

The psychologist must at all times be aware of what can be expected of the normal person. In his eagerness to rule out one classification or another, he may forget that there is also the category of normalcy. Psychologists who work in psychiatric clinics or hospitals may succumb to a mental set where they exclude normalcy as a possibility. This is because the so-called "base rate" or rate of expectancy does not include completely normal people in the zone of consideration. Nevertheless, if one fails to be aware of normalcy, can one be truly cognizant of abnormalcy? What, then, can a psychologist expect as signs or evidence of normalcy on the part of a client?

NORMALS AND NORMALCY

Normals are people who conform to "normalcy." Normalcy is defined by each individual culture or social milieu. It is easy to recognize the fact that normalcy among people in a Brazilian jungle differs from normalcy in New York City. It is more difficult to remember that there can also be a wide spread in the definition of normalcy within the same national boundaries or even within the limits of the same city, such as New York's Park Avenue and its Lower East Side. A person who is well-adjusted in the hill country may test as schizoid when compared to people living in an adjacent valley. In considering normalcy, therefore, it is important that the psychological examiner is acquainted with concepts drawn from sociology and anthropology. In some universities the emphasis in training psychologists is placed on the physical sciences, mathematics, and statistics, sometimes at the expense of the all-important social sciences. The authors believe that the understanding of an individual requires the understanding of the culture in which he lives. This can be facilitated by a knowledge of history and by the exploration of other cultures, past and present.

Within our own culture, "normal" implies capacity to effectively function and obtain satisfaction in three primary life areas: (1) home area, including marriage, sex, children; (2) job or vocational area, enabling a person to obtain a feeling of contribution to society through work; and (3) community area local, national, and international—ranging from the satisfaction derived from friendships with neighbors to concern regarding the welfare of the entire human species. Normalcy can also be conceptualized negatively. We can say that an individual is normal if he functions in a given society without getting into trouble; if neither he nor anyone else feels that he should be treated for a psychological disorder; and if he is able to refrain from the use of psychotic defenses and the overuse of neurotic ones. In short, we could call a person normal if he remains psychiatrically asymptomatic.

By virtue of the negative definition, the psychologist faces a dilemma when testing for normalcy. On psychological tests, a normal person may occasionally show neurotic and even some psychotic signs. This usually is unexpected by psychologists who have never had occasion to thoroughly test a group of persons judged to be normal. The authors have experienced this situation when one of the research projects in which they participated called for the examination of normal populations. When reviewing the records of such persons, one had the feeling that some of the members of these groups should not have been included in a normal population in view of the fact that their test records elicited a number of pathological responses. It is easy for the psychologist, under such circumstances, to think, "Ah, wait and see—some day they will have their nervous breakdowns." But a follow-up at a later date might show that the prediction was wrong. The authors have long ago come to the conclusion that "normal is what normal does," regardless of the disturbing images reflected on the psychological tests, as long as these are not expressed in terms of overt behavioral manifestations. Differentiation between normals and psychotics is possible, however, because of the signs of strength in normal test records that are lacking among psychotics. In our present limited state of knowledge, we must define being normal as *acting* normal even if this "normalcy" is only a mask that successfully hides from view a multitude of inner pathological impulses. If it were not for this point of view, we might have to admit that normalcy represents one of the rarest of the behavioral categories.

Rorschach [317] Indicators of Normalcy

We must not consider the task of delineating the normal or normal-acting individual as something current psychological tests are not designed to do. Although psychologists are generally trained to detect pathology, almost every psychological instrument can be used to give an indication of normalcy. At times, the psychologist himself may become the subjective yardstick of normal behavior. If a client's actions and test responses match his own, the client may be called mentally "healthy" by the psychologist. To avoid such pitfalls, Klopfer [217] and others have described the expected Rorschach pattern of the normal person in Fig. 5.1 and have justified this pattern with good logical theory but with little empirical support.

Analyzing Fig. 5.1, we note that the normal person is pictured as having a goodly amount of creative imagination and capacity for forming interpersonal relationships (M, human movement). He is able to express primitive instinctual drives (FM, animal movement), but these expressions do not outweigh the indices for control (M and F, good form) as is the case among persons who are emotionally immature. Emotional tensions (m, inanimate movement) are minimal. Signs of basic instability (K, shading such as clouds) and anxiety (k, shading such as X-ray) are absent. There are no responses suggestive of gross sensuality and nonsocialized behavior (c,

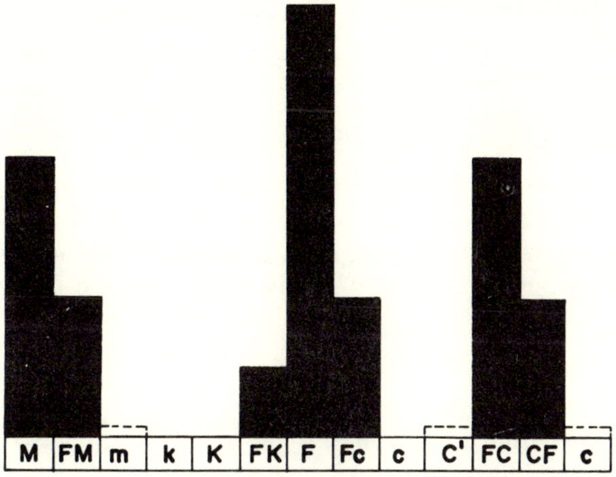

Fig. 5.1 The normal Rorschach psychogram. From T. C. Kahn and M. B. Giffen. *Psychological Techniques in Diagnosis and Evaluation.* Oxford: Pergamon Press, 1960.

shading as texture). Past emotional trauma leave their traces lightly (C′, achromatic color). As a whole, the normal personality is dominated by perceptual level, contact with reality, stability, and basic intelligence (F, good form). There is also a capacity for insight and introspection (FK, shading as vistas or reflections) as well as tact and an awareness of the environment (F, shading as surface appearance, fur, rug, etc.). Finally, the normal person is expected to demonstrate ability for appropriate affective response without loss of spontaneity, warmth, and artistic creativity (CF, color with good form). He can be impulsive and explosive (C, color with form disregarded), although this trend is minimal and held in check by controls that were discussed previously.

The Kahn Test of Symbol Arrangement (KTSA) [197]

It has recently been found by Craddick and L'Abate [89] that this test describes the normal person in a somewhat different manner than other tests. The two basic approaches to performance on the KTSA consist of emphasis on form and meaning. Three main types of form orientations are possible:

1. Form concept confined to the objects used on the test only ("D").
2. Form of the test objects applied to things in the world outside the test ("X").

3. Form consideration with emphasis on the colors ("F") or shape and appearance of the test objects ("E"). These represent sensual subjective reaction to appearance.

Also, there are three basic meaning orientations:

1. Meaning with substance, representing partial emancipation from form ("Y").
2. Pure meaning, representing total emancipation from form ("Z").
3. Autistic meaning, representing distortion of form concepts ("A").

Autistic meaning represents conceptualizations that are unintelligible because they are private to the person having them. Since the common symbolic meanings of the test objects are generally used as a way of communication within a given culture, the client's responses on the KTSA reflect his acceptance of cultural norms unless he deliberately ignores cultural tradition or is incapable of grasping the significance of these norms. Normalcy, therefore, excludes the use of "A" responses except among young children, where autism represents the development of early psychic ideational processes. Empirical evidence indicates that "Z" responses are common among intelligent normals [89]. "D" is seldom used; "Y" is present, with a moderate number of perceptive "E" and artistic "F" responses. As will be mentioned in the chapter on neurosis, an overabundance of "Y" is not a sign of good adjustment. Reality discernment "Y" should not outweigh idealism and active imagination "Z."

The Minnesota Multiphasic Personality Inventory (MMPI) [173]

Primarily, the MMPI is a measure used for the screening of emotionally disturbed individuals, the assessment of symptoms and the severity of symptoms in pathology. Therefore, little research has been carried out on the test on normal profiles and personality characteristics. Kleinmuntz [216] notes that the MMPI has been used in a variety of settings: educational (high school and college), military, industrial, etc. However, most of the studies deal with the prediction or analysis of emotional disorders or adjustment problems. The quantitative scoring system on the MMPI utilizes a mean of 50 and a standard deviation of 10; therefore, a scale score of 50 would indicate a hypothetical average or "normal" score. As a rule of thumb, T scores above 70 reflect pathology; therefore, the range for normals would be T scores ranging from 50 to 70. T scores falling below 50 must be interpreted according to the individual scale[156]. The 70 cut-off is certainly not a hard and fast rule, as many normals have at least one scale above 70[156]. Guedre and Reed state that one normal in 33 receives a T score above 70 on any single scale, although the chance of a normal receiving two scores above 70 is less than one in 1000, and the probability of three scores above 70 for a normal is one in 35,937[156]. As the number of T scores above 70 increases, the probability of pathology increases, although even at this score normality cannot be totally rejected.

One new trend in profile analysis—computer interpretation—has the potentiality for normal profile assessment. The capacity of computers to handle data lends itself to the construction of norms for general (normal) profile populations. Such programs as the Mayo Clinic Automated MMPI, currently produces descriptions of normal personality characteristics from profile scores. For example, a male with a raw score (K corrected) of 19 (T = 56) is described as a person "with normal energy and activity levels"[286]. A general description is also available for other clinical scales. There are several experimental scales reported by this computer service and, while most of these are oriented toward pathology, they do provide such scales as "Social Responsibility" and "Status," which seem to reflect normal personality characteristics. Thus, it appears that it may be possible to build new scales for normals.

It should also be noted that other tests have been derived from the MMPI with some designed for normal populations, such as the California Psychological Inventory (CPI)[151]. Gough developed this test specifically as a measure of normal personality characteristics. He selected roughly half of the test items used in the CPI from the MMPI, utilizing objective scoring procedures, standard score format for profiles, and other characteristics of the MMPI. (He actually made improvements over many MMPI procedures.) The CPI has been called possibly the best personality measure of its type[216]. Perhaps the efforts that would be involved in producing normal profiles utilizing the MMPI may be of little value since other comparable measures designed specifically for this purpose are available.

CREATIVITY

If "normal" means "average"—or behavior that approximates a norm—then "abnormal" includes above average as well as below average. Because of this, the term "normal" has come into disrepute. There is increasing evidence that future testing will concentrate on the abnormal person who falls to the right of the average or middle, as it has in the past concerned itself almost exclusively with those who fell to the left of this hypothetical midpoint. In a highly specialized civilization such as ours, there is increasing need to identify and attempt to understand the intellectually and creatively superior person.

It may be interesting to observe at the present juncture what psychologists can offer in their attempt to discover the talent of creative leadership. One of the first things that might come to mind is the idea of high IQ. There is considerable evidence to show that exceptionally brilliant persons do not score particularly high on standard intelligence tests. Some talents are so specialized that an IQ test is unable to measure them. It has been found that projective tests such as the Rorschach, Mosaic, Thematic Apperception, and the KTSA are more sensitive instruments for the identification of genius. (We do not mean "genius" as defined by high scores on IQ tests.) Some tentative signs suggestive of exceptional intellectual brilliance follow.

The Rorschach

1. A large percentage of whole card responses when these responses represent effective integration of smaller detail concepts. This is sometimes called "Z" tendency on the Rorschach Test and is not usually reflected in formal scoring.

2. A large percentage of good original responses. Original responses or non-populars are those that are not seen by the average person.

Either one of the above patterns may be suggestive of unusual ability. In each case, we would expect the presence of some color-dominated responses (CF), which would indicate sufficient lability and drive stemming from instinctual needs (FM). This creates sufficient tension to motivate the person to seek release through creative activity (M).

The Lowenfeld Mosaic Test [240] and Thematic Apperception Test (TAT) [272]

On the Mosaic Test, we would expect the use of many colors and the construction of a complete and highly imaginative scene. Thematic Tests also permit free reign of the imagination. Both kinds of tests are capable of eliciting a range of imaginative conceptualizations verbally expressed.

The Kahn Test of Symbol Arrangement

In general, on this test we would expect greatest emphasis to be on "Z" (highest level of abstraction) in the symbolization. Among creative physical scientists, "E" (form and construction of the test objects) would probably be prominent. Color "F" would be present among creative artists. The exceptionally gifted individual would have a minimum number of "C" (same as before) responses, since his versatility would enable him to vary his performance creatively. He might connect the various objects logically to make a story or to describe some events in his life. At least one of the arrangements would probably be based on similar shapes "E" but usually another concept would be incorporated into this idea so that similar shapes would be only one of the factors contributing to the type of arrangement made. "I put all similar shapes *and* colors together." Since there are thousands of different ways in which the objects can be combined on the strip, the client has considerable opportunity to use his imagination and demonstrate his individuality [200].

In spite of the theoretical considerations of how the person with superior creative endowment may act when confronted with psychological tests, there is no real evidence available as yet on this subject. The isolated studies that have been made on creativity manifested on tests are too few in number and too limited in scope to be conclusive. More research is needed in order to fully explore the study of superior creative ability.

BEHAVIORAL DISORDERS

We must not assume that a person with high intellectual endowment will necessarily be motivated to use it for the benefit of mankind. A consideration of the manner in which we use our abilities brings us face to face with another area of psychological exploration. At the risk of oversimplication, we may say that the normal person directs his aggressive drives primarily toward the outside world and in the process diverts them into socially acceptable outlets and activities. The neurotic tends to invert these drives so that they are directed at the self instead of at the outside world and they become self-punishing with resulting symptomatology. If the neurotic mechanisms are non-somatizing, the expression of the neurotic impulses may be reflected outwardly as projections of the self. Manifestations of these impulses are found in obsessions, over-identifications, compulsions, repressions, and emotional blockings.

Among nonpsychotics who do not use self as a target, there remains only one other avenue for the dissipation of psychic pressure. For these people, society or the representatives of society become the primary target of their drives. Kindled by anxieties and nurtured by aggression, they spend themselves in seeking retribution for the frustration that life imposes. Those who use society instead of self as their target are referred to as having a behavioral or character disorder. They are sometimes visualized as lacking a superego or conscience. They are amoral, opportunistic, and can be quite clever. The range of behavioral symptomatology of behavioral disorders is vast.

Most projective and some objective tests offer signs typical of behavioral disorders. However, the client's case history is the most effective tool for the identification of these conditions. One danger of relying solely on the interview and the case history is that some of these persons are able to dissimulate their true nature. As a matter of fact, this very act of dissimulating and denying or disguising aggression constitutes one of the recognized symptoms of a specific sociopathic personality type.

The Wechsler Scales [385, 387]

The practical matter of identifying persons with behavioral defects by psychological tests involves speculations regarding how humans develop behavioral problems. One explanation is that some types of behavioral symptoms stem from mental deficiency. On the Wechsler Scales, the expected psychograph for adolescent delinquents has low scores in the following subtests: information, comprehension, arithmetic, digit span, similarity. This contrasts with relatively high scores on the performance tasks. Mental defectives without prominent behavioral symptoms appear to obtain relatively higher verbal subscores (compared to the average of all their subscores) than delinquents. Wechsler points out that "the most outstanding single feature of the sociopath's (delinquent) test profile is his systematic high score of performance as compared to the verbal part of the scale" [387]. Wechsler also noted that "comparison is frequently made between intellectual understanding and affective acceptance of conventional behavior" [387].

The Kahn Test of Symbol Arrangement

Since acceptance of the norms of conventional behavior is reflected by the acceptance or rejection of socially formed symbols, it is not surprising to discover that tests such as the KTSA elicit typical response patterns from sociopaths. The manual for the test[198] lists 20 symbolizations commonly used by persons having behavioral disorders. When taking this test, this group is apt to slant the objects when placing them on the strip. The composite test score falls into a characteristic symbol pattern in which "X" responses dominate. Thus, "X" responses are more frequent than "Y" or "Z" responses—the latter categories representing higher forms of abstractions. It is of interest to note that the symbol pattern most frequently produced by persons suffering from behavioral disorders resembles the one associated with children eight to 12 years of age. This raises the question as to whether the social development of the sociopaths was arrested at this level of maturity. Kipper[214] has done some revealing work using this test with habitual criminals by comparing them to non-criminal groups. Wagner[378] has done research with the levels of symbolizations in adolescent adjustment problems and has identified typical symbol patterns of youngsters with behavioral difficulties.

The Rorschach

The sociopath shows his lack of motivation by his typically low number of responses on this test. The record is often constricted by emphasis on form (usually poor form) given with little elaboration. "Maps," "designs," and other evasive responses are frequent. Primitive concepts such as "clouds," "rocks," or "scenery" are also encountered. Often there are no human concepts, but, if present, animal movement almost always outnumbers human movement. Responses in which color dominates (CF) are more frequent than those in which color is incidental to form (FC). Callous use of color or color-naming may occur. Sociopaths seldom give any well-thought-out original responses on the Rorschach. Instead, they may see the common, popular, and banal things. They emphasize very obvious forms such as the wings on Card V or the animals on Card VIII. Anatomical responses seen by these persons often take the form of crude sexual preoccupations, such as an X-ray of the pelvis or a "rear end." These may take on a sadomasochistic coloring in cases where there are acting-out potentialities. Frequently, they reject one or more cards with verbalizations suggesting suspiciousness or egocentricity. The use of white areas on the cards to form concepts is sometimes associated with oppositional and negativistic feelings on the part of the client.

The Thematic Apperception Test

Just as the sociopath performs the "easy way," expending a minimum of effort on the Rorschach, he describes effortless accomplishments on the part of the figures he sees in the Thematic Apperception Test. On this test, he indicates his conviction that this is a "dog-eat-dog" world and that ruthlessness and strength lead to success. There is no place for ethics in this world; people suffer solely because they fail to use their wits in destroying the evidence of their antisocial acts. High ambitions may be ascribed to the central figure. These ambitions will not be achieved by hard work but by "getting the breaks" or "knowing the right people." Sociopaths show little emotion or concern with the fate of persons depicted as grief-stricken or forlorn. Instead, emphasis is always on how these people got into trouble and what means they find to extricate themselves. Authority figures are typically seen as cynical and selfish, and women are seen as weak or despicable. However, much depends on the type of behavioral difficulty with which we are dealing. Sociopaths with prominent passive or dependent orientations will offer concepts that are quite different from those with aggressive acting-out potential. These, in turn, will differ from the concepts of persons who cover their antisocial feelings by a screen of overconformity to social norms. In the latter case, the heroes depicted on the TAT are often true Sir Galahads who are too noble and free from fault to be realistically human.

The Minnesota Multiphasic Personality Inventory

The MMPI has been used effectively to screen this type of population. As with all paper-and-pencil questionnaires, the possibility exists that the client may slant his responses in order to make the best impression on the examiner. On the MMPI, there are certain built-in safeguards to warn the interpreter that the responses lack validity. Nevertheless, there is the question of how effectively the safeguards operate. When the test signs indicate that the client has faked, we are left with little to guide us in regard to the direction and nature of the malingering. In spite of these objections, a high Pd (psychopathic deviate) score on the MMPI and projective test indicators of antisocial personality are frequently found together in clinical experience. According to Hathaway and McKinley, the Pd scale on the MMPI "measures the similarity of the subject to a group of persons whose main difficulty lies in their absence of deep emotional responses, their inability to profit from experience, and their disregard of social mores"[172]. This description fits the picture of the sociopath as identified by other tests. Social development has been defective because of a specific type of intellectual lag or because of faulty symbol formation involving cultural norms.

DIFFERENTIAL DIAGNOSIS

The questions that psychologists are required to help answer usually consist of locating one of several possible underlying causes for the client's symptoms or behavioral characteristics. For example, psychiatrists who refer cases for psychological evaluation may be looking for evidence to help decide whether their client has primarily a behavioral problem or a neurotic one. Or the question may be asked whether a client's excitement is part of a schizophrenic process or a manic-depressive psychosis. Other common questions are: Can the symptoms be explained on the basis of neurosis or is there an incipient psychosis present that may become more virulent with time? Can the client's behavior be attributed to schizophrenia alone or are there some organic concomitants? Similarly, the teacher referring a child to the school psychologist may ask: Is the boy's troublesome behavior in the classroom ascribable to emotional immaturity, to lack of sufficient intelligence to keep up with the class work, or to serious family problems at home?

Because there is always a qualitative factor involved in the evaluation of a human being, psychologists cannot dispense with personal judgment. The trouble with the strictly quantitative "cookbook" approach to human evaluation is that we are dealing with the cooks themselves rather than with the ingredients of their stews and puddings. No mechanical guide exists that can tell the psychologist what resources he must draw on to extract a sound clinical impression. Variation of methods frequently occurs from client to client, depending on individual circumstances. When the total resources available to the psychologist are used, overlapping signs are not as perplexing as they might appear at first. For example, clients with brain damage and certain types of schizophrenics may offer similar concrete behavior in their solution to the Goldstein-Scheerer Tests of Abstract and Concrete Thinking[147]. Although test performance of these two groups is at times indistinguishable, a differential impression may be obtained by the fact that this concreteness by organics exists among those who show relatively few other clinical signs of disturbed personality and little general deterioration behaviorally. Schizophrenics who exhibit this identical degree of concreteness on the test behaviorally demonstrate considerable deterioration. In order to form an impression in cases such as these, the psychologist must be aware of the client's case history and his observed behavior.

Consistency

Consistency of evidence presents somewhat less of a problem. Let us assume that six tests are administered in a psychological battery and on all but one of these the responses indicate signs of behavioral disorder. No signs are found indicating pathology of a more serious nature. Signs of other conditions such as neurosis are scattered and weak. The psychologist can then report that the testing elicited responses suggestive of a behavioral condition and that the test battery was consistent with the exception of one test in reflecting the expected indicators of this condition. He must account for the presence of the inconclusive signs and offer an explanation for the fact that one of the tests failed to suggest any signs of behavioral disorder. Perhaps the psychologist had noted that the client was getting tired when this test was given. Perhaps rapport had not yet been established. It is also possible that the test was not sophisticated enough to pick up the condition.

In spite of the fact that consistency of trends is an important requirement for the formulation of clinical impressions, relatively little research has been done in this area. Most psychological test research concerns itself solely with one test at a time. Tests are then criticized if they fail to measure up to statistical expectations. However, even trends that are not statistically significant in themselves may be valuable in diagnosis when the information they provide is integrated into a diagnostic impression involving not one but several different kinds of psychological tests.

Test Battery

The test battery must be chosen with care and the materials used for testing must represent sufficient variety to enable an assessment of different approaches to the study of the client's personality. It is suggested that the battery include objects that the client can freely manipulate—for example, the three-dimensional materials that some tests provide. These should be utilized in addition to paper-and-pencil and visually oriented tests printed on cards such as the Rorschach and Thematic Apperception Test. A variety of materials is important since persons react differently to different kinds of stimuli. Physiological and psychological factors determine whether verbal, visual, or manipulative tests are most suitable for eliciting information from a specific client. When the test situation is limited to one medium or dimension, opportunities for obtaining accurate results may have been minimized.

The evaluator should not hesitate to admit that signs are inconclusive and conflicting. Psychologists realize that sometimes they can only confirm the therapist's dilemma in regard to formulating a diagnosis and suggestions for subsequent treatment. However, even this has its value, for it will establish the presence of conflicting and puzzling aspects in the case and will suggest that the therapist has not overlooked anything that could have contributed to a diagnostic solution. It rarely occurs that the psychologist is unable to throw some light on the problem. Even if a client fails to respond to the majority of the test stimuli that the psychologist offers, this unwillingness or lack of capacity to respond constitutes a valuable diagnostic aid. This is especially true if the client reacts to some stimuli but not to others.

Finally, the psychologist should use caution in coming to any conclusion on the basis of his expectations of what kinds of responses the client "ought" to produce. On the Rorschach, the assumption that the client will respond in a stereotyped manner to such stimuli on Cards IV and VII (so-called Father and Mother image cards) is one of the many concepts in impressionistic psychology that should be regarded with caution. If we consider only what is referred to as "card-pull" (the power of the materials to stimulate characteristic responses), we would not have sufficient grounds for assuming that certain cards represent parental or authority figures. Neither the hugeness, blackness, and strength implied in Card IV nor the vague femininity reflected on Card VII would be enough to elicit the expected responses were it not for "client-push," which is independent of "card-pull." Every person has a need to give expression to emotional drives and release disturbing thoughts. The "client-push" reinforced by "card-pull" (or its equivalent in other tests than the Rorschach) combine forces to give significant meaning to the test responses. It is the pressure of psychic drives or "client-push" seeking an outlet that causes the client to give expression to his fears, anxieties, and resentments. His needs are like those of a river pursuing a course down a mountain without a suitable path in which to run. The river flows even in the absence of a good river bed. So it is with the client's stream of thoughts. His need to express himself often causes him to offer dynamically meaningful responses even when the pull of the materials used may be relatively weak or unsuitable. However, this in no way implies that the choice of stimuli materials is not important. Even the pull of gravity cannot overcome some obstacles. A careful selection of test materials is essential to insure the smooth and unhampered flow of dynamically significant material.

BEHAVIORAL ASSESSMENT

The medically oriented diagnostic nomenclature utilized by the American Psychiatric Association (APA) has long been the accepted terminology of psychological assessment. The APA's elaborate system of pathological typologies sometimes supported by specific dynamic characteristics has generally been accepted as the proper method of diagnosis. This has led to the creation of a language peculiar to the mental health profession and has added a certain character of mystique to therapeutic practice.

Within the last two decades, there has been increasing interest in the evolution of an alternative method of assessment. This is particularly true among psychologists who identify with learning theory and a behaviorally oriented model. The inception of this movement was reviewed by Brown[58]. He mentions that *The Annual Review of Psychology* published in 1950 shows that early efforts were directed toward the explanation of a therapeutic approach based on specific learning theories. The following year Hathaway made the prediction that "if psychotherapy were to be identified as an educative process,... psychology might undergo a kind of renaissance as a basic science to the practice of psychological healing" [58]. As Brown[58] points out, this may have been an accurate prediction of the current popularity of behavioral assessment and the treatment methods of behavior modification.

In 1952 Eysenck[114] published his article on the evaluation of psychotherapy, which touched off a professional tumult that still continues to ferment and grow. This and other subsequent publications by Eysenck provided much impetus for the continuing development of behavioral assessment and treatment. Wolpe's work was recognized in the 1950s although, as one author noted, it probably had little input on the practitioners who were still mainly involved with more traditional approaches. It was not until the late 1950s that learning-theory-based assessment and methods of psychotherapy became recognized as a total treatment modality. At that time, this approach was still out of the mainstream of psychological practice and the more traditional psychoanalytical methods continued to be widely used. Behavioral approaches became more accepted in the middle 1960s. Data were being amassed that challenged the accuracy of the typological diagnoses and the universality of the analytic personality theories; studies measuring the evaluation and effectiveness of a variety of treatments seemed to give some support to the behavioral approach.

As mentioned previously, behaviorists have frequently attacked traditional therapy systems, claiming the following:

1. Failure of the traditional model to demonstrate a universal diagnostic procedure; experienced diagnosticians using the American Psychological Association format have demonstrated difficulty concurring on a diagnosis when rating the same clients [382].
2. Failure of the nosological model to relate directly to prognosis and treatment procedures.
3. Failure of the model to provide a functional theory of personality that allows for prediction of behavior. The typical dynamic theory is not particularly designed for prediction of specific behavior, whereas the learning theory model specifies behavior in such a way that prediction is possible.
4. Failure of the medical model to clearly delineate diagnostic typologies with the use of symptomatologies unique to the particular diagnosis. The amount of overlap of stated symptoms shared by various diagnostic categories can be extremely confusing. When describing a certain client, it may be necessary to add so many qualifying statements to the diagnosis that the original etiological definition may be lost in the addendums. Clear-cut behavioral symptoms that manifest themselves in the environment are rare and this leads to scorer confusion in view of the artificial boundaries of the diagnosis [291].
5. Failure to provide specified criteria for evaluation of the therapeutic process. This would include such areas as outcome (were the results effective?), process (what happens during therapy?), and the interrelationships between client and therapist.

The behaviorists claim that assessment programs based on learning theory have the following attributes, as summarized by Brown [58]:

1. Greater effectiveness as a treatment method; better chances for success.

2. Greater efficiency as a treatment method; providing results in fewer sessions.
3. Greater specificity in establishing goals and outcomes of therapy; predicted goals are established before onset of therapy.
4. Greater applicability to a larger population since the approach is useful in changing all learned maladaptive behaviors.
5. Greater utilization as a treatment method because of the simplicity of techniques.

The criticism and claims of behavioral therapists are particularly cogent considering the virtual infancy of the movement. There is little doubt that the behavioral concept to evaluation and treatment provides a serious challenge to the more traditional methods of assessment and therapy. At this point, it would be helpful to review some of the basic premises of the model and to describe the methods of behavioral assessment.

Behaviorists start with the assumption that virtually all behavior (whether it be considered adaptive or maladaptive) is learned in accordance with basic principles established by various learning theories [327]. A behavior is defined as adaptive or maladaptive by the environmental milieu in which it is emitted. This is why universal terms that describe a pathological typology by established symptoms become virtually meaningless.

The behaviorists have designed a method of assessment unique to the learning theory model. The major goal is to rid the client of maladaptive behavior, which the therapist categorizes as surplus or deficient [327]. He may also add together the client's behavioral assets—those behaviors that bring about reinforcement from his environment and are already part of the client's present repertoire of behaviors.

If the client has demeaned himself by actions that were inappropriate, irresponsible, or ineffective (typically resulting in sanctions), then the behavior is classified as superfluous, excessive, or maladaptive. The client's behavior must then be changed. This requires a form of extinction of inappropriate responses and the relearning of more suitable methods of responding. Behavioral deficits are usually observed in situations where the client fails to demonstrate an approved behavioral pattern. This is a result of his failure to learn appropriate responses. Thus, the absence of these behaviors prevents the client from acting in an appropriate manner and these acts are then viewed as maladaptive [327]. Behavioral assets can be identified by noting what the client does well and using these particular traits or talents that he demonstrates as behavior that could be termed "adequate" within his social milieu.

The behavioral therapist usually begins with a thorough study of his client, collecting demographic data primarily through interviews and observations. The focus of the interview does not follow the general pattern of a traditional psychiatric method. Information is gathered about the client's problem as it is seen within an environmental setting. In other words, an evaluation of the existing behavior is made and the maladaptive behavior is identified with recommendations regarding what specific changes are needed to correct this situation. No effort is made to discover underlying "causes" or hidden, repressed meanings. Behaviorists simply concentrate on the observable maladaptive behavior (sometimes referred to as symptoms).

Observations are made by the therapist during initial interviews; however, most observational information is collected by cooperative individuals who have direct contact with the client (such as parents, spouse, employer, friends, etc.), including all those who might be considered important in the client's life and who, in fact, will become sources of reinforcement during treatment. Some behaviorists, such as Wolpe, have been known to utilize psychological tests to add and support many of these naturalistic findings, although this is not, at present, a common practice.

When these data are assimilated and synthesized, a behavioral assessment is made and a treatment program is initiated. The specific technique that the therapist will use depends somewhat on his theoretical orientation and his designed treatment program. Generally, he first peruses the antecedents of the maladaptive behavior. This is done to discover environmental conditions that have led to these deviant responses. He investigates the conditions under which the behavior is emitted, thus observing those factors that reinforce and maintain the undesirable responses. Finally, he considers the consequences of the maladaptive behavior so that he may select a treatment program that will rid his client of unwanted responses while introducing acceptable ones. There is little doubt that the keys to the assessment are the reinforcing agents that propagate the maladaptive behavior. Without a knowledge of their interaction, it would be extremely difficult to bring about an appropriate change.

Examples of Behavioral Assessment Systems

With this general outline as a guide, it would now seem useful to explain two different approaches that utilize behavioral assessment. We will not go into treatment procedures in order to avoid repetition, since an example is given in Chapter 9. These approaches have no formal names and their selection should not be considered as suggesting that they are "the" most acceptable. They were chosen to give the reader an idea of how such an assessment is carried out.

One such program has been described by Peterson in his book, *The Clinical Study of Social Behavior* [291]. He suggests that the therapist can first initiate an assessment program by utilizing observational techniques. Behavioral observations are typically done with the use of rating scales or check lists by observers who have close contact with the client. The combined ratings are then compared for commonality and occurrence of problem behaviors in environmental situations. Peterson points out that the goal of this type of observation is a record of the functional analysis of behavior of the client. A functional analysis requires both the identification of dependent variables (behavior of the client) and independent variables (the external conditions of which behavior is a function) [291]. In a clinical setting, a functional analysis requires systematic reports of observation of the problem behavior as it existed prior to treatment and, specifically, the stimulus conditions preceding and following the maladaptive behavior. After the identification of these criteria, manipulation of conditions related to the behavior is attempted and, finally, changes in behaviors following treatment are recorded [291].

A second procedure of behavioral assessment is the interview. This appears to be a technique used by most therapists, although the structure of the interview varies. Peterson lists three basic facets of clinical interviewing: the form, the content, and the relationship between client and therapist. The behaviorally oriented practitioner usually uses a semistructured interview that allows some client spontaneity yet provides enough guidance for specified information gathering. The content of the interview must elicit explicit information concerning the antecedent, current, and predicted conditions in which the maladaptive behavior has been learned [291]. Peterson points out that the interview extends to "significant others." This group provides information about the client and gives the therapist additional knowledge of his client's environment and the important others that interact within these surroundings. Peterson points out that this may be a long and tedious process, but it is ultimately worthwhile.

The internal content of the interview is separated into four phases: the scanning operation—which is basically information gathered from the client and significant others; the extended inquiry—which includes more detail about the client and significant others; and the periodic reappraisal—which functions as a measure and direction of change during treatment. A follow-up is used to test the effect and permanence of the behavioral modification.

The interpersonal relationship between client and therapist is extremely important. Peterson feels that the therapist should consult a demographic profile of his client prior to an interview. According to him, failure to do this reflects a lack of interest and affects the harmony of the interview. He feels that the therapist must have a quality of expertise, honest interest, and must establish an atmosphere of common courtesy. The therapist should try to gain the most accurate account of the maladaptive behavior as reported by the client.

The final phase of behavioral assessment as described by Peterson is defined as experimental analysis of behavior. This implies that behavior will be deliberately and systematically changed. The actual techniques to bring this about vary, depending on the orientation of the behavioral therapist; however, in most cases, observations are made, interviews are completed, behavior to be changed is specified, and stimulus conditions are manipulated to bring about more acceptable responses. (See section on behavior modification in Chapter 9.)

Peterson cautions that this particular model is limited by the complexity of the client's behavioral repertoire. The identification of stimuli that are maintaining the maladaptive behavior probably is intertwined in the client's environmental milieu. Another limitation is classified as ethical, since the experimental changes brought about by the therapist must be beneficial to the client and to the society of which the client is a part. In summary, the strengths of this approach appear to be in the unification of assessment and treatment, where maladaptive behaviors are explained in terms of learning principles and, in turn, the new behaviors are established utilizing the identical learning principles that were used in identifying the original maladaptive behavior.

Another approach that appears to be more technical in procedure is that devised by Kanfer and Saslow. Kanfer first defined behavior with the use of a sophisticated operant stimulus-response model:

(S)—Stimulus: antecedent events
(R)—Response: observed behaviors
(K)—Contingency: schedules of contingency-related conditions
(C)—Consequence: events following R
(O)—Organism: biological condition of the organism [207]

Other characteristics of behavior are also stated as support and explanations of the basic model. Utilizing this approach to understand the behavior, a program is then constructed to "control the patient's environment, or one which enables the client to control his own behavior . . . so that the present problem is resolved" [208].

Typical of the operant model is an additional step that includes an evaluation of the client's ability to continue his readjustment within the environment without the aid of therapeutic treatment. This may necessitate changing the behavior of "important others" and placing control on the sources of reinforcement found in this environment. Thus, the approach demands a more active involvement by the therapist, particularly outside the therapeutic setting. As Kanfer and Saslow point out, the therapist is not only involved in treatment, he also plays an active role in environmental intervention and the total life pattern of the client. This action may, in fact, be more economical and less time-consuming than traditional methods since the therapist can utilize other treatment sources in the client's environment that can continue intervention and control after formal therapy has terminated. This approach functions primarily as a basis for "making decisions on specific therapeutic interventions regardless of the presenting problem" [208]. Such assessment systems allow the therapist to make decisions on the type and pattern of intervention, goals for treatment, and specific methods to be used. The following is an outline and brief discussion of this behavioral assessment system.

Much like Peterson, these authors begin with a preliminary or, as they term it, an initial analysis of the problem. Precipitating behaviors (problematic) are determined and are classified as to whether they are excessive or defective. If a behavior is termed excessive, the therapist determines frequency, intensity, and duration, and what behaviors successfully sanction the excessive behavior. If the behavior fails to occur (deficit), the therapist must determine societal expectations, needed frequency of response, and the appropriate form of the behavior. While classifying behaviors, the therapist also notes behavioral assets in the client's repertoire that can be used as sources of reinforcement or as vehicles for obtaining social reinforcement.

Specific problems are studied according to intensity and how objectionable the behavior has become. The therapist may also determine the "important others" who find the behavior objectionable and the consequences that have come about because of it. He must also weigh the effect of removal of the problem behavior (as this may be more detrimental than the precipitating problem) and decide whether the removal might lead to new and more devastating behavioral consequences. Finally, the therapist must determine just how much responsibility the client can share in planning the treatment procedure.

As a problem analysis, the therapist then studies the motivational level of his client to discover what kinds of things will maintain new behavior in order to utilize their reinforcing capacity. He must objectively measure the frequency and regularity of these stimuli and in what environmental situations they occur. Depending upon the problem, the therapist might want to use aversive stimuli that exist in the client's present repertoire to extinguish maladaptive behavior or his goal may be to remove current aversive stimuli that maintain the behavioral problem. In either case, these are sources of motivation and must be catalogued.

The next step in this behavioral assessment system measures the developmental functions of the client. This is divided into three categories: biological, sociological, and behavioral functions. Probably the most limiting in treatment as far as the therapist is concerned is biological function. He must take into account his client's biological limitations and resources. If there have been severe physical limitations, the consequences must be weighed in the client's life-style and self-attitude.

Since treatment is contingent upon understanding the environment, the therapist must take into account the characteristics of the client's social structure. Probably the most important feature is the congruency of the client's attitudes and those of his environment. He must determine if the precipitating problems are directly affected by the culture and, if so, whether corrections can be introduced in the total treatment modality.

Within the realm of developmental analysis, the therapist also scrutinizes specific behavioral changes that are deviant from social norms or those that are uncharacteristic of previous behavioral patterns: Were there extenuating environmental circumstances that existed when this deviant behavior was first noted or were there new "significant others" in the environment who were present at the onset of this behavior? Therefore, the developmental analysis takes into account biological limitations and benefits, the sociological structure of the client's milieu, and specific behavioral changes that could cause problems [208].

Upon completion of the developmental analysis, the therapist shifts to the client's sources of internal strength; this is termed analysis of self-control. This is, basically, a process of noting in which situations the client controls his behavioral problems and how he is able to bring this about. The therapist makes a careful study of the behaviors preceding and following the problem so that he can judge the possible aversive consequences of the acquired responses used by the client to avoid the problem behavior. Also, at this point, he can discuss the control of the behavior with his client and weigh the client's self-perceived control against outside observations of significant others in the environment. In summary, the therapist must be able to gauge how much use he can make of the self-controlling behaviors and what role the client can play in the actual treatment process.

Finally, all of the data that have been collected have to be synthesized into a total picture of the client in order to determine how he interacts in his environment. Kanfer and Saslow term these last steps "analysis of social relationships" and "analysis of the social-cultural-physical environment." Persons significant to the client will be identified and recruited in the treatment process. Norm groups are checked for compatibility with the client's own values and attitudes. It must be determined whether the environment will be amenable to psychological treatment and whether it will support the changes to be made. The collection of the data is similar to that presented in the discussion of the first assessment method and need not be repeated. However, Kanfer and Saslow do recognize the use of standardized psychological tests as providing quantitative scores and creating a miniature life experience.

This assessment system is considered by Kanfer and Saslow to be action oriented. It functions as a guide to data collection, as a method of synthesizing and organizing a variety of information, and, finally, as an outline or procedure for treatment. They suggest that this sets the stage for treatment since it provides knowledge of reinforcing conditions, motivation exercised by the client, and it defines specific goals (behavioral change) that in turn provide built-in criteria for evaluation[208]. This assessment approach also gives the clinician an overall picture of the client's environmental milieu, sources of reinforcement, limitations, etc.

Kanfer and Saslow have designed a stimulus-response behavioral assessment system that is technical in design and thorough in data collection. The structure is sophisticated and seems to require a therapist skilled in observation and interview, but, probably more important, one that possesses skills in data collection, environmental organization of people and objects, and one who is able to process and synthesize results, and, finally, organize the significant variables into a unified treatment procedure.

ALTERNATE POINTS OF VIEW

It should be mentioned that a number of psychologists have reservations regarding the growing popularity and ever-wider application of behavioral assessment and operant conditioning as a method for manipulating behavior. They contend that learning theory and habit formations fail to offer a well-balanced concept of the underlying causes of psychopathology and maladjustment. A number of physiologically oriented psychologists are investigating specific chemico-electronic and hormonal techniques that could analyze and create physiologically induced variations capable of improving behavior. Some of them are of the opinion that modification therapy and assessment based on it fail to sufficiently take into account physiological factors that affect brain function.

The increasing number of psychologists who are involved with biofeedback methods (that include changing brain-wave patterns and teaching clients how to adjust physiological processes in order to create therapeutic behavioral changes) claim that assessment of mental states, such as relaxation, cannot be determined merely by what the client reports. The criticism of much of the assessment of the client's condition by behavioral modifiers is that there should be concomitant physiological evidence to support the client's self-appraisal and the behavioral modifiers assessment of relaxation, improvement, and tension states.

Another group of psychologists does not believe that learning theory offers a valid rationale for meaningful and lasting personality change in spite of the successes it has demonstrated in changing specific habit patterns that were considered maladaptive behavior. As mentioned in Chapter 1, Frankl [126], after living through the horrors of a concentration camp, insisted that values and goals rather than conditioning are the primary forces in life and that these values can be taught and transmitted in order to achieve desirable personality changes. It follows from this that assessment methods must probe into this area of human concern in order to obtain a valid picture of what the client's problems are and what his needs consist of. Some of those who practice Frankl's logotherapy believe that all evaluations of human beings must take into account the client's long-range hopes, aspirations, ambitions, and, above all, basic concepts of moral values. They claim that without such in-depth consideration of life goals, assessments of any type are shallow and distorted. To some extent, their criticisms are directed at the assessment techniques used by behavioral modification therapists.

Admitting the success of operant conditioning and behavioral assessment applied to some types of habit maladjustments and recommending their use with specific clients, Kahn[202] maintains that these methods should not be used for certain other types of adjustment problems. He feels that methods employed to evaluate a client depend on many factors, one of which is the type of therapy that will be used. Conversely, Kahn points out, eclectically selected assessment can assist the therapist in ascertaining which kind of treatment may be the most appropriate. One of the purposes of this book is to describe a variety of such assessment methods and how they are utilized.

C. D. Jones[193] remains one of the severest critics of the basic idea of operant conditioning and behavioral assessment. He questions whether therapists have the right to determine for the client what "improvement" consists of and how it should be defined in any given situation in a person's life. He believes that, all too often, in operant conditioning (except when used with mental retardates) there may be a lack of understanding when therapists define for patients what "detrimental" behavior is or is not. In his controversial book, *Hominology—Psychiatry's Newest Frontier* [193], Jones claims that psychological benefits derived from such methods could lead to an abortion of self-actualization in a way not always evident to behavioral modifiers attempting to evaluate the advantages of their methods. He maintains that, except in very limited circumstances, the psychological benefits that might be derived from modification therapy are more than offset by the potential sociological harm *inherent in the methods behavioral modifiers use.*

Jones makes it clear that "efficiency" in "retraining" an individual to conform to existing norms may not be everything that counts in the life of an individual even if it succeeds in solving some of his immediate problems. He predicts that the concept inherent in operational conditioning could lead to the maintenance of an undesirable *status quo* which, in turn, could create social stagnation and, finally, to a degradation of the client's self-concept. He claims that the client does not become aware of this covert loss of self-esteem immediately, but that it is possible that it will affect him over a period of time measured in several years—perhaps as many as five, ten, and even longer. Such time periods are not used by those who maintain that the beneficial effects of operant conditioning are lasting and that possible side-effects are not harmful.

The followers of Dr. Jones' theories further explain that in adjusting an individual to his social milieu through operant conditioning there is a failure to consider the rights of persons with atypical value systems and of individuals with differences in racial, ethnic, national, sex-role, and cultural concepts from those of the behavioral modifiers. In spite of ethical cautions and the evaluation of consequences and intended considerations of the social milieu by the therapist, any concept based on learning theory is apt to fail to take into proper account the possibility that it may sometimes be society rather than the individual that requires modification for the sake of human progress. Jones' colleagues see the danger that behavioral modifiers might fall into the trap of viewing themselves as "gods" whose manipulation of other human beings reflects only their own "conditioned" value systems. They believe that operant conditioning, even among the most socially progressive and highly motivated therapists, might tend to create a social homogeneity among mankind at the expense of social improvement—especially that kind of improvement that runs counter to the contemporary values of the therapist's milieu. Therefore, they reject assessment methods based on modification therapy.

Jones describes methods used in his clinic, which he claims are successful in changing undesirable behavior, that lean neither on the old medical model nor upon learning-theory-derived concepts such as operant conditioning[193]. He insists that therapists must not employ techniques of even "proven success" that fail to permit the client to maintain his "human dignity" since, in the long run, such methods are self-defeating. These divergent views are presented to illustrate the controversial nature of human assessment and evaluation.

SUMMARY

The clinical psychologist is called on to obtain a diagnostic impression and to evaluate the complex traits that make up the human personality. He must be able to distinguish normal from pathological behavior and provide differential assessments that will aid in diagnosis and treatment. Some of the methods used by the clinical psychologist to accomplish this are described in this chapter. Behavioral assessment techniques and their therapeutic counterpart provide an alternate to traditional diagnostic medical models, which are believed by many psychologists to be outdated and of questionable value. Currently there is wide acceptance of these ideas but one should take note that a number of therapists have questioned certain aspects of behavioral assessment as well as its underlying theoretical rationale.

CHAPTER 6

Neuroses

Neurotic disorders are usually described and categorized by symptomatology. Classification systems such as these have always been a source of semantic problems in the field of mental health and much effort has been expended in attempting to arrive at acceptable diagnostic classifications. In Chapter 7 we will discuss some of the types of criticisms commonly raised. To date, the issue of diagnostic terminology is far from resolved. We will follow the *Diagnostic and Statistical Manual of Mental Disorders* (DSM-II, 1968)[8] by the American Psychiatric Association as a guide for the classification of neuroses currently accepted by many diagnosticians. However, it is recognized that there are other systems of classification that could have been used in this chapter.

Neuroses are usually classified as functional disorders although many physical symptoms may be precipitated. These classifications of emotional dysfunctions have always been defined by comparing and differentiating them from the general category of psychoses. There is no clear evidence whether these two groups are discrete and independent from each other, share a common causal relationship placing both on a pathological continuum, or have a direct cause-effect relationships with neurosis leading to psychosis. As was pointed out in Chapter 5 there is a high probability that pathological behavior is multifaceted, thus providing a variety of behavioral entities that make many combinations possible.

There are some common features found in all neuroses but these are not totally exclusive of neuroses alone. For example, most authorities feel that anxiety is present in all neuroses and is a major contribution to the formation of observable symptoms[100, 130, 403]. There are numerous hypotheses concerning the source of anxiety but most theories utilize the idea that it is the result of conflict. Analytic theories mention conflict between instinctual drives and societal controls. Rogerians explain disorder through conflict between perceived self and reality; Berne talks of conflict in transactional communications; Glasser concerns himself with conflict between irresponsible and responsible behavior; and Ellis speaks of irrational versus rational ways of behaving. Learning theorists differ in their explanations of neurotic behavior—to them it is simply learned behavior. They feel that an anxiety response becomes associated (conditioned) with a stimulus that originally was not considered harmful to the client. Later, the person tries to avoid the anxiety-producing stimuli and this does not permit new learning to occur that could extinguish the anxiety. In all of these situations, anxiety limits potential for new experience. As the neurotic uses more energy to avoid conflict stemming from exposure to the anxiety-producing stimuli, he continues to restrict his life-style, consuming energies to control the anxiety that could have been more effectively utilized for experiencing (learning). Even though specific symptoms may vary, there are other general consequences resulting from the neurotic paradigm.

When a disproportionate amount of energy is used to maintain the maladjusted pattern (or avoid it, as the case may be), the neurotic will suffer from chronic fatigue. White[392] defines fatigue as an unpleasant and inefficient state. Everything the person does seems to require a major effort and life becomes a continual struggle. Fatigue may be reflected in sleep habits, lack of physical stamina, and withdrawal from social contact.

Persons suffering from neuroses never seem to be satisfied with their accomplishments. They appear to live in a state of depression and dissatisfaction with themselves and the world around them. This unhappiness may prevent the neurotic from meeting his needs, which in turn leads to more dissatisfaction and consternation. Whether the anxiety is controlled by defense mechanisms or avoided by escaping cue-laden stimuli, the client must pay for this restriction by feelings of tensions. Since cues in the environment cannot be permanently avoided, the system used by the neurotic to safeguard himself from feelings of anxiety is not efficient. The resulting pressure is reflected in chronic irritation, frustration, fatigue, restlessness, and insomnia. Thus, the neurotic can be characterized as a deeply troubled person, rigidly controlled, severely restricted in experiencing and learning, yet continuing to function in his limited life-style.

The *Diagnostic and Statistical Manual of Mental Disorders* (DSM-II,

1968) lists eight categories of neuroses. These are classified on the basis of symptomatology and general behavior patterns. The following are short descriptions of each neurosis:

1. Anxiety Neurosis. This neurosis is characterized by anxious overconcern, extending to panic and frequently associated with somatic symptoms. Unlike phobic neurosis, anxiety may occur under any circumstances and is not restricted to specific situations or objects. This disorder must be distinguished from normal apprehension or fear, which occurs in realistically dangerous situations.

2. Hysterical Neurosis, Conversion Type. In the conversion type, the special senses or voluntary nervous system are affected, causing such symptoms as blindness, deafness, anosmia, anaesthesias, paraesthesias, paralysis, ataxias, akinesias, and dyskinesias. Often the patient shows an inappropriate lack of concern or *belle indifference* about these symptoms, which may actually provide secondary gains by winning him sympathy or relieving him of unpleasant responsibilities. This type of hysterical neurosis must be distinguished from psychophysiologic disorders (which are mediated by the autonomic nervous system), from malingering (which is done consciously), and from neurological lesions (which cause anatomically circumscribed symptoms).

Hysterical Neurosis, Dissociative Type. In the dissociative type, alterations may occur in the patient's state of consciousness or in his identity to produce such symptoms as amnesia, somnambulism, fugue, and multiple personality.

3. Phobic Neurosis. This condition is characterized by intense fear of an object or situation that the patient consciously recognizes as no real danger to him. His apprehension may be experienced as faintness, fatigue, palpitations, perspiration, nausea, tremor, and even panic. Phobias are generally attributed to fears displaced to the phobic object or situation from some other object of which the patient is unaware. A wide range of phobias has been described in the literature.

4. Obsessive-Compulsive Neurosis. This disorder is characterized by the persistent intrusion of unwanted thoughts, urges, or actions that the patient is unable to stop. The thoughts may consist of single words or ideas, ruminations, or trains of thought often perceived by the patient as nonsensical. The actions vary from simple movements to complex rituals, such as repeated handwashing. Anxiety and distress are often present, either if the patient is prevented from completing his compulsive ritual or if he is concerned about being unable to control it himself.

5. Depressive Neurosis. This disorder is manifested by an excessive reaction of depression due to an internal conflict or to an identifiable event such as the loss of a loved object or cherished possession. It is to be distinguished from involutional melancholia and manic-depressive illness. Reactive depressions or depressive reactions are to be classified here.

6. Neurasthenic Neurosis. This condition is characterized by complaints of chronic weakness, easy fatigability, and sometimes exhaustion. Unlike hysterical neurosis, the patient's complaints are genuinely distressing to him and there is no evidence of secondary gain. It differs from anxiety neurosis and from the psychophysiologic disorders in the nature of the predominant complaint. It differs from depressive neurosis in the moderateness of the depression and in the chronicity of its course.

7. Depersonalization Neurosis. This syndrome is dominated by a feeling of unreality and of estrangement from the self, body, or surroundings. This diagnosis should not be used if the condition is part of some other mental disorder, such as an acute situational reaction. A brief experience of depersonalization is not necessarily a symptom of illness.

8. Hypochondriacal Neurosis. This condition is dominated by preoccupation with the body and with fear of presumed diseases of various organs. Though the fears are not of delusional quality, as in psychotic depressions, they persist despite reassurance. The condition differs from hysterical neurosis in that there are no actual losses or distortions of function.

It is helpful to the therapist in the treatment of the neurotic to have arrived at some conclusion about a diagnosis of his client. However, it is of considerably more value to have an evaluation and assessment of the dynamic factors responsible for the development of the neuroses. Utilizing these, clinical psychologists can provide an estimate of the strength and weaknesses of the ego defenses, the levels of anxiety experienced by the client, and a general description of his ability to function. If the therapist is behaviorally oriented, he can gain knowledge of reinforcement contingencies in the client's environment, fear responses, and anxiety-producing stimuli.

A number of tests are available to the clinician for assessment. If the purpose is general screening and diagnosis, he may utilize one of the paper-and-pencil self-report measures such as the Minnesota Multiphasic Personality Inventory. If a more in-depth assessment is desired, projective tests may be better suited for the clinical evaluation. A test battery combining both approaches would more likely yield maximum information. This chapter will demonstrate the assessment of neuroses with the use of the Rorschach, Thematic Apperception Test, Kahn Test of Symbol Arrangement, Minnesota Multiphasic Personality Inventory, Draw-A-Person Test, sentence completion tests, and word association tests.

THE RORSCHACH [317]

There are a number of Rorschach signs designed to elicit the presence and strength of the ego defenses that are manifested on the Rorschach by negation and avoidance. The psychotic may respond immediately to a difficult card such as IX, whereas the neurotic may reveal the activity of his ego defenses by his hesitation in responding. The "witch-like" figures on this card are threatening to the neurotic and the color organization is difficult for him. The neurotic does not respond as the psychotic would by color-naming, perseverating a previous concept, or giving a bizarre response. He shows his discomfort by uncertainty, increased vascular pressure, perspiration, and other physiological evidence of stress or anxiety. The neurotic blocks when called on to respond to color since this seems to stimulate his easily aroused anxiety.

The Psychoneurotic Indicators on the Rorschach

1. Rejection of one or more cards.
2. Few, if any, responses in which form and color are present with form dominating.
3. Increased reaction time and hesitation before responding for those cards where shading is present.
4. "Color shock" manifested by discomfort at the presence of colors on the cards. There may be increased volubility, decreased number of responses, increased reaction time, expressed dislike or other comments on the color of the cards. This may also be manifested by excessive turning of the color cards and by physiological signs of increased stress.
5. Greater than average number of responses based solely on form of the blots, ignoring shading, color, and other factors.
6. Over 50 percent of animal and anatomical responses.
7. Not over 25 responses.
8. Few, if any, human movement responses with a relatively high number of animal responses.

Hysterical neuroses are differentiated from other types by the fact that color is prominent in these records, especially color responses in which form is a secondary consideration. In contrast with obsessive-compulsives, who offer a large number of responses, the records of hysterics are usually short. If a pure color response is given by hysterics, it is often seen as "blood"; they would be prone to describe the blots as either "weird," "horrid," or to exclaim, "How lovely! I like these colors." The obsessive-compulsive seldom gives a color-dominant response. He is more apt to describe his own responses as "imperfect" and seems to be doubt-ridden. He may attempt to be methodical, but often has difficulty in separating two adjacent areas appearing on the cards. The obsessive-compulsive is the only neurotic who, like the schizophrenic, uses contamination—such as "green worms seem to be coming out of the rabbit eyes," Card X. Some compulsives feel it is necessary to mention all parts of the blot, even when these are not used in concepts.

Persons with hypochondriasis, like compulsive neurotics, are likely to be over-attentive to details. On their psychograph, one finds a plethora of anatomical responses, X-rays, and, for reasons that are not entirely clear, one or more responses in which a "flower" or other botanical concepts are seen. Clients in anxiety states may show preoccupation with shading on the blots, focus on midline details, and exhibit an overawareness of symmetry. Depressed clients usually give few responses and then only after prolonged reaction time. These clients are not apt to give whole card responses and seem to be particularly aware of the dark shading on the black-and-white cards. Self-deprecatory remarks concerning their responses reflect their impoverished self-confidence, and slow reaction time corresponds with the general inhibition of physiological processes. In contrast, hyperactive clients may have many responses and their reaction time is fast. Whole card responses are common, but the quality of these responses is generally poor. A description of blot areas as "deteriorated, falling apart, or barely hanging on" may be a projection of dysphoria, fear of disease, or aging processes. Where the depressed client may often be preoccupied with the blackness of the cards, the hyperactive frequently responds with excitement to the colors, ignoring the more subtle aspects such as the intensity of the black-and-white shading and texture. Extroverts, who react quickly to the environment, usually have more color than human movement responses. The reverse is true among introverts and persons who habitually use considerable self-control. Color responses without presence of form may be suggestive of impulsive acting-out of drives. The absence or dearth of color responses sometimes may indicate lack of capacity to utilize emotional outlets constructively.

Other characteristics of the neurotic personality may be revealed on the Rorschach by the client's use of the blot areas in formulating his concepts. A preponderance of whole card responses is usually related to good intelligence but an artificial and strained attempt to use whole blots is considered a sign of status drive and a need for achievement. Preoccupation with small details on the cards is seen most often among compulsive, depressed or fault-finding individuals. Clients who are prone to use the white spaces are often oppositional. Diffused shading such as smoke or clouds as well as a greater than average number of concepts seen as three-dimensional vista or mirrored reflections as implied by shading are commonly associated with the presence of diffuse anxiety (that is, anxiety not channeled into areas where it can produce organic symptoms or specific fears). A prevalence of animal movement concepts is thought to be related to primitive instinctual drives and indicates regression when elicited on adult records. Too much awareness of texture on the cards seems to be related to hypersensitivity. Too little may indicate a personality that is emotionally obtuse, lacking refinements, and low in capacity to establish rapport.

The emotional and intellectual counterparts of the Rorschach determinants are summarized.

Rorschach Determinants Related to Personality Characteristics

Movement—Psychic energy

Human—creative imagination, intelligence, capacity for interpersonal relationships and identification with others, inner fantasy life and emotional maturity. Introversion is indicated when human movement responses significantly outweight responses utilizing color.

Animal—spontaneity, potential maturity, need for satisfaction of primitive instinctual drives.

Shading—Deep inner feelings

Three-dimensional—self-awareness, insight, introspection. As surface appearance and texture—"hairy," "fur," "rough," indicates sensitivity and tact. In the absence of form, excessive texture may imply lack of inhibitions and sensuality.

Form—Intellectual control

Good form—contact with reality, stability, intelligence.

Poor form—disorganized thoughts, lack of critical appraisal, distorted perception.

Color—Emotions

With form dominating—ability for appropriate affective responses, adaptiveness, good emotional control.

With form present, but color dominating—affective lability, seen in hysterical neurotics, emotionally unstable, but also can be creativeness or artistic temperament if some control factors are present in the psychograph.

Without any form—explosive, impulsive temperament, uncontrolled emotion, acting-out potential.

Another method of assessment is to interpret the Rorschach responses symbolically. Concepts are related to the client's symbolic framework, producing results similar to the therapeutic technique of free association. Some advocates of this method translate concepts such as seeing bugs and spiders as suggestive of hostility, a calf or a puppy as reflecting an immature and childlike orientation.

Proponents of the symbol interpretation method of the Rorschach offer hundreds of symbolic concepts and give possible personality correlates. Although some practitioners utilize symbols universally, the clinical psychologist should exercise extreme caution when interpreting symbols, since the generalizability of these cannot be supported by research. Each of the ten cards has its own concentration of symbols and it is possible to obtain personality dynamics from the client's differential reaction to the individual cards. The cards may be characterized as follows:

Card I.	Initial reaction toward life; symbolic of earliest genetic experiences.
Card II.	Elicits intensity and presence of uncontrolled, destructive impulses. Also gives first indication of color shock.
Card III.	Capacity for interpersonal relations, identification with humans.
Card IV.	Reaction toward authority and father figures.
Card V.	The so-called "reality" card. The easiest card for forming the acceptable concept of a bird, bat, or butterfly.
Card VI.	Sexual symbolization stimulus card. Reaction toward this card suggests attitudes toward sex.

Card VII. This is often thought of as the "mother image" card, and reflects feelings toward females, especially mother figures.

Card VIII. Because of the good definition of the animals on either side of this blot, it may also be considered a "reality card." However, it is in color, and therefore reality discernment must occur in the presence of emotional stimuli.

Card IX. Stimulates phobic thoughts and neurotics have difficulty responding to this card. This may differentiate them from psychotics. Because of the colors and threatening forms that they envision, some neurotics refuse to respond, saying that they "see nothing in it."

Card X. This is thought of as the "frustration tolerance card." Some also regard reaction toward this card as an indication of capacity for social adaptation. The many individual blots on this card require that the test subject be able and willing to respond to stimuli of varying size, color, and dimension.

THEMATIC APPERCEPTION TEST (TAT) [272]

The authors of this thematic scheme of eliciting projections evaluated the responses by a procedure sometimes referred to as the "Need-Press" method. Every sentence was analyzed to ascertain the hero's (main character of the story) needs in terms of the pressure or "press" of the environment. Weighted scores were then given to these two factors according to the types of needs and presses that were assigned to the central characters by the client. Clinicians, however, found this method of evaluating the TAT cumbersome and there followed a period of exploration by a number of psychologists in order to simplify the scoring. Actually, many clinicians with experience do not formally score the test. However, they keep several categories in mind, such as the adequacy of the hero, objects introduced and omitted, attribution of blame, signs of conflict, attitudes, types of inhibition, aggression, the outcome of the dilemma or conflict situation in which the hero finds himself, and repetitious themes occurring throughout the test. The psychologist then draws generalized conclusions from his observations and the client's responses.

Neurotics reveal their own impulses, fears, ambitions, and aggressions by projecting them onto the characters depicted in the drawings. The decision of whether these projected feelings are acceptable evidence of the presence of a neurosis is a subjective one. Therein lies the danger inherent in the interpretation. The diagnosis depends not only on the perspicacity of the evaluator in recognizing neurotic projections, but also on the evaluator's own dynamics, which may be introjected. Thus, it is possible for him to erroneously interpret as neurotic projections what other psychologists might consider normal. It is safer to employ the TAT as a method of discovering themes that are preoccupying the client after the diagnosis of neurosis has already been established. For example, Card 3GF shows a girl by an open door, hand over her face, in a position of emotional depression and apparently crying. The client who sees this situation as a girl "contemplating or thinking," and upon inquiry states that the girl probably is quite happy, reveals that he uses the ego defense of denial and may not be able to admit subjective feelings of depression.

A client may be projecting thoughts of suicide or death wishes if he sees a person about to jump out of a window on Card 14. He may state that the person in the drawing no longer wishes to live and may describe him as having lost hope and welcoming death. Several other cards lend themselves equally well to eliciting suicidal ideation. The clinician notes carefully which of the pictures are rejected by the client, what kind of activities or situations seem to interest or disturb the client, his attitude toward males and females, and his assignment of roles to the characters he describes. A relationship appears to exist between the outcome of conflicts, as envisioned by the client, and the prognosis of therapy. On Card 12M, showing a boy being hypnotized, the client may predict a favorable outcome or may decide that the results of the hypnosis are not going to be beneficial. By these reflections, the client may be projecting his own motivation for improvement or recovery. It has been found that clients who consistently suggest an unfavorable outcome of TAT situations have a guarded prognosis in terms of success of therapy.

A number of the TAT figures have a masked sexual identity, making it difficult at first glance to readily assign them a masculine or feminine role. The figure on Card 3BM, for example, could conceivably be called a boy or a girl. Insecurity and conflicts regarding sexual identification are mirrored in the perplexity and anxiety exhibited by certain clients when confronted by such figures. They express distress at being unable to decide whether the representation is male or female. They may have a similar dilemma in deciding whether the figures on Card III of the Rorschach are male or female. Overt and latent homosexual drives lend themselves to projection by the client on a number of cards. The TAT is often used as an accompaniment of psychotherapy in order to determine whether there are concomitant role shifts reflecting improvement of function and reduction of symptoms.

KAHN TEST OF SYMBOL ARRANGEMENT (KTSA)[197]

Indicators of Neurosis on the KTSA

Anxiety Reaction

1. Evidence of need for reassurance as manifested by anxious questioning: "How did I do?" "Did I do everything right?"
2. Self-deprecatory remarks: "I didn't do a good job." "I should have done it differently."
3. Excessive contact. Handling, turning, and fingering the object beyond normal curiosity.
4. Particular dislike of transparent objects, with remarks showing concern with their lack of substance and their transparency. Difficulty placing these transparent objects over other objects as required in Arrangements II and III.
5. Difficulty in giving reasons for liking and especially for disliking objects.
6. Lower estimate of recall ability than actual number of objects recalled.
7. Expressing concern at not knowing what "P" (parrot) shape represents. This object was deliberately designed to be amorphous.
8. Changing objects after placing them. The more frequent the changes, the greater the anxiety.
9. Discrepancy between reason given for the arrangement and performance of the arrangement—for example, client states "no reason" but the arrangement is obviously by color of objects.
10. High "B," "C," "E," or "F" scores depending upon how the client handles his anxiety. (Explanation of these is given on pages 67 through 68.)

Obsessive-Compulsive Reaction

1. Systematically arranging objects on table before placing them on the strip; also may have difficulty in sorting and refuse to sort one or more objects.

2. Excessive meticulousness in naming objects. "A red small heart, smaller than the other ones, about one-quarter inch thick."
3. High "C" score. "C" among first three letters of symbol pattern.
4. Good recall scores.
5. Higher numerical element on symbol pattern than other types of neurotics.
6. Extremes in contact—either excessive or none.
7. Excessive attempts to straighten objects—no slants or reversal of objects on the strip, unless slants are consistently the same in all arrangements.
8. Often an "E" score for first Reason for Arrangement and then "C" scores for the others. Design or balance emphasis in arrangement. May separate similarly shaped objects.
9. Reason for liking or disliking objects frequently is "well made" or "not well made," "good" or "poor workmanship."
10. Usually there is no variation in Direction of Arrangements; some start arrangement by placing objects at center of strip.

Hysterical Neurosis

1. "F" present in letter element of symbol pattern.
2. "D" often prominent.
3. Seven to nine different letters in the letter element of the symbol pattern.
4. No objects placed in HATE, BAD, or DEAD
5. Low recall (generally less than six objects correctly placed.)
6. Evades or denies disliking objects.

In addition to the above signs, it has been found that the depressed client is apt to have a slow arrangement time, to place some object or objects in DEAD in sorting, and may resort to excessive straightening of objects on the strip. His symbolization may indicate subjective feelings of hopelessness and he may place objects that he associates with himself in BAD or HATE. The hypochondrical neurotic is apt to remark about heart-shaped objects, "we need it to live," "health," "sickness." This type of client may also place objects in DEAD in sorting, but not in HATE or BAD.

Dependency is a component of certain types of adjustment disorders. Some neurotics are also excessively dependent and this is manifested by difficulty with the freedom of choice in making the arrangement. This type

Fig. 6.1 Administration of the Kahn Test of Symbolization.

of client may ask, "Arrange them any way at all?" seeking some help or guidance from the psychologist. Hyperactive clients have fast reaction times, offer more than one reason for each arrangement, or tell "stories" connecting one object with another to explain their arrangements.

The KTSA symbol pattern yields an index of the condition and flexibility of the ego defenses. Lack of flexibility or weakness of ego defenses may be indicated by having five or fewer letters in the symbol pattern. This usually implies acting-out potential. Signs of the presence of active ego defenses are:

1. Slow reaction time.
2. Asking questions or seeking reassurance during test.
3. Changing objects after placing them.
4. Excessive contact or no contact.
5. Critical remarks regarding the test or test objects.
6. Color and form details in naming task.
7. Hesitations, vacillations in placing, symbolizing, and sorting objects.
8. Higher recall performance than estimated.
9. Difficulty (such as "no reason") in sorting objects according to Liking and Disliking (Arrangement IV) if concurrent with good reasons for arrangement of objects in Arrangements I, II, and V.
10. Six or more letters in the letter element of the symbol pattern with an absence of any "A" scores. High "Y" and low "Z" scores.

In addition to the above, any of the previously mentioned signs of neurosis must be considered as a possible indication of active ego defenses.

MINNESOTA MULTIPHASIC PERSONALITY INVENTORY (MMPI) [173]

The MMPI and other paper-and-pencil self-report methods are utilized by some clinicians because of their controlled standardization procedures and the relative ease with which these tests can be administered and scored objectively. Additionally, interpretation of these tests are simplified since they yield standard scores. Other psychologists object to the self-report measure because the client can intentionally alter the results, although the MMPI has internal validity scales to detect conscious and unconscious fabrication. Another criticism is that these tests depend entirely on verbal self-evaluation on the part of the client and probably are not sensitive to certain aspects of his personality. Needless to say, such tests should never be used as the single psychometric indicator in any given situation. They may be best utilized to add objective support to diagnostic impressions that have been arrived at subjectively or as an addition to individually administered personality assessments.

The MMPI was originally designed for specific clinical diagnosis based on discrete scales. This function of the test has been replaced by pattern analyses that utilize combinations of scales reported by a numerical coding system. (See discussion on the MMPI in Chapter 7.) It should be remembered that T scores of 70 or greater may reflect pathology and that there is a relationship between the number of scales above 70 and the probability of an emotional disturbance.

Scales 1 through 5 and 7 on the MMPI psychograph are usually associated with the measurement of neuroses although other scales may add information to the analysis. The most commonly recorded neurotic profile is the classical "neurotic triad," which is classified as a 213 or 231. The 213 code replaces the traditional clinical scales of depression (2), hypochondriasis (1), and hysteria (3). Another common profile is referred to as the inverted triad (312 or 132). This profile is usually characteristic of neurotics suffering from psychosomatic reactions and hysteria. Supporting scales are 6 (paranoia, which in this case does not imply psychosis), which may indicate hostility in the client and, when elevated, 7 (psychasthenia), which may reflect an obsessive-compulsive syndrome [156]. A more detailed description of these and other neurotic profiles can be found in handbooks, atlases, and automated computer programs available for MMPI interpretation [174, 93, 286].

DRAW-A-PERSON TEST (D-A-P) [244]

Neurotic manifestations on the D-A-P include frequent erasures, shading, and reinforcement of lines. As one would expect, obsessive-compulsives show a tendency to overdo details; thus, shoes may be shown with eyelets, laces, and bows, hands and arms with details including fingernails. These persons may pay particular attention to midline emphasis, details of pockets, neckties, and clothing in general. Often there is much erasing in an attempt by the client to meet his own high standards of performance. Hysterical neurotics are prone to produce empty-looking drawings with eyes that are shown closed or that lack pupils. A prominent Adam's apple is sometimes seen in the drawings and occasionally parts of the body are left off. Omissions are most frequent among hysterics having conversion reactions. The drawings of clients suffering from neurotic depression are almost always small, projecting inferiority and low affect. The omission of arms in the drawings suggests withdrawal or feeling of extreme helplessness on the part of the depressed client.

OTHER TECHNIQUES

Utilizing the same general principles described in the D-A-P, psychologists may use a large variety of materials in order to measure and evaluate neurotic behavior. The Make-A-Picture Story Test (MAPS) [330] utilizes a miniature theater and various types of cut-out cardboard figures that can be manipulated separately (description—Chapter 4). Although the MAPS is more cumbersome and complicated to administer than the TAT, it permits a freer exercise of the imagination.

The House-Tree-Person (H-T-P) [60] technique is both qualitatively and quantitatively scored. In the appendix of the test manual an analysis of chromatic drawings is offered.

Sentence completion and word association tests are widely used for eliciting neurotic thinking patterns and for providing evidence of emotional blocking. This blocking is interpreted as indicating areas of guilt, anxiety, and repression. Among the areas most frequently tapped by word association and sentence completion techniques are:

Area	*Stimulus Phrase or Word*
Interpersonal Relationships	People . . . What annoys me . . .
	Dancing . . . Most women . . .

Area	*Stimulus Phrase or Word*
Parental Relationships	My mother . . . My father . . .
	Back home . . . House . . .
Psychosexual Relationships and Marriage	My wife . . . Marriage . . .
	Penis . . . Masturbation . . .
Self	I secretly . . . I wish . . .
	I . . . I hate . . . I need . . .
	I am best when . . . My greatest worry is . . .
	I can't . . . I regret . . .
Past Developmental History	In school . . . When I was a child . . .
	I failed . . . Back home . . .

Word association tests such as the one by Rapaport *et al.*[301] use a wide variety of words and are so constructed that the "loaded" word (the one designed to stimulate a reaction) is placed near an innocuous word in order to catch the client off guard and enable the clinician to observe difference in reaction. A few of the 60 words offered by Rapaport *et al.* are: book, father, paper, breast, curtains, trunk, doctor, dirt, cut, movies, cockroach, bite, frame, suicide, mountain, snake, house, vagina.

SUMMARY

This chapter reviews the basic characteristics of the neurotic personality and an assessment of these characteristics. The neurotic appears to suffer from continual anxiety, which restricts his experiences and limits his ability to function. Generally, the neurotic is an unhappy, guilt-ridden, depressed individual who is restricted in his outlook on life and develops pathological symptoms as a means of coping with his anxiety. Psychological tests are useful in helping the psychologist to understand the nature of the dynamics of his client's behavior and to assess weaknesses and strengths for utilization in the selection of the type of therapy that can be most effectively used to assist the client in making a better adjustment.

CHAPTER 7

Psychoses

There is a revolt against the use of diagnostic labels in psychiatry and, perhaps even more so, in clinical psychology. Some authorities in these fields believe that terms such as "psychotic" and "neurotic" stamp a client indelibly with identifications that potentially handicap the labeled person in future social and vocational contacts.

Others insist that those who work in the mental health field must have a structured vocabulary if they are going to communicate effectively with each other. Without this, they feel, they would be apt to talk in circles, using confusing and incomplete descriptive phrases when a simple term such as "schizophrenic," for example, can describe a client's condition less ambiguously. If descriptive phrases were to be substituted for diagnostic terms, so much semantic variation might be developed in time that meaning could not be clearly transmitted. If, on the other hand, phrases describing pathological behavior were to be standardized, one would simply be substituting phrases for the diagnostic terms in present use. This would make the effort to communicate more awkward without avoiding the problem of labeling the client.

Nevertheless, the concern for not stigmatizing a client by a label that might cling to him throughout his life is a valid one. In spite of all efforts in the past several decades to make "having a mental illness" acceptable, persons who have suffered such illness continue to find themselves socially and vocationally handicapped. Perhaps this stems from a deep-seated, irrational fear by the general public of contamination, even though mental illness does not fall into the category of infectious diseases. There lingers in the human psyche an atavistic fear of anything that society views as abnormal and this fear is not easily eradicated by reason. The existence of such conditions as *folie à deux* suggests that in some instances "contamination" may not be entirely without a basis. Perhaps, also, so-called "normal" people realize that they carry within themselves psychic impulses that they repress but that, nevertheless, are similar to those the mentally ill person expresses and dramatizes. If this is true, it would be a fallacy to expect that the mere change from diagnostic terms to descriptive phrases would substantially help to bring about social acceptance of persons who have suffered from mental illness.

The term *psychotic* suggests that the impairment from which the patient suffers is sufficiently severe as to disable him in meeting the ordinary requirements of the society within which he lives. This definition implies that there may be cultural differences in defining mental illness. In some simple societies persons with hallucinations were regarded as capable of interpreting the wishes of the gods. However, in general, as one travels in different countries, one is struck by the similarity in the behavior of the mentally ill in such diverse places as Panama, Japan, Switzerland, and the United States.

It may be incorrect to consider psychosis to be a more aggravated form of neurosis. These two conditions are not only quantitatively different (in terms of severity) but also qualitatively different. Neurotic behavior may actually be viewed as a "substitute" for a psychotic reaction. Thus, a person who utilizes neurotic ego defenses may be less prone to succumb to a major psychotic thinking disturbance than one whose ego defenses are rigidly held in check.

This does not mean that a neurosis cannot lead to a psychosis when there is additional stress, but usually this occurs only in cases where a prior psychotic potential existed within the personality. Not everyone agrees with this distinction between neurosis and psychosis. Some psychologists in the mental health field prefer to put all pathological behavior into a one-dimensional continuum stretching from mild to severe. However, it seems more logical to assume that human pathological behavior is a multifaceted phenomenon that includes among its facets one entity representative of the neurotic tendency to use the ego defenses excessively and an entirely different facet consisting of a predisposition to utilize psychotic defenses that entails a major break with reality. There are certain behaviors that differentiate psychoses from neuroses and other mental disorders.

Unpredictability is an outstanding behavioral characteristic of the psychotic personality. Hallucinations and delusions are other manifestations of this thinking disturbance. Inappropriate responses, ideas of reference, bizarre and regressive behavior, loose and *non sequitur* verbalizations, constricted and inappropriate reactions to stimuli, and severe mood disturbances are other symptoms commonly encountered.

FUNCTIONAL AND ORGANIC

The two main classifications most often used in the nomenclature of mental disorders are "functional" and "organic." The term "functional" implies that the disorder is one of dysfunction in psychological adaptation and, therefore, differs from "organic," which represents a condition whose origins may be traced to a physiological disease or to actual tissue damage. However, the question of whether or not the origin of so-called functional disorders are really independent of somatic causes represents a lively controversy that has been gathering momentum in the last decade. Psychiatric research continues to supply us with a variety of possible physiological conditions that reportedly accompany functional diseases.

Physiological deviations involving glandular, hematologic, and urinary factors have been associated by some researchers with the presence of specific mental disorders. To date, however, none of this research has had sufficiently solid statistical support to be totally accepted. Nevertheless, in view of the accumulating evidence, one cannot help considering the possibility that physiological malfunctionings and chemical imbalances may play a subtle role in the etiology of the so-called functional mental conditions. At least one should keep an open mind in this matter.

The problem is even more complicated by the fact that when two conditions coexist one does not know which one is primary and which one secondary. It is possible that a concomitant deviant physiological state may be the result of (rather than a contributing cause of) a so-called functional disease. And here we come to the core of the difficulty. It is undeniably true that every "purely" emotional response in a human being has a concomitant physiological parallel even if it is only a slight increase in pulse rate or skin conductivity. Conversely, every physiological reaction has its psychological counterpart even if it is only minutely registered within the consciousness. We cannot completely isolate the functional from the organic conditions since they are, to some extent, interdependent in every case. Therefore, for the purposes of this book, "functional" will be defined as referring to those conditions in which our knowledge of the organic factors is still vague and unreliable. As we use it, "functional" will mean that this lack of understanding limits us to placing the emphasis on the behavioral or functional aspects of the disturbance. In other words, it could be said that the term "functional" may be a reflection of our present ignorance.

A similar unclear situation exists in regard to the question of whether functional diseases are primarily inherited or culturally produced. In exploring that question, one is again in an area where there is much vagueness and uncertainty. To what extent, if at all, is there a tendency for mental disorders to follow familial blood lines? If there are predisposing genetic factors, how can these be isolated from social and cultural factors so that one may have a reasonable understanding of the weight of each in any given situation? Twins have been studied to try to throw some light on this subject as they have been utilized in probing the roles of genetic and cultural factors in intelligence. As in the matter of intelligence, studies of twins have failed to solve the vexing problem of determining with any certainty whether genetic or cultural factors play the dominant role. Although strong opinions are expressed on this subject, they are based largely on interpretation of data that is inconclusive. As is true in most controversial matters, at least two schools of thought exist today. Some maintain that the evidence can best be interpreted as showing that the major psychoses can be ascribed to cultural causes. Others lean toward genetic predispositions and "poor protoplasm" (except for the reactive psychoses), placing correspondingly less emphasis on the environment.

FORENSIC PSYCHIATRY

In most nations a person who commits a crime may be judged innocent by reason of "insanity." In this usage, "insanity" is a legal term that means a lack of ability to distinguish right from wrong and to adhere to right behavior. A client declared by a court as having been legally insane at the time that he committed a crime is incarcerated in a mental institution instead of a prison. The defense must prove that the defendant was specifically incapable of knowing right from wrong in regard to the particular criminal act he committed. Even if he is found to have been legally insane at the time the crime took place, he may still be considered guilty if, in spite of his illness, it can be shown that he retained the capacity to realize that the act he committed was illegal.

One can see that the terms "psychosis" and "legal insanity" are not identical. Juries at sanity hearings are confused when the defendant has been diagnosed as suffering from a disease described as an incipient psychosis (such as incipient schizophrenia, for example) and is, nevertheless, psychiatrically described as "not psychotic." A situation like this cannot be found anywhere else in medicine. One would hardly consider a woman to be "not pregnant" simply because she is only a *little* pregnant. Yet clients have been diagnosed as "schizophrenic, not psychotic," even though schizophrenia is the most common form of psychosis.

The explanation of this dilemma lies in the fact that in mild forms and incipient or convalescent stages of certain mental illnesses, severe symptoms are absent, making the descriptive term "psychotic" misleading. Thus, the American Psychiatric Association suggests that an organic condition be classified as psychotic only if the client is psychotic during the episode being diagnosed. It is unfortunate that in addition to representing a diagnostic category in American psychiatric nomenclature, the term "psychotic" does double duty by also indicating severity of symptoms. One can understand why some are tempted to avoid the use of such ambiguous labels, advocating descriptive phrases instead. As discussed earlier in this chapter, labeling a mental condition is, at best, fraught with difficulties but when a label serves two masters (as "psychotic" does) justification for its use loses additional ground.

IDENTIFICATION OF SCHIZOPHRENIA

Few medical entities have been subject to more speculation and controversy than the diagnostic category "schizophrenia." It is a recognizable behavioral syndrome, which can be identified by its symptoms even when the etiology—physiological or psychological factors that may be involved in the genesis and development—vary considerably. It is the presence of this syndrome that the psychologist attempts to probe, utilizing psychological tests. Accordingly, in test evaluation, we shall confine our consideration to the terminology in current use. By "schizophrenia" we mean the *behavior* that caused a diagnostician in his clinical appraisal to apply this term to his client.

It follows that psychological testing in cases where schizophrenia is suspected attempts to elicit test behavior that corresponds with schizophrenic symptoms—that is, delusions, hallucinations, paranoid ideation as well as the more subtle manifestations of increased rigidity, concreteness, autism, depersonalization, and loosening of anchorage to reality. In schizophrenia, as in other mental disease entities, the premorbid behavior in life can often be artificially sustained by habits and circumscribed by conventional surroundings to the extent that the clinical manifestations are repressed, internalized, or disguised, making them difficult to recognize. Some clients develop acute symptoms upon admission to the hospital where they can "let go" and be their "psychotic selves" while others seem to improve with hospitalization simply because they have been removed from the stresses of the outside world. Others may not manifest their psychopathology until its presence is detected by a psychological test. Testing creates a new, unfamiliar situation for most clients and for this reason deprives some of them of their accustomed defenses, making the pathological aspects of the personality more accessible. In addition to the obvious fact that testing gives the psychiatrist objective confirmation of his clinical judgment, in borderline cases psychological testing also can identify the presence of a psychotic process when it is still in a prodromal or incipient state. Thus, testing, at times, elicits signs of the disease before it can be detected in the diagnostic interview. Testing is also valuable when overlapping symptoms exist in which the client's behavior could clinically fit into several different categories. For example, psychological testing often can differentiate between pseudo-schizophrenic neurosis and pseudo-neurotic schizophrenia. The psychiatrist who wishes to know all he can about the etiology of a condition, the psychodynamics involved, the extent of deterioration caused by the pathology, the islands of strength remaining within the personality, and the possible prognosis often can rely on psychological testing to assist him in obtaining this information.

Tests used for the evaluation of schizophrenia are many and varied. In the limited treatment of this book only a few techniques utilized in testing for schizophrenia are presented. The tests described are: the Rorschach, the Thematic Apperception Test, the Bender Motor Gestalt Test, the Kahn Test of Symbol Arrangement, the Draw-A-Person Test, the Lowenfeld Mosaic Test, the Minnesota Multiphasic Personality Inventory, and the Wechsler Adult Intelligence Scale. These are the tests primarily utilized in the clinics and hospitals with which the authors have been associated and they are the ones that have proven the most useful. All of these tests except the Mosaic Test were listed as among the most often used tests in hospitals and clinics throughout the United States [242].

The Rorschach [317]

Although the original test by Hermann Rorschach [316] was published in 1921, not much work was done utilizing the Rorschach with schizophrenics until 1935. At this time a number of papers appeared describing how the test was used to help determine whether or not schizophrenia was an accentuation of a non-psychotic schizothymic type of personality or an actual disease process provoking qualitative changes in the personality. Various investigators noted that one of the most striking changes found among schizophrenics on the Rorschach was a decrease of human movement responses and a corresponding increase in responses approaching pure color.

Pure entities of clinical schizophrenia are rare. Often, cases show an admixture of hebephrenic, catatonic, and paranoid syndromes and may have affective or psychoneurotic coloration. Since clinical behavior patterns labeled schizophrenia are tremendously varied, rarely will a single personality picture typical of schizophrenia emerge on the Rorschach. There are, however, some signs that seem to be almost pathognomic of the schizophrenic process and there are response combinations that point to such a diagnosis. Each case must be evaluated separately and the number and value of the schizophrenic signs must be carefully weighed. The psychologist must seek corroborating evidence on other tests used in the psychological battery.

Specific Rorschach Indicators of Schizophrenia

The following are some Rorschach signs of schizophrenia. Careful evaluation is required even when pathognomic signs are present.

Deviant verbalization. Example: Card I (often seen as a butterfly or bat). "Man carrying a bag of frogs in the desert." Caution: The examiner must be alert to factors that would influence a client to deviate from the norms of the general population. Malingering must also be ruled out. Therefore, inquiry into the background of the deviant verbalization is recommended.

Confabulation. Illogical expansion of perceived concept. Example: The whole of Card IX is "a bear because I see claws here" (in the lower third of the card—upper pink area).

Fabulation (contamination). Arbitrary combinations of concepts. Such combinations do not exist in nature and are made only because of special positions on the blots or because of colors. Example: Card VII. "Two rabbits sitting on a large butterfly." Two rabbits are seen in the top half of the blot; a butterfly is seen on the bottom half. The two concepts are combined by the client only because they are adjacent. Caution: This is sometimes seen among obsessive-compulsives. Card I. "Bat-woman" because "the card looks like a bat and also looks like a woman—therefore, it is a bat-woman." Card X. "A caterpillar crawling in the grass; caterpillar because of its shape and it is on the grass because the caterpillar itself is green." Caution: Sometimes seen among schizoids and hysterics.

Perseveration. Automatic repetitions. Example: Card I. "Bat." Card II. "Bat." Card III. "Bat." Caution: Sometimes seen in organic brain disease.

Projected inferences. This category includes assigning emotional or threatening characteristics to the conceptualizations. Example: Card VIII (harmless animals are often seen). "A beast of prey ready to tear you to pieces." Card VII. "Two women—one laughing and the other one crying because she can't stand being laughed at." Caution: This response sometimes occurs among paranoid personalities suffering from behavioral disorders. Also seen among some normals who wish to share or divulge their dynamics to the examiner.

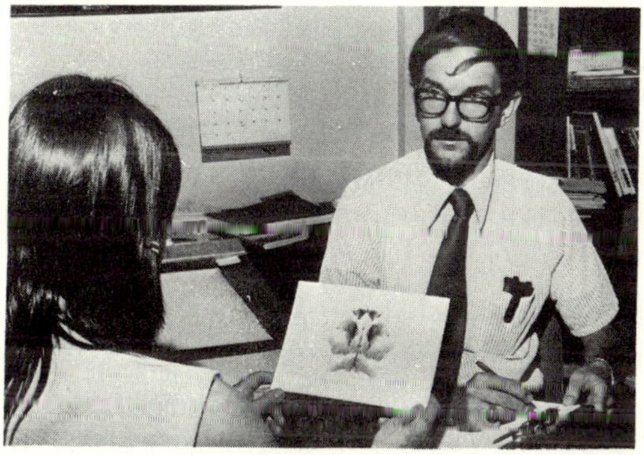

Fig. 7.1 Administration of a Rorschach Card Facsimile.

Summary and Discussion of Important Rorschach Signs

A study of the signs of schizophrenia on the Rorschach shows that the interpretation of a record and its evaluation for schizophrenia requires more than a mechanical approach to the task. The intensity of the sign is an important consideration. For example, on Card VII it makes a difference whether the client sees the "two women" as being jealous of each other—a relatively benign form of projective inference—or whether he sees them as "planning to exterminate each other," which is obviously more pathological. Likewise, a "rabbit's head [lower center of Card X] with green tears coming out of his eyes," is a less pathological combination than "a rabbit's head with green snakes devouring the rabbit's eyes." In the latter response, a projective inference is added to the fabulation. The impression of schizophrenia is more solidly supported when signs are strongly and persistently manifested on the record.

Less Specific Rorschach Indicators of Schizophrenia

Poor form conceptions. Example: Card V (usually seen as a winged creature). "A piece of cloth." Card III (often viewed as two humans in motion). "A chair." Caution: Also seen among clients with brain damage, malingerers, extremely hostile clients, or those suffering from visual difficulties.

Poor color responses. Exclusive or predominant use of color in the formation of concepts, including a mere naming of the colors on the cards. Example: "Red paint." "Grass because it is green." Caution: These signs are seen in organic brain disease and among hysterical personalities.

Few or no human movement responses. Example: Card III. "Two chickens." Caution: Paranoid and "over-ideational schizophrenics" often have more than the average number of human responses. This is one of the means for differentiating paranoid schizophrenics from other forms of the disease.

Rejection. Schizophrenics sometimes reject two, three, and more of the cards saying that they see "nothing," "can't make out anything." Caution: Rejection of cards also occurs among emotionally blocked hysterics, hostile persons with personality disorders, malingerers, and normals who resent the test situation. Neurotics who are overwhelmed by the anxiety-provoking aspects of the stimulus material sometimes reject cards, especially the colored ones.

Variability. Shifts from good form to poor form or vice versa. Variation in reaction time. Variability must be extreme before this becomes a significant sign; two or three seconds on one card and over 40 seconds on another card. Form fidelity must range from very good to quite poor. If the record is long, allowance must be made for a corresponding increase in variability in regard to form and reaction time. Caution: Anxiety neurotics are sometimes variable in their response patterns because they find some of the cards, notably those with color, more threatening.

Differential Diagnosis on the Rorschach

Hebephrenic Schizophrenia—Response Pattern

1. Numerous poor form responses.
2. Absence of shading, such as "fur," "texture."
3. Bizarre or "explosive" responses: "something breaking up," "a piece of dirt falling down," "oh, look at Dippy Do eating his pie."
4. Fixed concept perseveration.
5. Negativism, blocking, occasional white card area responses. Record not as constricted as seen in catatonics.
6. Color emphasis.

Catatonics—Response Pattern

1. Restricted in withdrawn states of the disease and expansive in catatonic excitement states.
2. Bizarre, explosive.
3. Usually no shading.
4. Color-naming.
5. Blocking more severe than in hebephrenics.
6. Fewer signs of regression than in some other forms of schizophrenia. Such responses as "eating something," "babies," "excreta" are usually absent.

Simple Schizophrenia—Response Pattern

1. Usually less than 12 responses.
2. No human movement, color, or shading.
3. One or more absurd form responses.
4. High animal content.
5. Perseveration.
6. The relative absence of bizarre responses differentiates this form of the disease from the more florid forms of schizophrenia.

Paranoid Schizophrenia—Response Pattern

Because much of the personality structure remains intact in this disease, evidence must be discerned and weighed with special care.

Recognition of the condition by psychologists depends on careful assessment of projected grandiose or persecutory delusions. Caution: Paranoid schizophrenics will sometimes attempt to avoid projecting their delusions and, not knowing how to handle the cards without projection, will refuse to take the test. Among the signs sometimes encountered are:

1. Usually one or more deviant verbalizations in which an animal or person seen on the cards will harm some other animal or person. "An eagle swooping down to kill something," "A witch about to kill a baby."
2. Projection of homosexual impulses or attributes. "That man with the moustache [Card IX] has a homosexual look."
3. Emphasis on eyes and mouths in the absence of other good responses. "Two eyes are staring in this card."
4. Usually less than 20 responses with occasionally only four or five responses.
5. One or more contaminations and confabulations.
6. Human movement (more than any other schizophrenic group).

Thematic Apperception Test (TAT) [272]

Schizophrenics who may be evasive or hostile on the Rorschach because they find the stimulus materials too threatening often react more favorably to the drawings of the TAT by Murray. This technique is designed for use with individuals seven years of age or older. It represents one of many methods in which drawings are utilized to elicit projections. The client is asked to tell a story about a picture.

Specific TAT Indicators of Schizophrenia

1. Rigidity and concreteness. The client relates only what is obvious in the picture. Refuses to elaborate. "Just a man and a woman there."
2. Negation. "I see nothing, except a drawing." I'd rather not tell you."
3. Perseveration. The client has a concept that may be relevant to one card. He responds with the same concept inappropriately to the other cards.
4. *Déjà Vu* reaction. The client feels that the card depicts a situation that is familiar to him or that he recognizes the persons in the drawings.

5. Projection of homosexual attributes. In paranoid schizophrenia, there is often a projection of homosexual intentions or fears; statements as, "The old woman is scheming a homosexual act with the young one" (Card 12F, which shows an old woman and a young one). Such projections may also be found among non-psychotics with homosexual wishes or fears. Schizophrenics often perseverate and are inappropriate in projecting homosexual intentions onto the figures on the cards. Psychotics may use an accusing voice when suggesting homosexual intentions or may indicate these intentions with a knowing look, revealing their feeling of omniscience.
6. Projection of threatening or evil intentions or of exaggerated fears. This sign applies primarily in cards where such projections would be inappropriate or farfetched. For example: "She is going to kill the other person" (roughly one-third of normal adults tested see aggression or violence) [273] is not necessarily a psychotic response for Card 18GF but it would be for Card 4, (commonly seen as a woman giving moral advice to an irrational man) [176]. Likewise, concepts involving death and destruction are not necessarily psychotic when elicited on Card 15 (usually depicted as sadness) [176]. When such projections are made inappropriately on Card 13G (often interpreted as exploration of the unknown) [176], they are suggestive of psychosis. This is especially true if they have a bizarre quality and if there is nothing in the client's recent background, such as death in the family or some other calamity, to induce such thoughts.
7. A grossly disproportionate emphasis on relatively insignificant factors on the cards. Example: The necktie on Card 18BM, the books on Card 13MF, the handkerchief on Card 6GF, and similar small details on the other cards.
8. Blandness and flattened effect. This is manifested in schizophrenia by complete lack of anxiety in reaction and description of the normally anxiety-provoking cards 18GF, 13MF, 18BM, 3BM, and 3GF. (All indicate scenes of possible violence or aggression.)
9. Frequent or prolonged perusal of the back of the cards. This suggests the possible presence of paranoid ideation and requires further probing.
10. Very prolonged reaction time: one or two minutes or more per card. This sign becomes more significant of schizophrenia (as differentiated from depressive psychosis) if there is considerable variation in the reaction time in responding to the series of cards.

The Bender Motor Gestalt Test [39]

Schizophrenia is manifested on the Bender primarily by disassociations, spatial separations, and tendencies of gestalt exaggeration. In florid forms of schizophrenia, there are often gross distortions with primitive scribbling and immature drawings. Among well-preserved paranoid schizophrenics, there is sometimes an exaggerated meticulousness and variation in size or position from the original drawings. When the client uses a separate sheet of paper for each design, often the reproductions are two or more times the size of designs on the cards, and this may reflect the client's inflated and unrealistic self-image. Our experience supports Bender's [38] own summary:

> In the visual motor gestalt function in schizophrenia, therefore, we find the fundamental disturbance of splitting expressing itself by dissociation in the gestalt figures which often distorts them fundamentally so that the gestalt principles are split . . . there is also failure to dissociate functions which tend to stick too closely together so that the experiences of the personality may be represented by any unwieldly conglomeration.

The Kahn Test of Symbol Arrangement (KTSA) [197]

Since schizophrenia is a disturbance in human communication resulting from a distortion of symbolic thinking, a test that probes the capacity for making abstractions with cultural symbols offers a means for identifying the disease. Signs of schizophrenia on this test were first identified by Fils [121] and his research was supported by subsequent studies [213].

The following are KTSA indicators of psychosis:

1. Number element of 50 or below. Exceptions: malingerers and mental defectives.
2. "A" in the first four letters of the Letter Element on the Symbol Pattern.
3. Very slow or very fast arrangement time. Exceptions: brain-damage.
4. Twenty or more objects slanted or inverted. Exceptions: malingerers, persons with considerable hostility toward testing, visually or physically handicapped persons, and organics with brain-damage.
5. Placing of more than one object in each segment. Exceptions: organic psychotics.
6. More than three deviations in naming the objects. Exceptions: malingerers and persons from different cultures or organics.
7. Twelve or more errors in recalling placement of objects in the previous arrangement. Exceptions: mental defectives, malingerers and brain-damage.

8. More than four objects placed (in the sorting of objects task) in: HATE, BAD, or DEAD. Exceptions: reactive depressives.

The following additional signs have been found to be suggestive of borderline schizophrenia[198]:

1. One or more "A" responses in combination with nine or more "Z" responses.
2. Perseverance of weak or borderlining "Z" responses. Example: heart: "good luck"; dogs: "good luck, too, since having dogs brings a person good luck"; cross: "good luck, because anyone believing in religion is lucky."
3. Refusal to utilize more than two or three objects in the sorting task.
4. Suspiciousness and hostility against the test and the examiner, especially after the client has taken other tests without showing these characteristics. This is because occasionally schizophrenics who use avoidance as a defense find the dual aspects of the KTSA (verbal and manipulative) a double threat in contrast with tests restricted to one-dimensional performance. Sometimes schizophrenics with insight and "holding-on" capacities may lavishly "praise" the test as a reaction formation to this hostility.
5. Exceptional difficulty in placement of one or more objects (exceptions, the "P" object), frequent changes in position after placing, difficulty in sorting.
6. Prolonged reaction time in the first arrangement with the placement of objects on the table first and exaggerated meticulousness in the arrangement of the objects on the strip.
7. One or more objects placed in HATE, BAD, or DEAD when the client is unable to give a logical explanation for such placement is a weak sign. The more objects placed in any of these categories during the sorting task, the stronger the sign, especially if a rational explanation for such placement cannot be elicited.
8. Holding one of the objects in the hand and showing reluctance in placing it on the strip. Putting an object to the lips or utilizing any other "magical" symbolic gestures in dealing with the objects.
9. Meticulous description of objects in the naming task such as: "A little red heart approximately the size of a penny, half the size of the blue heart and about one-quarter inch thick." This sign becomes stronger if the client also gives similar descriptions during the symbolizing task.

10. Gross verbal-motor inconsistencies. This includes denial of dislike of objects in Arrangement IV yet placing some in the HATE category in sorting. Gross misjudgment in estimating how many of the objects were placed right or wrong in Arrangement III. Giving a "B" (No reason) response for the arrangements when obviously a reason for the arrangement has been used—that is, color or form.

In general, it has been found that schizophrenics have fewer "Z" responses than neurotics (Exception: paranoid schizophrenics); more objects slanted than normals, but less than organics; and the highest number of "A" responses of all clinical groups. In contrast with brain-damaged clients, the schizophrenic is able to place similarly shaped objects together. In borderline and paranoid schizophrenia, the recall capacity (Arrangement III) often remains high with no errors in naming. The number and type of errors made in the naming task is a rough index of the extent of the deterioration caused by the psychotic process. Psychosis is suggested if the symbol pattern is below 50, except in paranoid or borderline cases. After psychosis has been established, the use of the table on pages 154–155 in the KTSA Manual [198] is helpful in differential diagnosis.

Draw-A-Person Test (D-A-P) [244]

The D-A-P is in many ways the easiest test to administer and the most difficult to interpret. Some persons rely on the manual to ascribe a "one-to-one" relationship between such responses as buttons and dependency needs, much hair and sexuality. This is misleading and should be avoided.

Although the D-A-P is, without question, one of the least valid tests when unsupported by other evidence, it is still a useful tool in the hands of well-trained psychologists who evaluate it cautiously and use it only in conjunction with other tests.

Indicators of Schizophrenia on the D-A-P

1. Omission of important parts, such as arms, hands, legs, or head. Exceptions: hysterical personalities, mental defectives, organic psychotics.
2. Bizarre additions, such as internal organs and scribbling that is not appropriate to the drawing.
3. Grossly exaggerated size or emphasis of any part of the drawing such as the ears, nose, and especially eyes.

4. Front-view profile confusion of face, such as two eyes or mouth and nose centrally placed in a profile drawing.
5. The presence of sexual organs in the drawings—especially when the rest of the body is dressed or partly dressed.
6. Tiny, empty drawings in the regressed forms of schizophrenia; large drawings with heavy-line emphasis in the grandiose and florid types of the disease.
7. A quality of remoteness and social distance in the drawing, which is difficult to define. This is usually accompanied with a bizarre elaboration. The figure of the nun shown in Fig. 7.2 is an example of this.

Fig. 7.2 These drawings show different responses of four male clients who were asked to draw a person. The male drawings reflect characterological disorders. One represents aggressiveness and over-confidence; the other helplessness and inadequacy. The female figures are the work of schizophrenics. One shows repression; the other loss of all inhibitory capacity. From T. C. Kahn and M. B. Giffen. *Psychological Techniques in Diagnosis and Evaluation.* Oxford: Pergamon Press, 1960.

In addition to these signs, which have been found to be most characteristic of schizophrenia, Karen Machover mentions others: "Joint emphasis in the simple kind of schizophrenia, rigidity in the paranoid types, erasures infrequent in the regressed types, and a diagrammatic quality and blocked movement" [244].

The Lowenfeld Mosaic Test [240]

Margaret Lowenfeld points out that the diagnostic potential of her Mosaic Test stems from its capacity to elicit what she calls the typical schizophrenic symptom—indifference to gestalt. This test enables the psychologist to compare a client's drawing with his constructions on the mosaic tray. Lowenfeld [240] describes the difference in the case of a schizophrenic woman as follows:

> . . . we asked her to draw a cat and she draws a cat that is recognizable and, among other details, possesses four paws. Comparing the mosaic and the drawing we find that a patient, who is perfectly able to draw a cat, makes a mosaic cat which resembles anything but a cat; that she knows this perfectly, but does not mind it in the least.

It appears, then, that some schizophrenics create conceptual designs that fail to correspond with reality in contrast with the greater reality awareness expressed by the client when dealing with the more conventional materials of paper and pencil. As with the KTSA, the client must manipulate individual solid objects that are combined into a symbolic expression and thus a level of organizational capacity is tapped. The KTSA and Mosaic Tests require the "bit-by-bit" construction of a gestalt, whereas such tests as the Rorschach and the TAT confront the client with a gestalt that is already present for him to accept or reject. The KTSA utilizes culturally formed symbols, each one of which represents a gestalt in itself. On the other hand, the geometric designs of the Mosaic Test offer no hint as to meaning and have no identification with anything except abstract designs. We agree with Lowenfeld's statement that "It is in the study of schizophrenia that the LMT [Lowenfeld Mosaic Test] has yielded by far the most interesting results" [240].

Indicators of Schizophrenia on the Mosaic Test

1. Preoccupation with symmetry and formal organization of the pieces with no attempt to construct any objects commonly seen in life.
2. Color is either over- or underemphasized or used unrealistically.

Lowenfeld cautions that these signs are not pathognomic. Instead, the test is best used in the investigation of clients whose diagnosis is already known. The Mosaic Test makes its greatest contribution in measuring the degree of disorganization. Four levels of performance are given to indicate this:*

1. Lowest level. Corresponds to performance of infants 16 or 18 months of age. Client looks at the pieces individually, turns them about in his hand, plays with them, may hold them up to the light, and occasionally may drop one on the tray with no attempt at placing the pieces to form anything.
2. One level above lowest level. Client can place objects on the tray but makes no effort at organization, no choice of color, no constructive use of figures.
3. Two levels above lowest level. Some fragmentary organization is achieved by client at this level as manifested by placing of pieces in twos or in a chain across the tray. This type of performance can best be described as automatic. Usually the client reacts with very little, if any, hesitation and performs quickly and mechanically. Occasionally there are some who respond with exaggerated care, slowly and meticulously placing the objects in a straight line or a curve. Slow reaction such as this is much more frequent among clients whose disorganization is due to brain damage.
4. Three levels above lowest level. The client organizes the pieces without fragmentation but with a compulsion for making diagrammatic and formalistic designs. Diamond shapes, hexagons, squares, or triangles are common among this group. In contrast to the preceding level, there are no loose ends. Performance is differentiated from that of normals by the rigidity of the designs, overemphasis on position of the pieces and absence of successful attempts to portray trees, people, houses, or like objects in a manner that utilizes both color and form realistically.

Minnesota Multiphasic Personality Inventory (MMPI) [173]

For general screening of psychological pathology, the MMPI is the most widely used objective personality measure. Although originally designed for differential diagnosis based on nine discrete clinical scales, research has shown the MMPI to be more accurate when combinations (pattern analyses) rather than single scales are used. Today, most MMPI systems have dropped the original separate clinical diagnostic categories and have substituted a numerical coding system.

*Adapted in part from Lowenfeld, Margaret [240].

When diagnosing psychoses utilizing the MMPI, the clinical psychologist works with scales 6 through 9, which are generally referred to as the psychotic group. In psychotic profiles there will usually be a moderate overall elevation of all scales, particularly 6 through 9, with a general positive slope (elevation) or a bimodal pattern on the right side of the profile[156]. Several patterns have been found to be suggestive of psychosis. For example, peaks on scales 6 (paranoia) and 8 (schizophrenia) with scales 7 (psychasthenia) and 9 (hypomania) depressed (although higher than scales 1 through 5), from what Dahlstrom and Welsh have referred to as the paranoid valley[93]. A number of publications are available for pattern analysis interpretation. Computer analysis is often used by the clinical psychologist in the interpretation of MMPI profiles. With the use of large data banks, these computer printouts can provide much information.

In summary, the MMPI is useful for the general screening of the mentally ill, especially where large populations must be processed. However, differential diagnosis based on a single clinical scale is no longer considered an accurate measure.

The Wechsler Scales

Controversy has accompanied the use of every psychological diagnostic tool, both individually and as a group, and the Wechsler Scales are no exception. In addition to establishing intelligence levels, the Wechsler may be useful for assisting in arriving at a diagnosis when it represents one of the several tests used as a battery[157, 253]. This use of the Wechsler has in recent years lost popularity among clinical psychologists.

THE EVALUATION OF SCHIZOPHRENIA

The psychologist's task is complicated by the fact that signs associated with schizophrenia on tests frequently overlap with signs characteristic of other pathologies. Few, if any, psychological test signs can be called truly pathognomic. It is only by the judicious use of several diagnostic methods, carefully interpreted and compared for common elements and consistent sign patterns, that the clinician can arrive at an impression of schizophrenia. Test signs for schizophrenia will be characteristic if the condition is obvious and unequivocal; but in that case there is less need for the use of psychological tests to arrive at a diagnosis. Psychological tests are valuable when the clinical report resolves the doubts that would have required prolonged client observation. Additionally, the strength and nature of the psychological signs are useful in arriving at conclusions regarding prognosis, type of therapy to be used, and the etiological dynamics of the condition. The psychological test signs may be used as a base line to mark progress in therapy and to establish the recovery of the client after treatment.

AFFECTIVE PSYCHOSES

Severe mood disorders in which the client experiences a loss of contact with his environment are often referred to as affective psychoses. Although these conditions represent a separate category, an admixture of schizophrenia and affective symptomatology is not unusual. Persons with such symptoms are described in the psychiatric literature as "schizo-affective types" with the primary diagnosis usually considered schizophrenia.

Major Types of Affective Psychoses

Involutional melancholia is a disorder that occurs among females during the menopausal years (usually between the ages of 45 and 55) and among males during the years of the male climateric (usually between the ages of 55 and 65). During these periods, obvious physiological changes occur but it is believed that these are not the primary cause of this disorder. Instead, the disorder appears to stem from the inability to accept the fact that one's major efforts in life have been accomplished and that the aging process can no longer be rationalized or denied. Especially prone to involutional melancholia are women whose life in earlier years centered primarily on their children and who, then, in middle age, are faced with the fact that now the children are no longer dependent on them. The condition is rare among women who have absorbing hobbies, maintain active interests in their husband's careers, continue their education, or are employed in a satisfying type of voluntary or paid work.

In most industrial nations males have been geared to be achievers. When they realize that in spite of all their struggles they have failed to reach their youthful goals, a disillusionment coupled with the fear of aging sometimes precipitates an involutional personality disintegration. It should be noted that some diagnosticians would place greater emphasis on metabolism, nutrition, and endocrine function in discussing the etiology of involutional melancholia.

Manic-depressive illness is divided into three major subtypes: depressed type, manic type, and cyclic type in which both mania and depression occur. These disorders are characterized by chronicity and a tendency for remission and recurrence. No obvious precipitating events can be identified as responsible for the onset of this disease. Instead, there appears to be a constitutional predisposition frequently accompanied by an obese, rotund, or sometimes stocky, body build. Familial trends have been noted in numerous cases. Additionally, there often is a history of childhood deprivation accompanied by such personality deviations as severe temper tantrums or self-imposed separation from peers.

Psychotic depressive reaction is a category used to describe a severe disabling behavior whose origin can be traced to a precipitating traumatic event in the client's life. It, therefore, does not usually have a long history marked by chronicity. Prognosis is considerably more favorable than in other types of depressive psychoses although recurrences are not uncommon.

These psychotic conditions can be distinguished from the depressive neuroses, hypomanic types, and cyclothymic personalities by the fact that the symptoms among affective psychoses are much more severe and of greater duration. Delusions or hallucinations are also apt to be present but these are usually circumscribed and transient in contrast with such symptoms in schizo-affective psychoses.

Testing Affective Psychoses

On the Rorschach the paucity and the morbid content of the responses are characteristic of the depressive stage. Often the responses will include concepts of decay and deterioration. The manic type of illness, on the other hand, is marked by overproduction with sometimes as many as 40 responses to one card. Poor form content with excessive color emphasis is characteristic.

When psychotic depression is present, the TAT usually elicits single word responses such as "death," "destruction," or, inappropriately, "fire." Sometimes there is merely a shake of the head and a sigh. There is a marked lack of interest on the part of the client in the test even when delusional material is expressed. As on the Rorschach, the manic client overproduces with florid and irrational elaborations. Thema involving violence—murder, killing, etc.—are not uncommon.

On the KTSA the performance of the client with depressive psychosis is characterized by a "slow" arrangement time. Usually no reasons are given for making the arrangements. However, when reasons are offered, they almost always reflect the delusionary content of the client's thinking processes, such as "all these objects are going to eat that little white dog." The client may place all the objects in the DEAD category during the sorting task. As is true of most psychoses (with the exception of paranoid disorders), the Numerical Element on the Symbol Pattern is likely to be no higher than 50 in both the depressive and manic stages of this disease. Since the Numerical Element is an index of the extent of the deterioration, it may, in very severe cases, be as low as ten or even zero. Slanting and overlapping of objects on the strip are suggestive of deterioration and characteristically occur in both the depressive and manic stages. The manic psychotic client will have a "fast" or "very fast" arrangement time. The explanations for the arrangements may amount to a gibberish with occasional bizarre and florid elaborations. On the sorting task, manic patients have been observed to change the position of a single object as many as 20 times. Surprisingly, the Left-Right directional approach to the arrangements is often maintained, as it is among normals, even though in making the arrangements the client may have practically thrown the objects on the strip in his haste to complete the task.

Drawings of figures as well as reproductions on the Bender Motor Gestalt Test tend toward micrographia in depression and macrographia in manic states. Bizarre elaborations reflecting the presence of delusions characterize the psychotic nature of the disease and differentiate it from the less serious affective disorders. It should be noted that both depressive and manic psychotic patients are apt to be uncooperative test subjects. Test rapport is extremely difficult to establish and attention span is usually markedly short. This reaction to psychological testing can usually be distinguished from the blocking, negativism, and evasiveness characteristic of other diagnostic conditions and, therefore, it may assist in the identification of major affective disorders.

PARANOID STATES

Paranoid states are characterized by well-systematized delusions, which may be grandiose or persecutory in nature. Psychiatric opinion is not in agreement regarding the question of whether these conditions constitute separate entities or are classified with the schizophrenias or paranoid personalities.

Paranoia is a rare disorder that mainly affects males over 40 years of age. It stubbornly resists treatment and, therefore, is considered one of the most serious of the psychoses. Diagnosis of paranoia is often delayed by the fact that the client's delusion is manifested only in a narrow band. In other respects he may appear rational and unimpaired. If the client's psychotic premise is granted, he can proceed logically to elaborate upon it. As can be imagined, detecting the presence of paranoia by psychological testing is a difficult undertaking.

Testing Paranoid States

The Rorschach is likely to elicit at least one if not several signs reflecting a client's delusion because the vagueness of the stimuli tends to encourage the client to rely upon his delusional system. Characteristically, all other responses on the test may reflect a normal personality. In many cases, however, there is a rigidity in the response pattern with a restriction in color production and a corresponding increase in static human figure or human detail responses.

Likewise, on the TAT there is apt to be constriction with a tendency to repeat with less than normal amount of variation. A dramatic change occurs when the client utilizes his delusional system to explain a situation depicted on the card. The client may suddenly become expansive and excited.

On the KTSA the delusional thought processes may come to light either during the explanation the client gives for arranging the objects on the strip or during the sorting task when he associates the objects with the stimulus words: LOVE, HATE, GOOD, BAD, LIVING, DEAD, SMALL, LARGE. Occasionally, the delusion is manifested in the third arrangement when the client is asked to place certain objects over other objects. Arrangement time and the order of arrangement almost always remains within expected normal limits. The Numerical Element on the Symbol Pattern is usually 100 or higher.

THE ORGANIC PSYCHOSES

In senile and pre-senile dementia there is emotionality, self-centeredness, and a steady decrease in the capacity to function adequately marked by difficulty in assimilating new experiences. The name implies that the deterioration is associated with age but the actual causes of senile dementia are largely unknown.

Alcoholic psychoses include a variety of disorders such as delirium tremens in which there are tremors of the limbs and body, disorientation, and terrifying hallucinations. Korsakov's psychosis is identified with the long-standing use of excessive alcohol and is characterized by memory impairment and thought disturbances.

Psychoses occur from intracranial infections such as syphilis of the central nervous system and occasionally encephalitis, pneumonia, typhoid fever, malaria, and acute rheumatic fever. Another class of organic diseases consists of those in which the vascular system plays a major role such as neuropathology associated with cerebral arteriosclerosis and cerebrovascular disturbances. With advancing cerebral arteriosclerosis, the blood vessels are narrowed and the flow of blood to the brain is impeded. Since blood carries oxygen, the supply required to nourish the cerebral cells is decreased, leading to cortical and subcortical tissue deterioration.

Conditions classified as psychosis with drug or poison intoxication (other than alcohol) include the use of psychedelic drugs—for example, prolonged glue-sniffing for so-called "kicks." Exposure to or ingestion of certain heavy metals, gases, and other toxins may lead to organic psychotic states that are categorized as "Acute Brain Syndrome."

Head trauma leading to brain damage has become more common with the increased use of automobiles, motorcycles, and snowmobiles. Brain injury is usually extensive if it results in psychosis; additionally, the location of the lesion is a very important factor. The client may have had a history of a circulatory disturbance before the accident and subsequently this may accelerate significant changes in sensorium and affect so that organic psychosis develops even when there is relatively little head trauma.

Finally, there are the intracranial neoplasms in which either benign or malignant tumors compress brain tissue causing behavioral changes severe enough to be classified as psychoses.

Testing Organic Psychoses

Psychological testing for organic psychosis is described in the chapter on brain damage (Chapter 8). The presence of an organic condition is suspected when deviations in behavior on the test are particularly severe. Examples of this are: drawing a figure out of proportion, devoid of detail, with perhaps some bizarre elaborations. Performance on the KTSA usually includes one or more bizarre responses with no meaningful reason given for the arrangements. The arrangement of the objects on the strip lacks precision and is usually disorderly. In placing certain objects over other objects as required in the third arrangement, the client will fail to associate similarly shaped objects. Instead, the association of objects will be made randomly. Recall of objects placed on the strip will be significantly low, usually no more than two or three objects correct. Symbolizations will consist of few if any abstractions ("Z" scores), but more likely the client will name what the objects are, or give their function—such as "dog runs"—or a description of the object's shape or color ("D" scores). In severe cases even naming of the objects may be too difficult for the client and in such cases bizarre or inappropriate responses will be given ("A" scores).

On the Rorschach, color-naming and card rejection are common. Perseveration is often so extensive that a client may only use one concept with minor variations in all of his responses. On the Goldstein-Scheerer Color Form Sorting Test the client will not be able to shift from color to form or vice versa. The distortion on the Bender Motor Gestalt Test will be severe with micrographia or macrographia, depending on whether there are withdrawal or expansive behavioral symptoms with the disease. Bizarre elaborations on this test may occur when the behavioral configuration has incorporated delusions or hallucinations.

SUMMARY

This chapter explains the overlapping nature of organic and functional mental diseases and offers a brief description of some of the major disease entities that are usually classified within the psychoses. The identification of the various psychotic conditions by means of psychological tests is illustrated. The controversies in dealing with labeling and nomenclature in psychiatry and clinical psychology are discussed, giving arguments for and against the use of current terminology.

CHAPTER 8

Methods for Testing and Evaluating Organic Brain Impairment

The clinical psychologist is often confronted with the task of assisting the neurologist and psychiatrist in the diagnosis of organic brain pathology. In general, there are three reasons for such referrals. First, neurological signs, if present, are sometimes inconclusive and contradictory. Second, somaticizing neurotics often present symptoms that are not easily distinguished from genuine brain damage. Third, there is an increasing awareness by members of the medical profession of the contributions that the well-trained clinical psychologist can make toward the identification of intracranial lesions.

No matter how adept the clinical psychologist is in the identification of cerebral damage, he represents the last resort in the collection of required evidence to make a neurological diagnosis. Too often, in small clinics where neurologists are not readily available or where there is a scarcity of EEG machines, psychiatrists are tempted to place a heavy burden of responsibility on psychologists in the evaluation of symptoms for organicity. The present level of efficiency of psychological techniques in identifying brain damage does not warrant this. Yates [407] has systematically evaluated current state of accuracy of psychological tests designed to identify organic brain damage and, in general, he finds them wanting. He suggests employing new techniques that would yield objective scoring criteria based on what he calls "a reasonable theory," supported by adequate statistical treatment. In his assessment of available techniques, he did not include the Bender Motor Gestalt Test, the Benton Revised Visual Retention Test, nor the Kahn Test of Symbol Arrangement. Yet these have shown the most promise and most nearly follow Yates' suggestion in regard to scoring theory and statistical treatment.

Tests utilized for identification of organic brain disease share conspicuously in the barrage of criticisms that are directed at psychological diagnostic instruments by some research psychologists. However, psychological methods for the identification of brain damage are being utilized more, rather than less, among neurosurgeons, neurologists, and psychiatrists. The authors can recall many cases where psychological testing alerted the attending physician to the presence of an organic-cerebral disease in what appeared to have been a purely functional condition. Follow-up studies proved that the psychological test indications of organic brain disease were correct. Most clinical psychologists in practice for any length of time can offer similar examples. It is difficult to say whether or not the tests for brain damage currently in use are inadequate or whether the shoe of inadequacy fits better the statistical techniques used in the assessment of their accuracy.

Psychological tests may also be employed to assay the extent of loss in cognitive and emotional areas when the presence of organic brain disease has already been established. Before we mention specific signs and indices of loss, it may be fruitful to consider briefly the theories underlying the use of psychological tests in diseases involving intracranial lesions.

In an analysis of such theories, there are two considerations. First, clients with organic brain damage tend to react psychologically to their pathology in a characteristic manner that is reflected and identifiable on psychological tests. Second, psychological tests are sensitive to early impairment of cerebral efficiency. Sometimes inability to meaningfully integrate psychological test stimuli (such as Rorschach blots) precludes the appearance of positive neurological signs. Likewise, some psychological tests in which blocks or designs are used are sensitive to damage in the psycho-motor-spatial area while others point out impairment in the visual and the retentive fields. Performance in these areas can be observed and measured conveniently and accurately by means of psychological tests. Deterioration may be estimated by comparison of performance in other areas of function. This can be accomplished in a relatively objective manner by using norm groups of clients with known damage as an experimental group and those without brain damage as controls. Then, any given individual performance may be evaluated in terms of these results.

Psychological reaction to an organic deficit has some general characteristics shared by a large number of organic clients. Typically, the brain-damaged client tends to feel insecure, be rigid in his behavior, perseverate in responses, and be slow in his reactions. Is this behavior due to cortical malfunction or is it primarily a psychological reaction to illness? A case may be made for either position. A person aware of a loss of skill due to an organic deficit is slow to respond to a test situation because his awareness of loss makes him insecure, hesitant, and cautious. On the other hand, this slowness may also be caused by a weakened capacity for cortical integration stemming from tissue damage. There is much to recommend the point of view that the weakness of the premorbid personality is accentuated among clients whose disease has made inroads in effective cortical functioning. Persons whose psychological homeostasis has been upset by any type of disease are less able to inhibit suppressed emotions or to effectively act a role in life that serves to disguise their true dynamic selves. This is also true of persons subjected to an increase of environmental situational stress and is, therefore, not necessarily confined to brain-damaged clients.

Other attempts to classify tests of brain damage into "quantitative" and "qualitative" types have failed since such a division is arbitrary and there is too much overlapping. Perhaps it is most practical, instead, to divide psychological instruments that measure brain damage into those designed explicitly for this purpose and those that are primarily personality or intelligence tests. In the latter, the brain-damage component is a secondary though not necessarily a less important function.

TESTS DESIGNED TO MEASURE BRAIN DAMAGE

The Hunt-Minnesota Test for Organic Brain Damage[190]

In the introduction to the test, Hunt writes: "The Hunt-Minnesota Test is specifically designed for routine clinical detection of organic brain damage, primarily where the damage has occurred after the person has reached the age of 14 or 15 years"[190]. In many ways this test is typical of a group of techniques that utilizes recall of designs, words, and numbers (recent memory) and matches this performance against vocabulary or general information representing early memory. An age factor is taken into account and a differential for deterioration is computed. A more detailed list from The Hunt-Minnesota Test follows:

1. Matching of designs.
2. Recall of words.
3. Saying the months of the year.

4. Counting from 1 to 20.
5. Counting from 3 to 30 by 3's.
6. The attention test.

The instructions for the attention test are: "I am going to read a long list of numbers and I want you to tap on the table with this pencil every time I read the number 3. Here is a short list for practice—5, 3, 6, 8, 3, 3. Now, listen carefully and be sure to tap the table every time I say the number 3." Other tasks on the test are:

7. Counting backward from 25 to 1.
8. Reversing digits.
9. Saying the months backward.
10. Serial subtraction of 3's from 79.

The instructions for the serial subtraction are: "Now, I want you to count backward from 79 to 1 by 3's as fast as you can. Now you start at 79 and count backward by 3's as fast as you can like this: 79, 76, 73, and so on back to 1. Ready, 79 . . ."

As the reader may recognize, the above is similar to the mental status examination routinely used by physicians. The difference is that here the task is part of a framework of a total recall situation in which it is compared to efficiency on other tasks and is statistically weighted and scored in accordance with total performance.

The Shipley Institute of Living Scale [329]

This test is based on the fact that brain-damaged persons deteriorate in their capacity for abstract thinking. Concreteness is a characteristic of the intellectual functioning of organic clients, although it is also seen in other mental pathological conditions. Shipley's test requires the client to make 20 abstract completions.

Instructions are: "Complete the following. Each dash calls for either a number or a letter to be filled in. Every line represents an item. You have ten minutes to finish." Examples of this task are:

1. White, black, short, long, down,__
2. NE/SW SE/NW E/W N/__
3. Surgeon 1234567 snore 17635 rouge/__ __ __ __ __
4. 3124 82 73 154 46 13/__
5. Two w four r one o three/__

Performance on this task is matched with a multiple-choice vocabulary test, which it is assumed represents the premorbid level of intellectual functioning. The ratio of abstract performance to vocabulary is developed into a percentage of deterioration score.

Goldstein–Scheerer Tests of Abstract and Concrete Thinking[147]

Another series that employs the principle of abstract and concrete thinking in the detection of organic brain disease is commonly referred to as the "Goldstein–Scheerer Tests." The chief difference between these tests and the foregoing is that Goldstein and Scheerer employ actual objects rather than words or numbers. For example, the Goldstein–Scheerer Cube Test uses four wooden blocks whose surfaces present different colors and color combinations. Two spiral-bound books show a series of 12 designs of increasing difficulty, which the client must copy using the colors on the blocks to make the designs. An ingenious aspect of the test is that the designs not only increase in difficulty as the client proceeds but, when failure occurs, a series of graduated hints are given. The amount of help required can be used as a quantitative measure of impairment. The type of hints offered may be of interest to the reader. They are as follows:

1. Printed design about one-fourth the size of the actual design to be reproduced with the blocks.
2. (If client fails above) Printed design exact size of the one to be reproduced with the blocks.
3. (If the above is failed) Printed design quarter size, with lines showing how the blocks must be fitted together.
4. (If this is failed) Printed design exact size of the one client must reproduce with blocks. Lines are also present showing how the blocks must be fitted together.

Thus, upon failure, the tasks become increasingly less abstract until (4) they represent pure visual-psycho-motor performance without abstraction.

The Goldstein–Scheerer Color Form Sorting Test consists of four triangular plastic objects and a like number of square and round plastic objects. All the objects that have a similar shape differ in color. The administration of the test is simple. The client is told to sort the objects, grouping together those that belong together. He may do this by grouping all similar shapes together or by placing together all objects having similar colors. No matter how he performs the tasks, he is asked subsequently to "sort them differently," requiring him to shift from a shape to color principle, or vice versa. Goldstein and Scheerer[147] give a behavioral analysis of performance of this task, describing two approaches: the abstract and the concrete. They point out that, in the former, the client

> assumes a conceptual attitude from the very start. He carries out the instructions by volitionally abstracting from various individual sense impressions and orients himself toward a conceptional frame of reference in the category of form or color.... In arranging the materials spatially, the subject will casually "throw" the forms he chooses in different heaps or "piles," not being particular about the spatial position of the individual figures within each heap[147].

This is contrasted with concrete performance where clients "with disturbance of cortical function are unable to assume the abstract approach and, therefore, discharge the task on an exclusively concrete level of responding"[147].

The client with organic brain damage has difficulty in abstracting color or form as a principle of sorting. He shows a preference for one way of grouping the figures and arranges them in designs or patterns as a substitute for abstraction. He is unable to shift volitionally from either color to form or form to color. Goldstein and Scheerer point out that "insofar as shifting occurs, it occurs passively under forcible experimental conditions"[147] that the test provides by means of the graduated hints. If the client perseverates in the use of color and seems unable to grasp the idea of form, the examiner can turn all the pieces upside-down and, thus reversed, they are all white. Since color is no longer evident, it is automatically eliminated as a sorting factor. In addition to being able to shift from color to form, the test requires that the client account for the principles he used to accomplish the task. Thus, the verbal-cortical areas as well as the psychomotor areas are tapped by this test.

The Goldstein–Scheerer Stick Test consists of 30 sticks of four lengths. The materials are used to determine whether the client is able to copy figures composed of sticks and reproduce them from memory. The test is divided into two parts, the first requiring the client to copy a sample figure, the second—to reproduce the figure once it has been removed after being exposed to it for five to 30 seconds.

The other tests of this series, the Gelb–Goldstein Color Sorting Test and the Goldstein–Scheerer Object Sorting Test, require the client to make color associations and, in the sorting test, to sort a variety of simultaneously presented objects according to general concepts and to shift frames of references volitionally and without assistance. Some of the objects used in the sorting test are a hammer, a pair of pliers, a pipe, a book, a pencil, a bicycle bell, matches, and a candle.

The Benton Revised Visual Retention Test[42]

This is one example of tests that rely exclusively on the client's ability to use visual memory effectively. The test can be given in one of four possible administrations or in combination of several administrations. The directions for administration are:

> The subject is given a blank sheet of paper, the dimensions of which correspond to the dimensions of the cards on which the designs are printed and a pencil with an eraser. He is told that he will be shown a card on which there are one or more figures, that he will study the card for 10 seconds, and that when the card is removed he will draw what he has seen[42].

Benton suggests both a quantitative and qualitative analysis of performance. The qualitative aspect is measured largely by the amount and kind of distortion (such as reversal), rotation of figures, and the general fidelity of the reproductions. The quantitative scoring follows the usual pattern for evaluating such tests. Table 8.1 indicates the number of errors made

Table 8.1 Distribution of performance levels in brain-injured and control patients.*

	"Number Correct" Scores	
Performance Level	Brain-injured (N-100)	Control (N-100)
2 points above expected level	2	4
1 point above expected level	4	17
Equal to	9	34
1 point below expected level	16	29
2 points below expected level	12	12
3 points below expected level	21	4
4 points below expected level	12	—
5 points below expected level	13	—
6 points below expected level	7	—
7 points below expected level	3	—
8 points below expected level	1	—
	100	100

*From *The Revised Visual Retention Test* by A. L. Benton[42].

by a brain-damaged group and by persons who have been screened for an absence of organic brain disease.

The Grassi Block Substitution Test [153]

Grassi requires the client to make copies of a set of blocks. The models are presented to the client at four levels of increasing complexity. These range from the simple concrete task in which the client copies only the top side of the model to the complex concrete task where he has to copy all six sides of the model correctly. He must produce it in a different color schema.

TESTS FOR SPECIFIC CEREBRAL CONDITIONS

Aphasia, Agnosia, and Apraxia

Eisenson's [109] technique continues to be one of the most comprehensive and popular psychological methods for examining for the presence of aphasia and associated disorders. The manual describes the nature of congenital and acquired aphasia as well as areas of disturbance and testing for intellectual changes. The materials in Eisenson's tests are a set of pictures, colors, geometric forms, and selected verbal items. Additionally, a kit is furnished consisting of such materials as a penknife, a teaspoon, a key, a shoelace, a comb, scissors, and a clock face with easily movable hands. The test is constructed for both screening and diagnosis. Evaluation of the following pathological conditions is possible.

1. Primarily for evaluative and receptive disturbances:
   - (a) Visual agnosia: recognition of common objects, pictures, colors, forms, numbers, letters, printed words, and printed sentences.
   - (b) Auditory agnosia: recognition of sounds such as coughing, humming, whistling, clapping, and word identification.
   - (c) Tactile agnosia: object identification while blindfolded using left and right hand.
   - (d) Auditory-verbal aphasia: verbal comprehension, oral sentences, reading comprehension, oral paragraphs.
   - (e) Silent-verbal aphasia: silent reading comprehension.
2. Primarily for productive and expressive disturbances:
   - (a) Non-verbal apraxia: body parts, simple skills, and pretended action.

(b) Verbal apraxia: numbers, words, and sentences.
(c) Automatic speech-counting: recitation of various types, singing.
(d) Writing: numbers and letters, spelling, naming, word-finding, arithmetic processes, and oral reading.
(e) Time recognition: clock setting.

In Eisenson's test, all areas are scored as to extent of loss in the following manner: complete, severe, moderate, little, or none.

A shorter method for the examination of agnosia, apraxia, and aphasia is offered in the *Mental Examiners' Handbook* [389]. Basically, this method is similar to the longer and more thorough Eisenson technique. Again we have naming objects, repetition of spoken words, writing from dictation, complicated actions (testing for ideational apraxia), tactile recognition of objects, plus special tests for agraphia, alexia, and Parkinson's disease. In addition, the authors have offered a method for estimating percentage of loss, although no data are given to show the validity or reliability of such an estimate. Loss in each area is computed by the percentage of answers that the client failed.

The Kahn Aphasia Test, Experimental (KAT) [203]

Another approach that claims to do no more than a rough screening is the KAT, which consists of a set of ten questions to be used with the same materials used in the KTSA. The test does not attempt to measure the finer differentiations of disease entities, but merely to detect their presence and roughly estimate the amount of loss. As a quick and convenient screening method, it has proven useful in alerting the psychologist to the possible presence of an organic condition and the need for a more thorough investigation of the client's symptoms.

1. Examiner places strip in front of the client and says: "Please read the numbers on this strip beginning with 1." Upon completion of this task, examiner says: "Now read the numbers backward beginning with 15."
2. Examiner points to number 13 and asks: "What number is this?" In the same manner examiner points to numbers 5, 7, 2, and 14, asking each time: "What number is this?"
3. Examiner places the following eleven test objects randomly on the table: three dogs, a cross, a circle, three hearts, a brown butterfly, two red stars, and asks the client to name each of the objects.

4. Using the same eleven objects as in (3), the examiner places them on the strip in any order on spaces 1, 2, 3, 5, 7, 9, 11, 13, 14, 15. Examiner says: "Now I will name each object and as I name it please pick it up in your hand. Then put your hand with the object in it behind your back and then put the object back where it was on the strip."
5. Examiner puts all of the test objects on the table and says: "Show me some objects that are red." After the client has complied, he asks: "Show me some objects that are black. Show me an object that is white and one that is green." Examiner asks: "What were the four colors of the objects that you have just shown me? Tell me what the colors were."
6. Examiner picks up the white dog and shows it to the client for about three seconds and places it in the box out of sight. Examiner asks: "What object did I just put into the box?" Examiner repeats this with a red star, the cross, and the circle.
7. Examiner places all the objects on the table so that they can be seen by the client and says: "Point to three objects that look like something that shines in the sky at night and tell me what shines in the sky at night." After the client has complied (or tried), examiner says: "Point to the objects that look like animals that can run and bark and tell me what you call those animals." After the client has complied, examiner says: "Point to the objects that look like something that can fly and tell me what it is that can fly."
8. Examiner gives the client both butterflies and says: "Give me the one that is heavier." Examiner gives the client the blue and red heart and says: "Give me the one that is lighter in weight." Examiner gives the client the large dog and a red star and says: "Give me the one that is heavier."
9. Examiner places any ten objects randomly on the table in front of the client and also places the box cover and box base in front of him. Examiner shows that both sections of the box are empty and says: "Put all of these objects in these boxes, placing half of them in this box (points to one section) and half of them in this box (points to the other section)."
10. Examiner points to one of the box sections and asks: "How many objects are in this box?" If the client fails, examiner tells the client "five." He then places these objects in the other box section and asks: "How many objects are in this box (the one with all the objects in it) now?" Examiner places the empty half of the box

over the box with the objects, thus hiding them from view and asks: "How many of the objects in this box can you recall?" A minimum of four objects should be recalled for a passing score.

The KAT is not designed to be used by clients with IQs below 70 or children under 7 years of age. The examiner must be certain that the client understands the test instructions and has sufficient verbal skill to comprehend them. Additionally, the examiner should be alert to the client's level of involvement in the testing situation, since malingering and a lack of interest can produce invalid results.

The KAT screens for the presence of agnosia, aphasia, and apraxia. Agnosia is indicated by many errors in a variety of tasks throughout the test. Aphasia is suggested by errors on parts 1, 2, 3, 6, 10, recall of colors on 5, and by failure in naming objects on 7. Apraxia is indicated by errors on parts 4, 5, 7, 8, and 9. It should be noted that there may be considerable overlapping. Loss due to aphasia, apraxia, or agnosia is considered moderate if there are one to four errors; moderately severe if there are four to eight errors; severe if there are over eight errors. Each task failed is counted as one error.

DETERMINING CEREBRAL DOMINANCE

The Harris Tests of Lateral Dominance [166]

This is used in speech and reading clinics with clients where lateral dominance may be a factor and for preschool age groups with motor handicaps. The test is also applicable to ages six and over. It yields 13 scores to determine which hemisphere is dominant. These are:

1 and 2. Knowledge of left- and right-hand performance
3. Simultaneous writing
4. Handwriting
5. Tapping
6. Dealing cards
7. Strength of grip
8. Total hand dominance
9. Monocular sighting
10. Binocular sighting
11. Visual acuity
12. Total eye dominance
13. Kicking

Peacher[285] writes:

> It is conceivable that this test [Harris Test of Lateral Dominance] might also be of value in the determination of laterality in cerebral lesions in adults with aphasia. This would concern the case of pathology in Broca's area in right-handed individuals in the absence of aphasia. Detailed testing, by revealing that such an individual may actually be predominantly left-handed, may obviate the production of aphasia in the anticipated dominant hemisphere.

The A-B-C Vision Test for Ocular Dominance[263]

This test was designed by Walter R. Miles and is applicable to ages of five years or over. It requires simultaneous and balanced use of the hands and gives the client the impression that he is using both eyes when in actuality he is employing unilateral vision. It is considered to be the "most satisfactory single test of ocular dominance presently available"[369]. Materials include three V-scopes, ten area-blackness comparison cards, and instructions for administration.

TESTS PRIMARILY DESIGNED FOR THE ASSESSMENT OF PERSONALITY OR INTELLIGENCE

The foregoing tests were designed specifically for the evaluation of organic conditions. The tests that follow are used just as frequently for determination of organic brain pathology, although their general function is a much broader one. The fact that they are not confined to any specific disease entity makes them, in some respect, more useful because they suggest other diagnostic categories in the event that organic pathology is not indicated. It is unlikely that a psychological method can identify only behavior due to cortical or motor neural tract deficiency without being sensitive to general personality characteristics.

The Bender Motor Gestalt Test[39]

This is a popular inclusion in the organic battery. Lauretta Bender devotes two chapters of her manual of the test to the clinical evaluation of organic factors. These deal with:

1. Sensory aphasia and cerebral localization of the visual motor gestalt function.
2. The disturbance in visual motor gestalten in different types of organic brain disease.

Although the author describes responses typical of other conditions (such as schizophrenia, manic depressive psychosis, mental defectiveness, and psychoneuroses), the test's greatest usefulness remains in the field of organic assessment and in the evaluation of developmental motor maturity levels. The materials consist of eight cards, each one presenting a geometric design that the client is asked to copy. Many psychologists simply have the client reproduce the figures as he sees them on the card. Others require the client to draw the figures from memory after a time lag. Figure 8.1 shows the designs as they appear on the cards. Nine of the designs are taken from Wertheimer's original patterns, which he used for research in visual Gestalt psychology [390].

In her discussion of *dementia paralytica*, Bender describes how persons with this condition are apt to make their figures very small, to fragment and separate parts. This is found to be associated with various diseases of the brain and occurs as a result of weakening or poverty of impulses. In cases where there is not much evidence of pathology and intelligence remains intact there are tendencies to revert to primitive groups. Such primitivization may be assessed by referring to Fig. 8.2. It

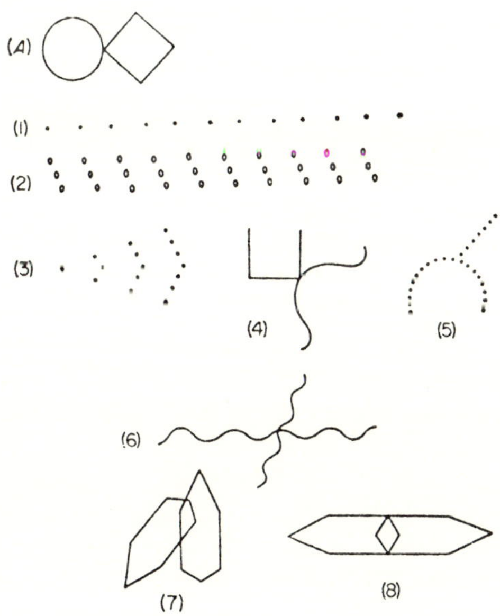

Fig. 8.1 Test figures. From T. C. Kahn and M. B. Giffen. *Psychological Techniques in Diagnosis and Evaluation.* Oxford: Pergamon Press, 1960.

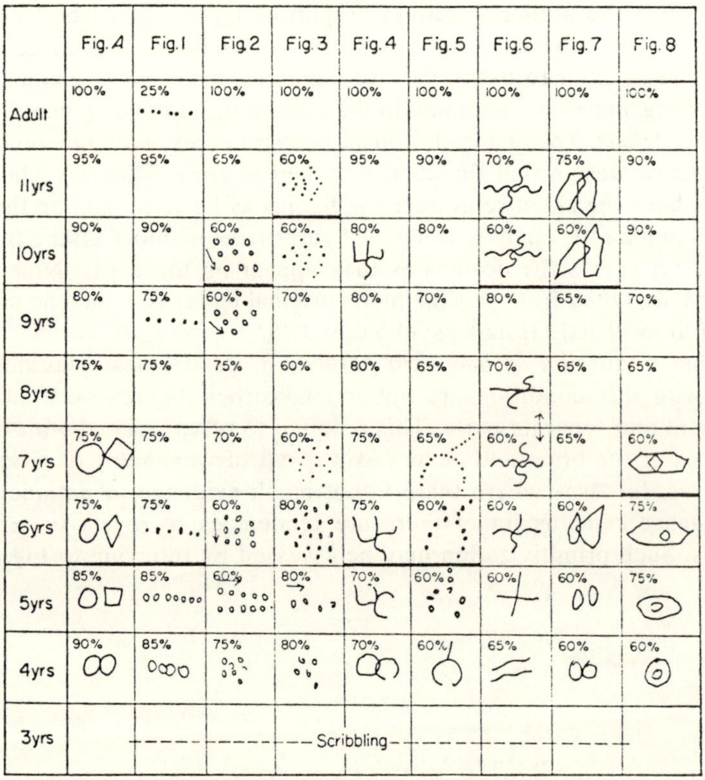

Fig. 8.2 Summary of responses for each year of age in developing children. It may be used for evaluating maturational norms and levels of retardation and regression. From T. C. Kahn and M. B. Giffen. *Psychological Techniques in Diagnosis and Evaluation.* Oxford: Pergamon Press, 1960.

shows what can be expected at various age levels. Regression to an early psychomotor developmental level is found to be associated with many diseases—functional as well as organic.

Clients having progressive encephalopathy (such as seen in alcoholic psychoses) often show a tendency to interrupt an incomplete figure by stroke-like perseverations. Those with traumatic psychoses sometimes produce bizarre forms. Disturbance in acute confusional states is reflected in poor integration of parts of the figures as compared to the whole with some confusion of background. In such cases, primitive regression is secondary to the primary difficulty. When the disease produces lethargy or dullness, micrographia is often noted on the Bender.

In general, psychologists consider the following as organic signs on the Bender:

1. Serious disturbance of internal gestalt.
2. Primitive features.
3. Modification or substitution of parts of figure.
4. Micrographia or macrographia.
5. Difficulty with angles.
6. Partial rotation (as compared with complete rotation believed to be more typical of schizophrenia).
7. Vagueness and sketchiness.
8. Loss of detail and fragmentation.
9. Perseveration, concreteness, overlapping, and oversimplification.
10. Manifestations of need for visual guidance, such as using the edge of the paper as a guide, drawing guide-lines, especially when associated with impotence and perplexity.

It is usual to find one or more of these organic signs among clients having brain damage. If only one sign is found, it is usually clearly and strongly manifested. If several signs are present, they may be correspondingly less obvious upon superficial inspection. To illustrate: a client in a psychiatric hospital ward was given a diagnosis of functional psychosis. On psychological testing, this client gave responses strongly suggestive of organic brain disease. The client died and, when autopsied later, the brain sections demonstrated extensive and diffuse cortical deterioration. This was consistent with his performance on the Bender Test, which had elicited unmistakable organic signs. Psychological findings of organic cortical involvement must be taken seriously since, occasionally, psychological signs of organicity may be the only available indicators of central nervous system involvement.

The Draw-A-Person Test (D-A-P) [244]

The D-A-P, as it is commonly called, simply requires that the client draw a person. He is free to draw any type of person, male or female. After the completion of the first drawing, he is asked to draw a person of the opposite sex. One of the pioneers in this method of appraisal, Karen Machover, has included in her book on human figure drawing characteristic responses of individuals suspected of organic brain pathology. She considers the following suggestive:

1. Lack of details.
2. Erasures infrequent.

3. Figures may be large.
4. Head large.
5. Lines heavy and simple.
6. Proportions poor.
7. Synthesis weak.
8. Omission of parts.

It has been found that tests that are easiest to administer are sometimes the most difficult to interpret. These signs, which Machover lists as characteristic of clients with brain lesions, are not easy to distinguish from similar performance by some types of neurotics and psychotics. However, if one has had extensive experience with the drawings of various types of clinical groups, one finds that they do follow recognizable patterns and, therefore, to the experienced eye, the D-A-P has a useful place in the organic battery. This is also true of drawings other than those involving persons as the theme. In general, the art production of persons with organic brain disease shows an emptiness with marked absence of detail and distortion of proportions. Bizarre features, the distinguishing mark of the florid schizophrenic, are seen among persons with organic brain pathology only when psychosis is also present. The brain-damaged client's integration of the parts of the drawing (his so-called gestalt formation) is apt to be weaker than that of the non-organic schizophrenic. (See Chapter 7 for a discussion of differential diagnosis with psychological tests.)

The Lowenfeld Mosaic Test [240]

The Lowenfeld method of examination was developed in England and is becoming more popular in the United States and other countries. It gets away from the paper-and-pencil aspect of psychological testing and allows the client to work with geometrically shaped plastic designs of various colors. The literature on the use of this test for organic brain disease is growing, although the test designer's own book remains as the classic. The chapter in the book written by Dr. Henri Ellenberger [240] describes the performance of clients with cerebral arteriosclerosis, cerebral atrophy, cerebral stroke with aphasia, traumatic brain damage, Korsakoff's Syndrome, general paresis, post-encephalitic syndromes, and epilepsy. Organic signs on the Mosaic Test are:

1. Lack of response to the test.
2. Lack of comprehension of test directions (advanced cases).

3. Lack of enjoyment in taking the test (in contrast to schizophrenics).
4. Irritation by difficulties of the test, often with an expression of dissatisfaction and feelings of having failed.
5. Difficulty and failure in achieving the gestalt the client has in mind.
6. Selection of a simpler design after failing the more complicated designs.

Organic signs in the mild forms of the disease:

1. Poorly executed construction of small geometric patterns.
2. Confusion of shapes of test objects. For example, a client may construct a design in which the use of a triangle would complete the picture. Instead, he attempts to use a square and does not seem to realize why it fails to fit into the picture.
3. After successful performance in making simple designs, the client fails when the examiner asks him to make a more complicated design.
4. Insensitivity to variations in color. The client may make a design using a color that does not fit with the others. He is usually unable to correct this even if the error is called to his attention.
5. An apparently senseless attempt on the part of the client to keep fitting pieces together in a meaningless manner, regardless of design. Automatic placement with no reference to design suggests the presence of more extensive damage.

A case from Dr. Ellenberger's files[240] illustrates the value of the technique.

> . . . Another of our female patients was diagnosed as paranoid schizophrenic. She had the delusion that she possessed a large fortune which the government had stolen from her. Invited to do an LMT, the patient said she wanted to make a cross—which, in view of her exalted religious beliefs, did not surprise us. But she could not succeed in arranging the arms of the cross. When she tried to correct what she had done wrong she only succeeded in making it worse . . . . The result of the test led us to suspect that the exalted or paranoid utterances of the patient were nothing more than an empty automatism which concealed an organic affection of the brain. She died of heart failure . . . a few weeks after the test, the autopsy disclosed the existence of generalized brain atrophy, without any focal lesion observable with the naked eye.

The Rorschach [317]

The Rorschach's use as a method for detecting organic brain disease is controversial. Nevertheless, it is sometimes used since under certain circumstances it appears to be helpful. The authors recall a case where a

40-year-old, single, white male had exhibited his genitals in a theater to a young girl sitting next to him. Psychiatric evaluation and complete social case history delineated an individual who suffered extensively from castration anxiety, feelings of sexual inferiority, and impotence; in general, he was chronically functioning on a schizoid level of adjustment. The manifestation of "exhibitionism" fitted precisely into the picture and the behavioral traits suggested a diagnosis of a personality disorder. However, psychological evaluation elicited classical signs of organic brain disease. Following this clue, pneumoencephographic studies were performed that outlined a central nervous system lesion.

Bell's book, *Projective Techniques* [36], lists ten signs of organic brain disease as originally formulated by Piotrowski. These have become known as the "Piotrowski signs" of organic brain damage. Bell describes them as "among the most valuable for clinical diagnosis, although their findings have not been entirely accepted by other experimenters" [36]. They have been rephrased so as to be more intelligible to persons not acquainted with Rorschach terminology.

Ten Piotrowski Signs of Organic Brain Disease

1. Number of responses less than 15.
2. Response time greater than 60 seconds.
3. Less than two M (Human Movement responses). More than two M may occur in post-traumatic organics with little personality change.
4. Less than 70 percent of the responses are of average form level.
5. Less than four popular responses.
6. One or more color-naming responses (this sign overlaps with schizophrenics, especially those with deterioration).
7. Perseveration of a response at least three times without regard to form accuracy (this particular type of perseveration overlaps only with schizophrenics and the feeble-minded).
8. Impotence—that is, the client gives a response he knows is a poor one, but still does not or cannot withdraw it.
9. Perplexity—that is, the client asks constantly for directions and assurance from the examiner. He asks things like: "Is that the right answer?" "Did I say the right thing?" "You see it, don't you?" This may occur persistently throughout the record.
10. Automatic phrases that are illogical and irrelevant to the task. (Certain types of neurotic clients, especially obsessive-compulsives, will exhibit automatic phrases, but they will be logically placed and pertinent to the testing situation.)

Seven Rorschach Signs of Nonpsychotic Organics—Idiopathic Epileptics [159]

1. Stickiness—that is, a modified perseveration in which the client changes the location variable and even subtly changes the concept itself. The perseveration is on a higher intellectual level than the organic perseveration and will not fall to a minus form level.
2. Pickiness—that is, a Detail (D) to a Small Detail (Dd) approach that results in a larger number of responses than in psychotic organics and is frequently accompanied by good form level.
3. Human Movement (M) responses are outweighed by the sum of color responses (C).
4. Human Movement (M) responses are frequently given in contrast to organics and schizophrenics, but many of the M's are poor form level and their number actually increases with the amount of pathology involved.
5. Fewer Animal Movement responses (FM) than normals (this may be due to the epileptic's preoccupation with the human body).
6. Responses with Color dominant but Form present (CF) plus Pure Color response (C) are greater than responses with Form dominant but Color present (FC). This sign has a total overlap with psychotics and neurotics, except psychopaths.
7. A staccato flow of interpretation—that is, an unsystematic blocking apparently unrelated to blot or concept variables; uneven sequence of response and reaction times with intra-card blockings.

The Kahn Test of Symbol Arrangement (KTSA) [197]

This technique, which utilizes recall ability and capacity to make space-color-form associations, has been found helpful in identifying clients with organic brain pathology. The test materials include 16 plastic objects having easily recognized shapes with the exception of one object, vaguely resembling a parrot (see Fig. 8.3). The objects used are: three hearts, three dogs, three stars, an anchor, a circle, a partial circle, a cross, a parrot, and two butterflies. Murphy *et al.* [270] call this method "a radically new approach to the problem of personality evaluation." In their study they were able to distinguish clients with organic impairment from a mixed group using this test. In another study, Kahn reports: "Cutoff scores were established for the four groups in the two studies . . . a cutoff score of 54 would separate 92 percent of the first organic group and 100 percent of the second organic group from all non-brain-damaged subjects in both groups" provided three "normal" subjects over 70 years old (in whom

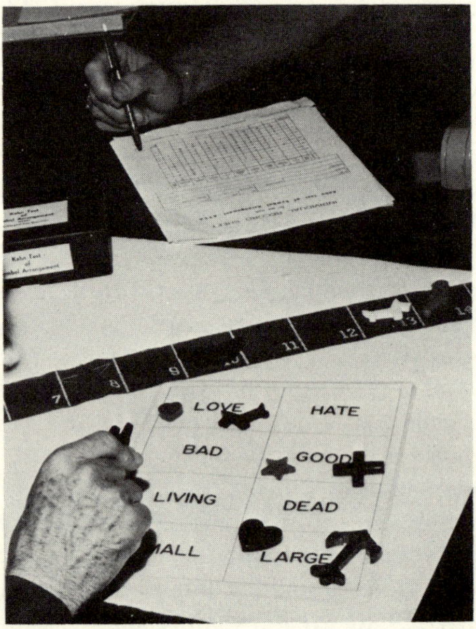

Fig. 8.3 Kahn Test of Symbol Arrangement.

some cortical damage may be suspected on the basis of age) are excluded from the study. In all, over 150 test subjects were involved in this investigation[196]. Goldenson writes: "The Kahn Test of Symbol Arrangement—can be employed with verbally blocked or unresponsive clients because of its manipulative aspects. Reliability and validity studies have yielded impressive results"[145]. Craddick and L'Abate[89] have written a monograph summarizing the most recent studies utilizing this test. They have several pages devoted to a description of the use of this test with clients having a variety of types of organic brain pathology.

Nonpsychotic Organic Signs

1. Slow, careful performance.
2. Similarly shaped objects carefully placed together; few slants becoming more frequent with increased pathology.
3. Reversals appear as pathology increases.
4. Meticulousness in the Naming task with many but usually not all of the objects.
5. Pointing out likenesses and differences of test objects.

6. Difficulty in recognizing transparent butterfly, or in naming circle.
7. High "C" score (same as before response).
8. As pathology increases, "D" score (naming or describing function of test objects) becomes more prominent, and "Z" (intangible abstraction) fades out.
9. Presence of "A" score (bizarre responses) suggests involvement of emotional or cognitive areas.
10. Number element usually between 50 and 70.

Psychotic Organic Signs

1. More slanted and inverted objects than any other group, disorderly arrangement on strip, objects out of segments, overlapping.
2. In severe pathology, two objects may be placed in one segment or objects may be crowded on the strip or fitted into each other.
3. Usually slow or very slow arrangement time.
4. May have bursts of high speed practically throwing objects down on strip.
5. Generally does not place star on star, or butterfly on butterfly in objects—over task, Arrangement III.
6. More divergencies from norms in Naming and in recall tasks than any other group.
7. Number Element above 50 is rare; usual range 15–50.
8. "D" (Naming or Function) is the typical Letter Element with "B" (No Reason, No Symbolization) and "X" (Concrete Association) also prominent; the occasional "Z" (Intangible Abstraction) indicates descent from a former intellectual level.
9. Seldom names "P" object as parrot.
10. Fails to place similarly shaped objects together in the arrangements, sorts objects automatically without reference to the meaning of the words printed in the rectangles.*

The KTSA also provides for an estimate of percentage loss due to deterioration by using the Numerical Element of the symbol pattern in the following formula:

$$\% \text{ of Loss} = 100 - \left(\frac{\text{Numerical Element}}{\text{IQ}} \times 100\right).$$

*Compare these signs with other types of indications of organic brain disease on the KTSA shown in the Kahn Manual [198] and the review by Craddick and L'Abate [89].

In other words, if a client obtains a Numerical Element of 90 and his IQ is 120, his loss of efficiency is estimated to be:

Numerical Element divided by IQ − 0.75
0.75 times 100 = 75
100 minus 75 = 25, indicating 25 percent loss.

This method is still experimental but in the absence of other test methods of estimating percent of loss of function, it is being used to assist clinical judgment of loss.

Wechsler Adult Intelligence Scale (WAIS) [386]

In recent years, the WAIS offered brain-damage deterioration scores by contrasting performance on "Hold" and "Don't Hold" subtests. For example, Vocabulary is a "Hold" subtest while Block Design is a "Don't Hold" one. The Wechsler deterioration scores have been largely discarded by psychologists as not being supported by the literature. However, deterioration indices such as these may be valuable since the amount of loss of cerebral efficiency is sometimes crucial in determining compensations where there is head trauma and impaired cortical functioning caused by accidents.

SUMMARY

Psychological tests are an important adjunct to the examination of clients suspected of having cerebral pathology. Their use, however, is justified only in conjunction with neurological and psychiatric examinations. When medical examinations are inconclusive with borderline signs, contradictory clinical manifestations, or overlapping symptomatology, psychological tests can be useful. They may affect the decision of the physician in performing further diagnostic procedures. Their use is also justified in screening clients for referral to medical specialists.

The use of psychological instruments for measuring the amount of mental and intellectual deterioration that has occurred is sometimes necessary. The increased use of psychological tests for assessment of intellectual loss and emotional changes is recommended.

CHAPTER 9

Approaches in Counseling and Psychotherapy

The utilization of psychological techniques with the emotionally disturbed was first systematized by Joseph Breuer and Freud in their treatment of hysterics. This monumental achievement led to the development of a large number of schools of therapy and counseling. The following is a list of some of the contributors to the therapy movement:

Neo-Freudian: A. Adler, E. Fromm, K. Horney, A. G. Jung, O. Rank, H. Sullivan.
Learning Theorists: H. J. Eysenck, E. J. Shoben, J. Dollard, N. E. Miller, A. Banduvra, J. B. Rotter, J. Wolpe.
Phenomenologists: C. R. Rogers, G. A. Kelly, C. H. Patterson, F. Perls.
Existentialists: V. Frankl, R. May, R. R. Grinker.
Eclectics: E. Berne, W. Glasser.
Rationalists: E. G. Williamson, A. Ellis

The overwhelming number of schools of therapy, each with its own techniques and methods, has caused considerable confusion. Each method usually purports to be the only approach for successful treatment, yet when asked which is the best, experts in the mental health profession are unable to give a satisfactory answer because there is no single approach in current therapies that has consistently proven to be superior to other methods.

The vast number of approaches available reflects the paucity of objective research measuring therapeutic processes and comparing the effectiveness of therapeutic procedures. It was not until the work of Carl Rogers that experimental methods were applied, to any extent, in measuring the process and results of counseling and psychotherapy [314]. It would seem that since clinical psychologists are trained as researchers and therapists they share the responsibility in both designing and carrying out more exacting research in the area of psychotherapy.

Another dimension of this problem is that schools of therapy are usually directly related to theories of personality, which are equally numerous in the field of psychology. Much of the controversy and confusion found in schools where therapy is taught stems from the basic personality theory utilized by that school. However, the cause-effect relationship is tenuous since notable fathers of therapy such as Freud and Rogers developed their personality theories from their therapeutic experiences. No matter which cart comes before which horse, personality theories and schools of therapy seem to be intertwined and tend to be ambiguous in regard to both theory and practice.

Whereas personality theories disagree, schools of counseling and psychotherapy do share in the goal of treatment and in their attempt to alleviate mental suffering. Since so many approaches and subsequent techniques are available to practitioners, the art of therapy seems to have produced an "eclectic" effect. Counselors and therapists tend to find approaches and techniques that best fit their counseling method and are appropriate to the problems presented by their clients. Thus, a counselor or therapist is usually not committed to any one school of therapy, although he probably has some allegiance to the basic tenets, particularly those explaining man's behavior, that he learned during his academic schooling and internship. Even this commitment is tenuous since the therapist's experience will cause him to modify, adapt, and substitute new ideas from his earlier position.

The adoption of the eclectic method by many therapists may help to explain studies that show that experienced therapists become more convergent in approach and techniques even though they are a product of different schools of therapy [347, 349]. These researchers also indicate that the methods of experienced therapists are different from those of neophyte therapists even when both are products of the same university. Results seem to point out that experience has a major effect on therapeutic procedure and that therapists do not necessarily remain within the school of therapy that they were exposed to during their clinical training.

It is conceivable that there is a relationship between survival in the profession and common personality characteristics shared by therapists. Thus, there may be a tendency toward finding methods and developing techniques that are similar. It also should be pointed out that today many academic programs are becoming eclectic in their training. As more practitioners graduate from these diversified programs, the differences between experienced practitioners and neophyte therapists may diminish.

Keeping in mind the variety of methods and techniques of therapy available and the arbitrariness of their selection by therapists, it would now seem useful to review some of the traditional schools of therapy to demonstrate some of their basic tenets and procedures. In a book of this limited scope it is impossible to give a representative picture of all therapies utilized today. The counseling and therapeutic approaches that have been selected hopefully will provide the core characteristics of the more popular methods presently in use. Of course, the selection is arbitrary and many worthy approaches may have been overlooked.

The approaches to therapy presented here and in the following chapter are grouped together according to major components, theory, style, and techniques. The first part of this chapter will emphasize the cognitive models, including the trait and factor school of E. G. Williamson and the rational-emotive methods of Albert Ellis. Those therapies subscribing to the basic tenets of learning theory usually classified as behavior modification will also be discussed. The second part of the chapter will present the traditional therapies, which stress the affective or emotional context. These are characterized by the probing of unconscious patterns of behavior, the phenomenological concept of the self, and the irrationality of man. Therapies represented in this section are also divided into two parts: the psychoanalytic methods and the client-centered approach. Chapter 10 will present some of the newer and more unusual procedures, including transactional analysis, reality therapy, homonological therapy, and an approach considered by many to be a preventive therapy for the normal person—sensitivity training. Most of these newer approaches could be considered eclectic since they combine many ideas and procedures from both the cognitive and affective schools.

No attempt has been made to present every aspect of the therapies in depth. Many sources are provided throughout these chapters for further information. We have also made no systematic effort to give examples of each of the different therapeutic processes since these can be found in the current literature; however, excerpts from sessions of a few new types of therapies not readily found are represented.

COGNITIVE APPROACHES

Traditionalist therapies appear to share some common characteristics. The climate of the client-therapist relationship is similar to that of the physician-patient. The counselor or therapist usually establishes himself as the expert in the relationship, imparting advice to the client. In fact, at times he may become a type of educator, giving information that extends choices for the client, suggesting "homework" assignments to be completed between counseling sessions, etc. The counselor or therapist usually takes a detailed history, analyzes the problem(s), supplies tentative solutions, and aids the client in making decisions.

Trait and Factor Approach

This rational view of therapy is a product of E. G. Williamson, Donald Paterson, and others at the University of Minnesota. The origins of this approach were founded in vocational counseling but it has since developed into a more general method of counseling and therapy.

Williamson sees man as having the capacity for both good and evil. He feels that man grows and develops as a result of interaction within his environment, that he strives for optimum potential, and that each person has the right for self-determination because he is unique and different[400]. However, this self-determination may not be acceptable to the therapist if the behavior is antisocial[397]. Williamson also states that counseling or therapy should ideally be voluntary, although it is not a necessary element for a therapeutic relationship to evolve[394].

Trait and factor therapy begins with an in-depth collection of background information from both the client and outside sources. Additionally, the counselor may choose to administer a series of appropriate psychological tests. The collected information is synthesized and the counselor then formulates some hypotheses concerning the causes of the client's problems. He also may set up a specific plan of action to overcome the client's difficulties, although this is usually done with the client participating.

When the actual therapeutic relationship begins, the counselor attempts to establish rapport by demonstrating a professional attitude and showing genuine interest and concern for the client. As the client's confidence is gained, the counselor centers on helping the client understand himself—his assets, liabilities, and the probable causes of his problems. He then attempts to aid his client in planning the proper course of action to alleviate the area of difficulty. Generally, the counselor follows up his client's activities to insure that the programs were carried out and the desired results achieved.

The trait and factor method is a very directive, tutorial approach. Stress is on the cognitive processes of the individual while deemphasizing his affective, emotional realms. Detailed data collection and use of objective tests give the trait and factor therapists a more objective, scientific orientation. Trait and factor therapists are often criticized for their direct control of the relationship.

Some critics feel that this approach does not allow the client to solve his own problems, thus creating a dependency relationship. The emphasis on cognitive processes overlooks the complex emotional affective world of the client and, therefore, this method may not help the client understand the many-faceted aspects of his behavior[280]. Thus, the approach appears to be most effective in situations where advice is needed, where emotions and feelings play a lesser role in the client's problems, and where there is need for an expert's "guiding hand."

Rational-Emotive Approach

Another cognitive approach popularized by Albert Ellis is what he terms rational-emotive therapy. Ellis feels that man is made up of both rational and irrational components. If he is rational, he is well-adjusted; if he is controlled by irrational thinking, then he experiences maladjustment or, as Ellis points out, he demonstrates deviant behavior[280]. He treats emotions as irrational thought since these detract from rational thinking. Therefore, the bases of maladjustment are irrational thought patterns that are maintained by internal verbalization. These irrational patterns can be eliminated by teaching the client to think rationally, thus making self-verbalizations rational and not illogical and self-defeating[111]. Ellis also identifies the ways that lead to neurotic behavior or irrational thinking. These include such concepts as:

1. "Everyone must love me and approve of what I do"[111]. Ellis feels that the need for approval is only necessary to achieve one's own purposes.
2. "There are bad and wicked people and they should be punished—this may include yourself"[111]. Ellis points out the relativity in moral right and wrong and judging the behavior of others may be an irrational process.
3. "Fearful or dangerous situations must receive constant attention"[111]. Ellis shows that an inordinate amount of time and energy is wasted on worry and that the rational person will deal with situations directly and reduce threat or accept it.
4. "One should rigidly adhere to lessons and experiences of the past"[111]. It is pointed out that the past experiences should not

necessarily affect one permanently; the past should be utilized, but one should be open to new experiences.

5. "There is a need to be dependent on others" and "we should be concerned about the problems of others"[111]. These two positions seem to go together since Ellis feels that the rational person will seek independence and will build on his own initiative. Also, the rational thinker is not overly concerned about the problems of others. Other peoples' problems are their own, and an over-concern adds little to one's well-being. If problems have a detrimental effect upon a person, he should make an effort to eliminate them.

The purpose of rational-emotive therapy is to substitute logical, rational thoughts for those that are illogical and irrational. The rational therapist carries this out through direct, frank attacks on the client's irrational thoughts. He may do this through confrontation, cajoling, and, at times, "teaching" the client. The therapist functions as the expert in the relationship and gives advice and subsequent direction to his client.

The effectiveness of the rational-emotive approach is highly speculative. Ellis reports a success rate of 90 percent, although this includes cases reported as improved as well as cured[111]. This figure is also affected by his arbitrary selection of clients. Ellis is quick to point out that the rational-emotive approach is best used with certain types of clients. For example, they must demonstrate at least average intelligence and have the ability to reason.

Behavior Therapy

Behavior modification or behavior therapy has been described as truly a psychologist's approach to treatment. This is supported by the fact that behavior therapy is grounded in learning theories that have been traditionally recognized as within the realm of psychology, even though several psychiatrists (particularly Joseph Wolpe) have had a great deal of influence in shaping basic methods. Although not a new form of treatment, it is only recently that behavior modification has gained recognition as a legitimate approach. Today it is becoming one of the more popular treatment techniques as demonstrated by the number of new texts in the field. Mikulas[262] states that more behavior modification texts have been published since 1969 than were written in all previous history.

Like many other therapeutic approaches, the impetus for behavior modification came about as a reaction to analytic procedures, although most behavior modifiers extend this criticism to include all affectively oriented therapies. An example of this was the vocal attacks by Eysenck who tried to show that the dynamic approach to therapy was little better than no treatment at all. Even though his research had many design errors, his basic findings have led to behavior modification therapists challenging their affective counterparts to demonstrate scientifically their effectiveness of treatment. Most behavior therapists feel that affectively oriented therapies, particularly psychoanalysis, are time consuming, expensive and usually available only to clients who represent the segment of society that has adequate intelligence, insight, and economic affluence. However, the major criticism voiced by behavior theorists is in the analytic premise of the intrapsychic powers or psychological constructs that control man's behavior. The constructs used by analysts to explain behavior have been ambiguous and difficult to objectively identify and measure. Most behavior modifiers object to the mystical realm of the intra-world where few predictable laws of current and future behavior can be stated and quantitatively tested. They also object to the definition of abnormal behavior, which is usually explained by the dynamic practitioners as some sort of intrapsychic conflict within the individual.

Behavior theorists place the emphasis on environmental stimuli and thus maladjustment comes about not from within the client but as a result of the interaction between client and environment. Since behavior is maintained through contingencies of reinforcement, and almost all behaviors are learned (including those which society considers maladjusted), behaviors can be unlearned, changed, modified, or substituted. These are usually chosen by the client, although it is possible that the stimulus for change comes directly from societal controls since it is society that maintains the reinforcers. The model for pathology is not medical or disease-oriented but based on the premise that the client failed to learn proper responses or that responses previously learned were problem creating. This assumes that there is no underlying cause of observed symptoms and no concealed conflict repressed in the psyche. The removal of inappropriate behavior is the sole concern of the behavior therapist; therefore, the obese client is treated for eating habits, the male impotent for his lack of erection at the appropriate time, and the homosexual for his socially disapproved interest in the same sex.

Behavior therapy or behavior modification is usually classified as a cognitive process although it differs from other cognitive models in its strict adherence to the theoretical systems of learning theories. A variety of behavioral approaches are available although most can be grouped into two general categories: the respondent or classical school, which follows the theory of Pavlov, and those favoring the model developed by Skinner, which is usually referred to as operant conditioning. Figure 9.1 represents these two basic models. In practice these two methods are many times combined to bring about behavior change. It might be mentioned that there has also been an effort to combine learning theory and the analytic process in therapy[100]. The practice of this third movement seems to have fallen into disuse although many of the hypotheses concerning complex behavior may prove to be quite valuable in the next decade as behavior therapy matures.

Probably the most popular therapeutic method in behavior modification is "Therapy by Reciprocal Inhibition" developed by Joseph Wolpe. Trained as a psychiatrist, he became discouraged with the analytic approach during World War II and turned his efforts to a study of the classical learning experiments of Pavlov and the animal studies of Hull. Wolpe studied Hull's work in inducing neurotic symptoms in animal subjects and many of his ideas reflect this influence.

Wolpe states that all neuroses are anxiety-based and are caused by a pairing of unconditioned responses with neutral (nonharmful) stimuli present at the time a client experiences a noxious or unpleasant stimulus. Since anxiety responses originate in the sympathetic nervous system, responses from the parasympathetic system would be most incompatible with anxiety responses[403]. A variety of methods are used to inhibit responses to noxious stimuli such as assertive training and deep muscle relaxation. Since its development in 1938 by Jacobson[191], deep muscle

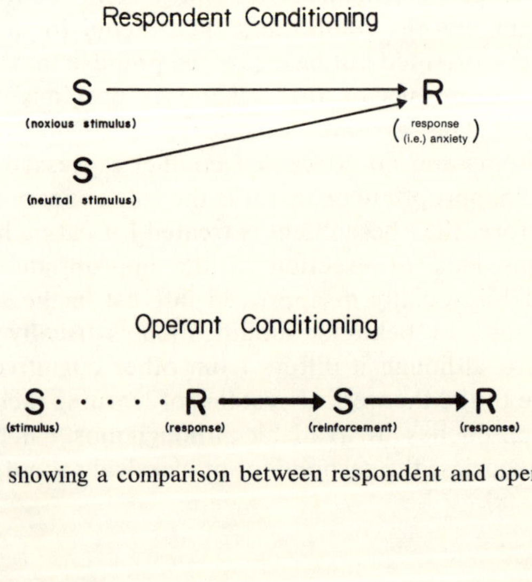

Fig. 9.1 Models showing a comparison between respondent and operant conditioning.

relaxation has become the most popular inhibiting response act. This process, called "systematic desensitization" by Wolpe, appears to be a useful inhibitor in a variety of situations.

Treatment Procedures

The initial effort in reciprocal inhibition therapy is to take a careful, detailed, case history since the therapist must be able to recognize the various reinforcing contingencies within the client's environment that maintain his behavior patterns. During this early phase, the therapist may also administer a battery of personality measurements to judge anxiety, level of neuroses, and strengths and weaknesses in the personality structure. For example, Wolpe reports that he uses the Bernreuter Personality Inventory and the Willoughby Personality Schedule to measure the level of neurotic anxiety existing in his client[403]. When sufficient information has been collected, the therapist discusses the treatment procedure with the client. A hierarchy of anxiety-provoking situations are then constructed with the most anxious situation placed at the highest point. Therapy is commenced with the introduction of deep muscle relaxation exercises. This relaxation training is utilized throughout therapy. Time given for relaxation training in the interview varies, but it decreases dramatically as the client becomes able to reach a state of relaxation within minutes or even seconds at the beginning of each therapy session. Most of the early relaxation training can take place in the privacy of a client's home aided by the use of training tapes.

When the therapist is convinced that the client has reached a state of relaxation (which can be objectively measured by using a Galvanic Skin Response Indicator—GSR), the therapist introduces anxiety-producing stimuli, beginning with those placed at the lower end of the hierarchy. The client is asked to imagine as vividly as possible (fantasize) the anxiety-producing situation. Many times the anxiety-provoking stimuli are in the environment and the therapist can create an actual situation, such as going into a crowded store or driving a car; if this is not practical, he may utilize models, replicas, and even pictures of anxiety-producing stimuli. Since the stimulus is introduced while the client is in a state of relaxation, the relaxation should theoretically inhibit the anxiety reaction and the client should continue to be relaxed rather than anxious in the presence of the stimulus that previously had been anxiety provoking. However, if the anxiety-producing stimulus overcomes relaxation, the therapist merely abandons the stimulus and takes his client back into a state of relaxation.

Most behavior modifiers utilize a nonverbal signal from the client when anxiety is experienced since it is felt that relaxation can be more readily reintroduced if no discussion takes place.

When the client reaches a state of deep relaxation again, the stimulus is reintroduced until the client experiences no anxiety. Once this is accomplished, the next stimulus on the hierarchy is presented, and so on, until the hierarchy has been completed. It should be pointed out that many times during therapy it may be necessary to alter, add new items, or even construct new hierarchies. At all times the therapist encourages his client to attempt to actually experience the anxiety-producing situations in real life *after* he has desensitized himself in the therapy sessions. Wolpe's use of counterconditioning (inhibiting a response) is not a new or unique method; however, he is one of the first to combine a theoretical model to explain behavior and a systemized procedure for treatment of maladjustment based on these learning principles.

Wolpe and his associates report a success rate of roughly 90 percent. Unfortunately, these figures suffer from some of the same criticisms as other statistics of therapies. The results are contaminated by arbitrary client selection, criteria for success, etc. Wolpe's deemphasis of the relationship of therapist and client may also be misleading[56, 215] and the dynamics of this relationship should be investigated. Even with these limitations, reciprocal inhibition appears to be a useful therapeutic procedure.

Operant Conditioning

When B. F. Skinner presented his theories on the control of society by operant means in *Walden Two* [339], he was stating a basic premise for the operant behavior modifiers; control of a client's behavior can be carried out by providing or eliminating reinforcement to bring about desired change. According to this position, behavior can be controlled through the manipulation of reinforcement. This "Law of Effect" presented by E. L. Thorndike in 1923, showed that behavior is more likely to be repeated if it is rewarded. Rewards can be either verbal expressions such as praise, intangibles such as love, or material items such as food, drink, or tokens.

The major role of the Skinnerian therapist is to observe the client's behavior, noting overt actions that should be changed and the possible consequences of this change. The therapist (or human engineer, as he is called) must also determine what the client finds reinforcing or punishing. Most operant conditioning programs have been developed in hospital settings, since this method requires a rigid control of the reinforcers in the environment of the client.

An example of operant procedure follows. The operant modifier carefully observes the client as he interacts within his environment, paying particular attention to the maladjusted behaviors (symptoms) and the reinforcers (positive and/or negative) that maintain the behavior. After consultation with the client and the people in the client's milieu who influence him, the therapist decides what behavior should be extinguished and what new behaviors should be learned. Operant therapists are quick to note that this last point demonstrates a distinct advantage of operant conditioning over respondent. Operant modifiers not only extinguish maladjusted behavior, they also teach or shape new, more appropriate behaviors.

Having reached this point, the therapist must control the environment of his client since improper behavior must receive no reinforcement (or, if necessary, should be punished). New behavior must be shaped through one or a combination of techniques available: successive approximations, modeling, fading, and/or discrimination training. Thus, the therapist designs and engineers a program to bring about behavior change. The program identifies contingencies for reinforcement, behavior to be extinguished, and new behavior to be learned or shaped. Many times this will involve several people (those controlling reinforcement in the client's environment) as well as the manipulation of the client's physical surroundings.

Operant techniques in behavior modification have radically changed procedures with the institutionalized, particularly where token economy systems have been established[24]. This procedure is also utilized in programs with the mentally retarded and with classroom behavior problems[230, 23, 187]. The operant approach has been tried with some success in bringing about behavior change in emotionally disturbed children[238]. Operant conditioning therapy provides a method for modification of behavior where analysis of specified, observable behaviors can be manipulated in a controlled environment.

The following case study represents a combination of behavior modification approaches.

Female, Age 11

Reason for referral. Betty was referred to the Mental Health Clinic by her mother. She suffered from a severe case of trichotillomania (hair-pulling), which had evolved over a five-year period and had recently grown considerably worse. Extensive scalp damage was evident where areas of her head had been completely balded. The client also experienced anxiety over her inability to interact with other people (particularly peers).

Summary of social history. The client's hair-pulling started approximately three months after the separation of her parents. It appears to have begun while the child was asleep or dreaming since hair was initially found around the bed area. As this became more severe, the child began pulling out hair during waking hours in the bedroom and bathroom when alone. Sharp increases were noted during anxiety-producing situations such as birthdays, parental fights, etc.

The parents' relationship prior to termination of their marriage was abusive and hostile. The father would often come home late after heavy drinking and was verbally hostile to the wife, threatening to kill her. (Many such scenes were witnessed by Betty.) He seemed to be indifferent to the children and refused to take part in his daughter's therapy. The mother appeared to be the dominant parental figure. She reported that at one time she was very close to Betty even to the point of being overprotective. However, her availability changed since the divorce and the child started to withdraw from her. She felt that the hair-pulling was probably her fault because she no longer had as much time for the children and had become very short tempered when she had to care for them.

Treatment. In order to modify Betty's behavior, it was first necessary to control her environmental behaviors. It was decided to utilize a strong aversive stimulus to extinguish the trichotillomania. The client was taught to self-condition any hair-pulling cravings by administering a shock whenever the desire appeared. The shock was administered by a portable hand-held shocking device. The client was instructed to go to the bedroom or bathroom, deliberately put her hand to her head, think about pulling hair, then shock herself. The client was also trained in chart-keeping and instructed to record the number of hairs pulled daily for a seven-day period (baseline) and collect and return these to the therapist. In addition, she was told to record the number of hair-pulling cravings that she felt daily on a wrist golf counter. The rationale behind the charting was to give the client immediate feedback about her behavior and also to serve as a stimulus for social reinforcement to be provided by the therapist. The feedback method was used because it made the client more aware of the consequences of her behavior and therefore made it easier to bring it under her control. Aversive training lasted for approximately four weeks. Inspection of the data gathered by the client indicated a definite reduction in hair-pulling behavior. The number of incidents recorded at baseline were 40 per day and this was decreased to 15 per day during training. When it became evident that aversive training was controlling the trichotillomania, the second phase of training was initiated.

Since Betty was particularly shy in the presence of people and was unable to express her feelings, assertion training was started. She was instructed in "feeling talk" behavior, which functioned as a reward when she asserted herself as well as inhibited the feelings of fear that she had first reported in interactions with others. During assertive training, hair-pulling all but ceased. She reported that she felt more confident and that she could control "her problem." Betty also found it easier to interact with her peers.

Follow-up: A follow-up visit took place three months and six months after termination. Betty seemed quite happy and far more outgoing. Trichotillomania had ceased and there was no indication of any symptom substitution.

SUMMARY—THE COGNITIVE MODEL

Cognitive methods of therapy encompass a variety of approaches and techniques. Stress is on the intellectual processes in overcoming maladjustment. Learning theory is basic to some approaches. The therapist perceives himself as an expert in the client-therapist relationship and controls much of the therapeutic process. Success rate is reportedly high although research design is questionable.

AFFECTIVE APPROACHES

It is extremely difficult to select therapeutic approaches that are representative of the affective model since no other area in therapy reflects so much diversity and contradiction. Affective approaches usually emphasize the underlying aspects of man's personality, the psychic processes that cannot be seen yet directly affect the very identity of the individual. Psychological constructs such as the unconscious, the ego, and the self-concept have been created in order to define and give meaning to these inner processes. In various affective methods, terminology may differ depending on the theoretical model used, yet actually the terms often have similar meanings. Thus, it is possible to identify a thread of common conceptualization in a number of the affective approaches. Much of the similarity can no doubt be traced to the original systematic affective approach developed by Freud, which was called "psychoanalysis." The basic premises of this approach molded many subsequent therapeutic models. Its influential status produced both positive and negative reactions and many theorists listed in the introduction founded schools of therapy as a result of, or a reaction to, analytic theory. Yet even within antithesis, the effect was paramount. Thus it seems appropriate to begin this section with a discussion of psychoanalytic therapy, followed by a presentation of the client-centered school, which was founded partly as a reaction to the analytic model. A variety of methods reflecting diversity in the affective approach will be discussed in Chapter 10.

Psychoanalysis

For more than a half century, psychoanalysis has dominated the field of psychotherapy. Its historical significance in psychology is unparalleled and this dynamic school, founded by Sigmund Freud, continues to help shape the therapeutic milieu. New approaches have significantly curtailed the practice of classical Freudian psychoanalysis, yet its influence is still strong in affective approaches.

The process of psychoanalysis is highly integrated with Freud's personality theory. His investigation of the unconscious mind, the instinctual drives of man, and his theory of infantile sexuality play major roles in therapeutic interpretation. It is beyond the scope of this book to trace the development of these theories as they emerged from Freud's practice. Original works are available [128, 131] as well as many excellent interpretations [165, 249].

The basic objective of psychoanalysis is to help the client better understand the inner processes (unconscious) that control much of his behavior. Some of these unconscious motivators may lead to conflict within the client. The roots of the conflict are found in his childhood experiences. The role of the therapist is to bring these conflicts to a conscious level and help the client understand and work them through so that he will make a better adjustment to his life-style.

The analytic school has not been technique-oriented. Freud never seemed to stress specific techniques in his writings and left much latitude to the therapist[128]. However, there are some generalized procedures that can be mentioned.

The preliminary stage in therapy usually involves an interview and the recording of background material. This so-called case work-up may range from superficial to quite extensive, depending on the therapist. In classical analysis, the client reclines in a position that maximizes relaxation while the therapist remains out of his direct view to prevent distraction. It should be noted that contemporary therapists seem to prefer face-to-face contact between the client and themselves. During the initial phase of therapy, the analyst establishes a permissive, nonthreatening environment, utilizing nondirective techniques. He attempts to be noncommittal and accepting of the client. It is during this early part of therapy that free association is encouraged.

The therapist instructs the client to verbalize his thoughts no matter how embarrassing or trivial. As the client attempts this, he experiences unconscious resistance and finds that he is unable to freely verbalize certain thoughts. The analyst helps his client understand this resistance and, through symbolic interpretation, brings to the surface unconscious causes of the resistance. Dreams are also commonly used in this initial interpretation. (Freud felt that dreams were often laden with the symbolic meaning of underlying conflicts.) Free association with interpretation of resistance often may have a cathartic effect on the client since he gains insight into some of his lesser unconscious conflicts. Also, during the period of free association, a relationship has been formed between analyst and client that must precede the next phase of the therapeutic process.

Transference may be the center of psychoanalytic therapy. It is hypothesized that the client will "transfer" to the analyst a role that is basic to the client's conflict. Thus, the analyst becomes the displaced source of frustration, hostility, wishes, etc. that the client has repressed since early childhood. This is called negative transference. The traditional analyst, in essence, loses his own identity in the eyes of his client and becomes this all-pervasive power. Many contemporary analysts do not accept this mirroring effect and feel that transference may be more of a generalized displacement. In this case, the therapist probably maintains at least some of his own unique personality in the relationship.

The analyst interprets the total transference relationship for his client. It is important that the client first accept and then work through this major emotional conflict with the aid of the analyst. This "working through" may be an extremely long, time-consuming process since the material is emotionally charged and deeply rooted within the personality. At termination, the client has an understanding of his unconscious drives and motives, can better control his instinctual urges, and should now make a better adjustment to his environment.

Many critics of analytic therapy feel that the relationship between client and therapist created around transference and interpretation leads to strong dependency ties. This type of criticism seems inappropriate when directed against an entire school of therapy and is probably more characteristic of specific therapists, no matter what their orientation. More valid criticisms are usually centered in such areas as length of time required for treatment and subsequent expense, limitations as to type of appropriate clients, lack of objective research on the effectiveness of the approach, and rigid adherence to a personality theory that makes many assumptions about human nature that have not been verified through research.

Client-Centered Therapy

As its name implies, the focus of this therapeutic process (which was founded by Carl Rogers) is on the client. Rogers became disenchanted with the analytic approach because of his own basic premises of man, his position concerning the self-worth of the individual, and his acceptance of the self-actualizing process proposed by Maslow.

It is interesting that Rogers strayed from the analytic path since his early background appeared to mold him into following tradition. Rogers first entered the Union Theological Seminary, but his interests took him into clinical work with children at Teachers College at Columbia and later at the Institute for Child Guidance. The divergency between his scientific training at Columbia and the analytic approach at the Institute led Rogers to formulate a new approach to therapy. He joined the staff at the University of Ohio in 1940 and two years later published his first major contribution, *Counseling and Psychotherapy* [306]. It was his investigations at the University of Chicago (1945–1957) that were probably the most productive in the development and research of his personality theory and therapeutic approach. More recently Roger's interests have shifted from individual therapy to group sensitivity training for "normal" persons learning interpersonal skills and self-acceptance.

Like other therapists who have developed personality theories from their practice, Rogers' theory of personality and the structure for client-centered therapy are closely interrelated. In his book, *Client-Centered*

Therapy, Rogers [307] published the 19 propositions* of his personality theory:

1. Every individual exists in a changing world of experience of which he is the center.
2. The organism reacts to the field as it is experienced and perceived. This perceptual field is, for the individual, "reality."
3. The organism reacts as an organized whole to this phenomenal field.
4. The organism has one basic tendency and striving—to actualize, maintain and enhance the experiencing organism.
5. Behavior is basically the goal-directed attempt of the organism to satisfy its needs as experienced in the field as perceived.
6. Emotion accompanies and in general facilitates such goal-directed behavior, the kind of emotion being related to the seeking versus the consummatory aspects of the behavior, and the intensity of the emotion being related to the perceived significance of the behavior for the maintenance and enhancement of the organism.
7. The best vantage point for understanding behavior is from the internal frame of reference of the individual himself.
8. A portion of the total perceptual field gradually becomes differentiated as the self.
9. As a result of interaction with the environment, and particularly as a result of evaluational interaction with others, the structure of self is formed—an organized, fluid, but consistent conceptual pattern of perceptions of characteristics and relationships of the "I" or the "me" together with values attached to these concepts.
10. The values attached to experiences, and values which are part of the self-structure, in some instances are values experienced directly by the organism, and in some instances are values introjected or taken over from others, but perceived in distorted fashion as if they had been experienced directly.
11. As experiences occur in the life of the individual, they are either (a) symbolized, perceived, and organized into some relationship to the self, (b) ignored because there is no perceived relationship to the self-structure, (c) denied symbolization or given distorted symbolization because the experience is inconsistent with the structure of the self.
12. Most of the ways of behaving which are adopted by the organism are those which are consistent with the concept of self.
13. Behavior may, in some instances, be brought about by organic experiences and needs which have not been symbolized. Such behavior may be inconsistent with the structure of the self, but in such instances, the behavior is not "owned" by the individual.
14. Psychological maladjustment exists when the organism denies to awareness significant sensory and visceral experiences, which consequently are not symbolized and organized into the gestalt of the self-structure. When this situation exists, there is a basic or potential psychological tension.
15. Psychological adjustment exists when the concept of the self is such that all sensory and visceral experiences of the organism are, or may be, assimilated on a symbolic level into a consistent relationship with the concept of self.

*From *Client-Centered Therapy*, Copyright © 1951 by Carl R. Rogers. Reprinted by permission of Houghton Mifflin Company.

16. Any experience which is inconsistent with the organization or structure of self may be perceived as a threat, and the more of these perceptions there are, the more rigidly the self-structure is organized to maintain itself.
17. Under certain conditions, involving primarily complete absence of any threat to the self-structure, experiences which are inconsistent with it may be perceived, and examined, and the structure of self revised to assimilate and include such experiences.
18. When the individual perceives and accepts into one consistent and integrated system all his sensory and visceral experiences, then he is necessarily more understanding of others and is more accepting of others as separate individuals.
19. As the individual perceives and accepts into his self-structure more of his organic experiences, he finds that he is replacing his present value system—based so largely upon introjections which have been distortedly symbolized—with a continuing organismic valuing process.

Thus, his perception of man is one of a positive, rational being striving toward actualization, or what Rogers terms the fully functioning man[310].

According to Rogers, maladjustment comes about when a person develops perceptual distortion or incongruence between his self-perceptions (self-concept) and his actual environmental experiences. This inconsistency leads to feelings of anxiety since his striving toward actualization has been interrupted and he becomes unsure of his life direction. He must now react to needs and behave in ways that are incongruent with the self[307]. When a person is in a state of incongruence he becomes vulnerable, perceptions become inaccurate, and his perceptual field narrows—giving him tunnel vision. His defenses, which are the distorting mechanisms, now can no longer create perceptual facades. As a result, the perceived self breaks down and self-rejection becomes severe. Rogers feels client-centered therapy is most useful when a person reaches this point of impasse.

Treatment

Like other affective approaches, therapeutic techniques in client-centered therapy are nonspecific. Rogers feels that the attitude of the therapist is singularly more important for success than any techniques the therapist possesses. It is the accepting attitude of the therapist that creates the climate or conditions needed for beneficial emotional growth. The following are the conditions stated by Rogers [308] that are required to bring about change:

1. Two persons are in psychological contact.
2. The first, whom we shall term the client, is in a state of incongruence, being vulnerable or anxious.

3. The second person, whom we shall term the therapist, is congruent or integrated in the relationship.
4. The therapist experiences unconditional positive regard for the client.
5. The therapist experiences an empathic understanding of the client's internal frame of reference and endeavors to communicate this experience to the client.
6. The communication to the client of the therapist's empathic understanding and unconditional positive regard is to a minimal degree achieved.

Rogers, in a recent publication[315] seems to have placed particular emphasis on three of these conditions for success in therapy: genuineness, unconditional positive regard, and empathy.

He describes genuineness as a trait that is central to the success of the therapeutic process. Genuineness requires an openness in the therapist, both toward his feelings for his client's experiences and toward himself as a worthy person. He enters into an honest relationship with his client where there are no pretenses, no roles, and no promises. This openness allows the therapist to "tune in" to and reflect his client's feelings which, in turn, helps the client build trust in his therapist. There is no professional facade and no false expertise on the part of the therapist. It is more an encounter between two individuals of equal status, where the therapist demonstrates a sincere effort to help his client explore the incongruence in the perceived self. The therapist is open to his client's feelings and to his own, which helps lead to a genuineness in the relationship.

It is felt that unconditional positive regard develops if the therapist is sincere in the relationship and communicates an accepting attitude to his client. No preconditions are established for this acceptance and there are no moral nor value judgments placed on the behavior of the client. This total prizing may be a difficult thing for the client to integrate since important people in his world have probably not given him this kind of acceptance. Once the client feels that the therapist is genuine, he is able to trust the therapist with his own feelings and thoughts. The unqualified acceptance of the client does not mean that the therapist approves or personally sanctions the behaviors of the client. Rogers notes that certain behaviors are inevitable under the consequences of situations or circumstances in the client's life-style[315]. The behaviors are understood but not necessarily approved of by the therapist, yet the client is still accepted as a valued person.

Accurate empathy is a characteristic of client-centered therapy that has been interpreted by some psychologists as a specific technique. When described, it does appear to be a type of process that a therapist could probably learn to apply. Empathy is defined by Rogers as the ability of the therapist to understand his client from the client's frame of reference. In order to help his client understand himself, the therapist must attempt to "reflect" the feelings, emotions, etc. that he receives from his client. This communication is kept within the framework of the client's perceptions, not the therapist's. It is basically saying to the client, "I feel as you feel, I am trying to understand what is going on in your world, and this is what I am hearing and feeling." As the therapist perceives his client's world, he does not lose the "as if" quality of the relationship that allows him to feel and see the incongruences yet frees him from the emotions that distort his client's perceptions. Therefore, the therapist's reflections may be, in reality, more basic to the problem than what the client is expressing. Reflection differs from interpretation in that the information comes from the client's frame of reference and not from the therapist's. The distinction is somewhat ambiguous and probably can only be determined through analysis of recorded sessions.

The selection of the conditions and processes that have been presented are those that are most commonly identified with Rogerian therapy [307, 315] and certainly do not exhaust the conditions and assumptions established by Rogers himself. A perusal of his work is necessary to fully appreciate the therapeutic process he tries to convey [307, 309, 310]. In essence, the reader must almost move into Rogers' phenomenological field to grasp his concepts since it is a very personal experience between the reader and the therapist. Rogers [315] sums up the process of therapy in the following statement:

> As he [client] finds someone listening to him with consistent acceptance while he expresses his thoughts and feelings, the client, little by little, becomes increasingly able to listen to communications from within himself .... slowly he moves toward greater congruence .... He is, at last, free to change and grow in the directions which are natural to the human organism.

Client-centered therapy has experienced wide acceptance particularly among American psychologists. Its stress on research and its more positive orientation to the nature of man no doubt appeals to what Harper calls the American democratic tradition [165]. Some of the other factors adding to this acceptance are the importance of the therapist's attitudes concerning defined techniques and placing responsibility on the client for his own behavior. This more simplistic approach to therapy appeals to a broader range of mental health workers, particularly inexperienced and lesser trained therapists.

The client-centered approach is not experiencing quite the acceptance it achieved in the last decade. Some of this loss is no doubt due to the lack of the leadership that was given by Rogers in the 1950s and early 1960s.

Critics of this therapy have also become more vocal. It is pointed out that the disregard for differential diagnosis hampers effective treatment and probably makes this approach only useful with mild adjustment problems [368, 353]. Research utilizing the client-centered approach tends to refute this criticism [315]. Some of the basic premises of Rogers' theories of personality have been heavily attacked [333, 261], which seems typical of theories developed from therapy experiences.

SUMMARY

This chapter reviews both cognitive and affective approaches to therapy. Cognitive therapies stress the rational, intellectual processes while affective methods emphasize the emotional aspects of personality. Both approaches report comparatively high rates of success although much of the research is speculative.

CHAPTER 10

New Approaches in Counseling and Psychotherapy

This chapter will review a few of the newer innovations in the practice of therapy. There are several new approaches whose acceptance currently ranges from limited to wide. Again, the authors do not claim to present a representative sample of new approaches but have selected some that appear to have wide applicability for present and anticipated demands. Transactional analysis, developed by Eric Berne, combines the affective and cognitive positions and establishes a contemporary approach that should have general appeal to practitioners. William Glasser developed his therapeutic procedures with delinquent females although the general methods have since gained wide appeal. Its unique stress on morality has gained acceptance throughout a variety of institutional settings. Hominological therapy stems from the work of Kahn. This approach encompasses the total person as he interacts with his environment. Finally, this chapter will conclude with a therapy concept for normals. Sensitivity training has been purported to be a method for preventive mental health by its supporters and has been described as an imminent danger to an unsuspecting public by its critics.

TRANSACTIONAL ANALYSIS

Eric Berne, the originator of this approach, achieved international fame from his best-selling book, *Games People Play* [46]. It was this work that brought to light his innovative approach to therapy. Until his untimely death in 1970, Dr. Berne had a distinguished career both as a practicing psychiatrist and as an author.

Like many other practitioners, Berne[46] developed his ideas from his actual practice of therapy. The basis of his approach seems to be what he terms "the transaction."

> If two or more people encounter each other . . . sooner or later one of them will speak or give some other indication of acknowledging the presence of the other. This is called the transactional stimulus. Another person will then say or do something which is in some way related to the stimulus and that is called a transactional response.

During a transactional interaction a person has several ego states available. Berne divides these ego states into three groups: (1) Parent—He imitates the behavior of the significant parental figures that he recalls from his childhood. (2) Adult—He makes an objective appraisal of his environment, weighing probabilities and possibilities by past experiences. (3) Child—He maintains child-like states similar to those he recalls from the ages of two through five. The three states compose a personality system and include everything a person feels, thinks, says, or does[49]. Berne also points out that there are subdivisions of the three primary states that help to explain more complex behavior.

When two human beings engage in a transaction, many possible combinations come into play. An example of an Adult to Adult transaction would be: "Wife: Will you drop me off at the store on your way to work? Husband: Yes, it is right on my way." Figure 10.1 illustrates an Adult to Adult transaction. The transaction response followed the same route as the transaction stimulus. This is termed a simple or complementary transaction. Complementary transactions insure a continued com-

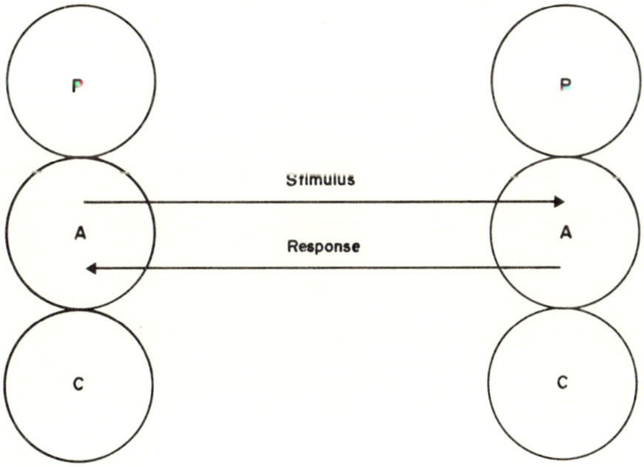

Fig. 10.1 Example of a complementary transaction.

munication. Unfortunately, complementary states may break down when a transaction becomes crossed. Figure 10.2 is an example of a crossed transaction. In this case, the transactional response does not parallel the transactional stimulus. "Wife: Would you mind picking up your shoes? Husband: That's your job and besides I'm too busy." Berne notes that there are 72 possible cross transactions but only four of these are of real concern to the therapist.

Type I is the Adult to Adult stimulus and the Child to Parent response (AA-CP). He refers to this in therapy as representative of a transference reaction. It is also the most common difficulty experienced in social interaction.

Type II represents the Adult to Adult, Parent to Child crossed transaction (AA-PC). Berne states that this is typical of a counter-transference experience between therapist and client.

Type III is the Child to Parent and Adult to Adult (CP-AA), called the "exasperating" response, where a search for sympathy by a person is rewarded with objective information by another.

Type IV is the Parent to Child and Adult to Adult (PC-AA), and this explains what Berne terms "impudence." A good example of this is a domineering boss who demands respect for his opinion but he receives factual answers from an employee that he considers out of place from such a young upstart. Berne goes on to describe numerous other combinations that may be therapeutically important in understanding a client [47].

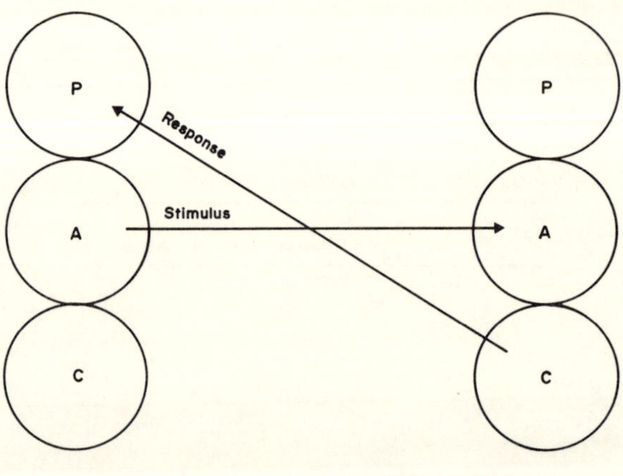

Fig. 10.2 Example of a crossed transaction.

Not only is the therapist concerned with simple and complex transactions, but he must be able to understand series of transactions that his client experiences. Berne has developed a unique vocabulary to explain these chains of transactions. He discusses these in terms of games that are transactive with concealed but defined results. Games, according to Berne, are well-defined procedures where motives are ulterior and where there are specified results and a definite payoff [46]. He also discusses the "Script," which is the unconscious life pattern established during early childhood. This pattern may be constructive or destructive; those with destructive styles are in need of therapy. Another term used by Berne to explain series of transactions is "time structuring." He shows that people have the need to structure time so that they seek out stimulating situations (sensation hunger). They will also search for specific sensations (recognition hunger) and finally gravitate into groups and organizations (structure hunger) [49].

Short-term structuring in social behavior is also discussed. Berne explains these short-term time structures as "withdrawal" (characterized by no overt communication), "rituals" (which are comparatively safe positions where people are wrapped up in their own thoughts and communicate little information), and "activities" (which Berne defines as work). These usually reflect external Adult to Adult complementary communications.

"Pastimes" are classified as sentence completion exchanges, where complementary transactions take place between people who do not know each other very well [49]. Pastimes would seem to reflect the "small talk" of social gatherings. Finally, Berne notes that pastimes lead to games, which were previously mentioned. This brief review hopefully stimulates those interested in transactional analysis to delve into the various works of Eric Berne, where his unique approach and personality theory is more thoroughly explained [46, 47, 49].

Treatment

No doubt some of Berne's early training in analytic therapy has influenced his treatment theory and procedures. There is emphasis on behaviors, thoughts, etc. from early childhood. His basic personality structure of the three ego states also resembles the Freudian model, although Berne makes some major distinctions [47]. He feels that the behaviors that are characterized by the Parent and Child ego structures reflect the past and generally show that the person has not learned to respond as an independent adult. Therefore, the major role of the therapist is to help the client identify the games that are inhibiting Adult transactions.

Berne lists eight steps or techniques of transactional analysis. As in most therapeutic approaches, these need not come in any particular order and all may not evolve in any one therapeutic experience. He states that the therapist first uses "interrogation" [47] to get factual information that may be important in the therapeutic process. This also helps to inform the therapist what ego states the client is using. "Specification" [47] usually follows interrogation and appears to be an identification of important behaviors or feelings that will be referred to at a later time. The information is made known both to client and therapist.

When information has been collected, Berne utilizes a technique, popular in sensitivity training, that attacks the client's inconsistencies. "Confrontation" [47] brings to light the behaviors that are causing the client to play rigid and inhibited games. It would seem that if the confrontation is successful, the client experiences insight into the Parent and Child ego states that have affected his behavior. The therapist then attempts to strengthen the Adult ego state by "explanation" [47]. At this point, the client is open to interpretation and is ready to experience complementary Adult transactions. "Illustration" [47] is the next step and is characterized by Berne as an interposition, a way of stabilizing and strengthening the client's Adult ego state so that the probability of his slipping back into the more primitive ego states are minimized. With the stability of the Adult state established, the therapist encourages the client to confirm the success of the confrontation and to confront other behaviors that the client utilizes to keep him from independent Adult transactions. Once it appears that the Adult state is in control, the therapist utilizes the technique of "interpretation," [47] taken from the classical psychoanalytic method. He attempts, through interpretation, the "deconfusion" [47] of the Child ego state. This appears to be an analysis of childhood problems. Berne puts considerable emphasis on this step although he points out that the interpretation of the Child is not absolutely necessary, nor is the establishment of Adult control required before completion of analysis. In fact there are three alternatives presented at this stage: Adult control without analysis of Child, analysis of Child before complete Adult control, and Adult control followed by analysis of Child.

The therapist has now brought the client to a point of "crystallization," [47] where the client has the ability for complementary Adult transactions. It is now up to the client to extinguish his game playing and move toward positive mental health. Berne points out that the transactional therapist does not greatly influence the behavior of his client. The client must make his own decision; if the therapist makes the decision, the Adult to Adult transaction becomes Parent to Child. "The therapist tells him when he is able to solo, but the patient decides when he will actually take off" [47]. A more detailed analysis of this therapeutic procedure can be found in *Principles of Group Treatment* [47] and *Transactional Analysis in Psychotherapy* [45].

Transactional analysis appears to be a novel approach when compared with the more traditional therapies, although many ideas presented are not unique. What may be appealing (or appalling, as the case may be) is Berne's vernacular vocabulary as he applies it to the process of therapy. His candid interpretation of this is refreshing and his ability to communicate his thoughts has been extremely successful to both laymen and professionals.

It is possible that Dr. Berne's work has come at an opportune time when a very complex society is in need of someone to understand and analyze behavior, but it is distressing to the research-oriented psychologist that studies testing the validity of these methods and theories are not forthcoming. His death in 1970 has no doubt taken away some of the impetus to future exploration of his theory. Therefore, it is the responsibility of the disciples of this approach to develop and objectively measure the effectiveness of transactional analysis.

HOMINOLOGICAL THERAPY

This type of therapy is an outgrowth of an approach to the understanding of human behavior developed by the study of hominology [201]. The term is derived from *hominidae*, which in biology means the family of mankind evolving through to modern man.

Hominological therapy is an experimental approach that has been used as a therapeutic technique with normals, both individuals and groups, and, also, as an adjunct to other psychotherapeutic methods. It hinges on a theory of personality that identifies eight different dimensions of development that are thought to play a crucial role in the maturation of both the individual human being and the human species. The concept of therapy is tied to this developmental maturation.

Within hominological therapy, self-actualization (the goal of a number of other therapies) is considered to be a trap that offers the client a false sense of security—one that is basically not therapeutic. Instead, hominology views behavior that is on a higher level of maturation (more therapeutic) as counter to self-actualization even if the concept of self-actualization includes creative and altruistic goals. This higher behavioral activity represents a different kind of maturation level and, within it, other-people-actualization becomes a more cogent consideration than self-actualization.

The dimensions of development that play a crucial role in maturation involve a person's understanding of his social potential. In order to comprehend his own unique social potential, the client must first understand himself (that is, he must recognize the component parts of his self-image). Only after this has been accomplished can he visualize his role as it pertains to the maturation process.

Life Areas

In hominological therapy the client or group explores its reality perception in the following life areas: Self, Other People, Government, Arts, Science, Material Goods, Ethics, and Religion. After instructions from the therapist, the client constructs the self-image chart called a "hominologram," in which he plots the combination of reality perceptions he believes he is using in each one of these life areas [201]: Authoritarianism (faith and trust in others); Intuitionism (feeling without external evidence); Rationalism (reasoning); Empiricism (scientific evidence); Pragmatism (utility in relation to a premise held by the client); and Verbal Structuralism (automatic responses to words or symbols). Figure 10.3 is an illustration of a hominologram. The client also may attempt to plot the reality sources of other persons who are important to him, using the same chart on which he plotted his own self-image.

Eight hypothetical developmental levels of behavior are defined and the behavioral characteristics of each is tied to mankind's emotional and mental potential. Each level has its own "action theme," leading to distinctive goals and moral commitments. The exploration of the levels that the client believes he utilizes for his own action themes enables him to evaluate the directional focus of his life. Thus, meaning and value in life are clarified for the client and a more satisfactory adjustment may then be achieved.

Experience has demonstrated that this is not only an intellectual experience for the client, but one that often evokes deep emotional concomitants. Hominological therapy differs from other methods in that it attempts to use a new dimension consisting of visual self-image charts drawn by the client himself to facilitate insights followed by an explora-

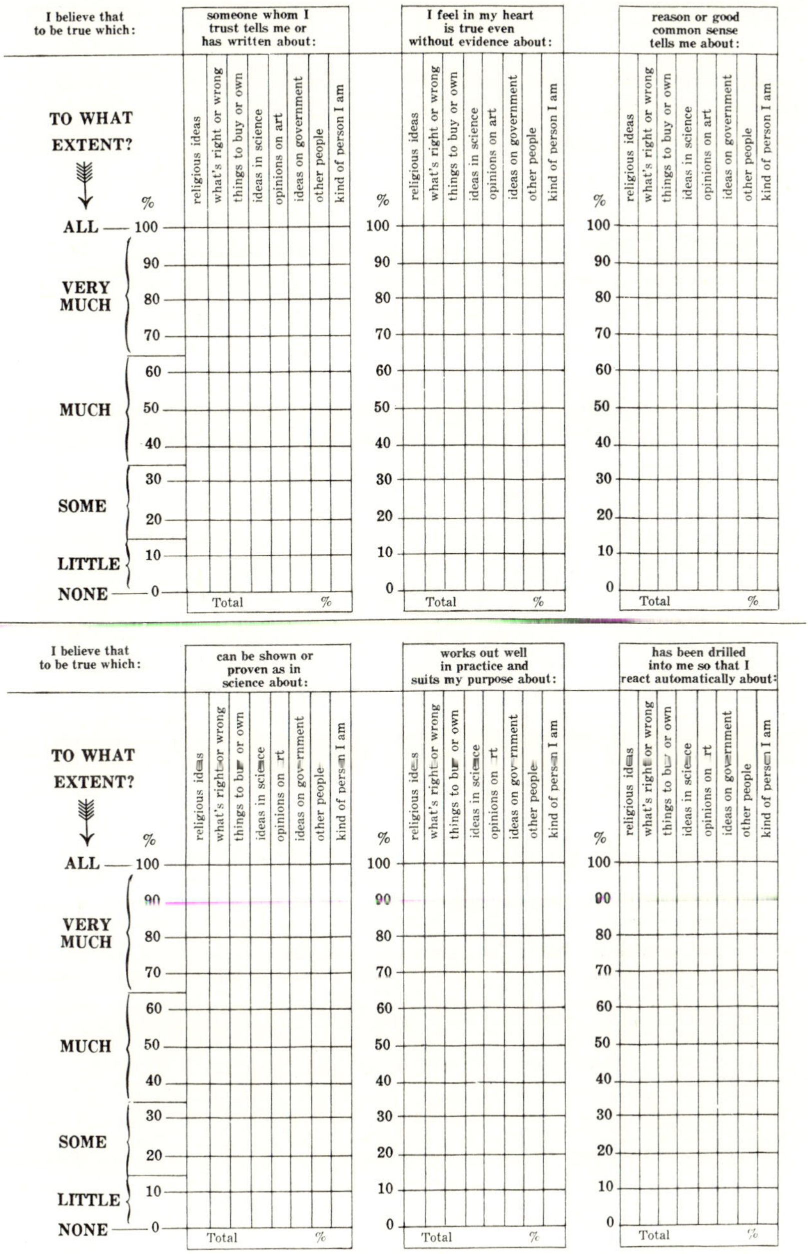

Fig. 10.3 Hominologram I—Charting the Self-Image.

tion of his goals and values. By providing clients with new self-insights and a deeper understanding of human differences and similarities, this approach has been found helpful in improving interpersonal relationships between individuals and groups. It has been used with drug addiction, marital problems, adolescent adjustment problems, race relations, rehabilitation efforts, and in establishing better communications.

Recognition of Alternatives

Hominological therapy is based on the concept that the client is capable of changing his outlook on life with subsequent improved adaptation by discarding the types of reality sources that are problem-creating and adopting other reality resources that are more problem-solving. However, he can do this only if he fully understands what the alternatives are and what they entail. Without such understanding of alternatives, the client is forced to remain as he is, without any options. After he has selected the reality sources that serve him best, he can recognize those life goals and human values that represent the highest level of maturation that he is capable of reaching.

Rapport and empathy should be developed between the client and therapist during the process of self-discovery. Self-actualization is not the client's goal but self-exploration is an essential prerequisite and a distinctive feature of this type of therapy.

The therapist usually assumes the role of "guide" or teacher in hominological therapy. His function is to assist the client in the reorganization of his newly discovered self, so that he can find purpose and goals in his life. When conducted as group therapy, the members participate in this role and help each other in probing the implications of their individual self-image charts.

A brief excerpt of client-counselor interaction in one aspect of hominological therapy is presented. The following is from the fifth meeting between client and therapist.

(Client has constructed Hominologram I—Criteria of Reality.)

Counselor: Do you see anything in the profile on your hominologram that could help us explain why some of your attitudes are problem-creating?

Client: I think that I tend to depend too much on Authoritarianism in the life area of Self.

Counselor: Could you explain that?

Client: Well, it seems that my self-image depends too much on what other people say about me. I take what they say too seriously.

Counselor: As we discussed last time, there is no right or wrong in this but it seems to be problem-creating for you to use Authoritarianism in this case. By examining your profile on the hominologram do you see any alternatives?

Client: I guess I could use more Rationalism and, perhaps, also more Intuitionism to restructure my ideas of who and what I am.

Counselor: How would you do it?

Client: That's what I don't know.

Counselor: As you know now, Rationalism in hominology means using reasoning and logic, whereas Intuitionism means inner feelings. Could you use reasoning and personal feelings as a substitute for accepting by faith the opinions of those people who work with you who are constantly annoying you?

Client: I wish I could. Even if someone who is a real nut criticizes me slightly I get all shook up. Then I hate myself and them too.

Counselor: Do you know why you react like that?

Client: Before, I used to think that I was too sensitive. Now I know it is because I still consider them an authority—a source of truth—even though I know that they have no real basis for what they say.

Counselor: O.K. With the knowledge you have gained from examining your hominologram, what would you like to do about this situation now?

Client: Well, I now see that there are a number of alternatives of which I have never before been aware. I can tell myself that I will not accept this or that guy as an authority. Instead, I will use reasoning to counteract remarks that hurt my feelings. I'll try to ignore some of my critics because I realize that I have been accepting them as if they were authorities on the subject of me—even though I know they aren't.

Counselor: How would you use Rationalism instead?

Client: I'd simply say that reason tells me they are wrong and that logic confirms that I'm a pretty good person simply on the basis of my job performance, which is a matter of record—I guess that's Empiricism—also because I know that I have genuine desires to be a decent kind of person. I feel that way and if I can use this feeling, it would be Intuitionism.

Counselor: Can Intuitionism be a substitute for some of the Authoritarianism you are now using?

Client: I think not. I don't trust my feelings sufficiently—I prefer to be wary of them. Every time that I've acted impulsively, I've been hurt. Maybe I should trust them more.

Counselor: Will you then attempt to substitute Rationalism for Authoritarianism in the life area of Self?

Client: Well, I could also use some Empiricism as you defined this kind of reality perception last time.

Counselor: But you scored low in Empiricism on the Self portion of the life area chart, didn't you?

Client: I guess that is because I don't know how to use Empiricism in relation to my self-image. How does one?

Counselor: As we have discussed, Empiricism within hominology represents the attempt to utilize scientific measurement in the perception of reality. How do you think it could be applied to you?

Client: Well, an IQ test is supposed to be scientific, isn't it? So is an impartial record of my work performance.

Counselor: I guess so. How did you make out on those possible sources of Empiricism?

Client: It didn't make me a genius but I'm no dummy either.

Counselor: I guess your college grades might perhaps be considered empirical, more or less.

Client: Perhaps if I were to use more Empiricism, not only college grades or IQ, but other things, too, it would show that I wasn't all bad or stupid.

Counselor: Would a self-image derived from these sources be acceptable to you and would this be more problem-solving?

Client: Maybe. But Empiricism doesn't turn me on enough. By the way, I just thought of something else. Couldn't I retain Authoritarianism as the source of my primary reality apperception but change my choice of authority? I mean, why couldn't I believe those who say *nice* things about me? I have been ignoring them and, instead, I'm having my feelings hurt all the time by those who say nasty things. Why couldn't I switch authorities and believe the nice guys and not give up Authoritarianism for any of the other reality perceptions?

Counselor: Then you could stay within your present framework as you have charted it on your hominologram.

Client: Yes, but nevertheless, I think that I want to utilize the other available reality perceptions to a greater extent than I am now doing. I mean Rationalism, Empiricism, and perhaps also some Intuitionism. Using Pragmatism, I could adopt the premise that if something makes me feel better and doesn't hurt other people, it is good for me.

Counselor: Do you think it would make life more pleasant for you to diversify your sources of self-perception?

Client: I think that it might enable me to live with less self-hate. At least I'll be using more of what is available to me for creating a self-image. Perhaps, I'd be foolish if I didn't.

Counselor: In view of our conversation today, will you construct another hominologram showing how you would like to redistribute your reality perceptions in the life area of Self? I think that this will help fix firmly in your mind the possible changes you could make if you wanted to.

In spite of favorable reports from those who are using hominological therapy, the authors are not convinced as yet that it has sufficiently demonstrated merit. This is because this approach is still too new to be adequately documented and to have enough data accumulated to enable an objective evaluation to be made. It is obvious from this that considerable research is necessary with this promising technique before it can be described as a successful method of psychotherapy. For further discussion of hominological therapy, see pages 281–287 of Appendix A.

REALITY THERAPY

It is not unusual to find critics of the psychoanalytic procedure of therapy in both the medical and psychological professions; however, it is rare to find a person who criticizes and then seeks out and develops new methods. William Glasser, the founder of reality therapy took this kind of initiative and has created a therapeutic process that appears to be highly successful. Glasser became disenchanted with conventional psychiatry while completing his psychiatric residency. According to personal accounts by Glasser[304], he was not overly popular with some of his supervisors, who did not approve of his innovative ideas and methods.

Glasser's ideas and hypotheses were tested while he was head psychiatrist at the Ventura School for Girls, a facility for delinquent adolescent females. The result of this crystallization was his book entitled, *Reality Therapy* [142]. Since the publication of this in 1965 and his subsequent popularity on the lecture circuit, Glasser has become a recognized figure in the field of therapy. His popularity also seems to cross other vocational boundaries, including those in correctional work and education, and this has led to much demand for training in reality therapy. As a result, the Institute for Reality Therapy was founded. According to one source, more than a thousand people of varied professions have received training in reality therapy at this center[304]. It appears that Glasser has developed a method of treating psychological maladjustment that appeals to a variety of people in and out of the field of mental health.

Treatment

The basic premise of Glasser's treatment model is his position on mental illness. He feels that being mentally ill is an excuse for irresponsible behavior and, no matter what the pathological symptoms are, every individual with this condition is unable to fulfill his essential needs [142]. He points out that when needs are met, symptoms disappear. The other common characteristic in the behavior of the emotionally disturbed is that "they all deny reality of the world around them" [142].

The establishment of reality is basic to the goal of Glasser's therapy because his approach reorients the client to reality and teaches him how to fulfill his needs. He feels that there is a commonality of needs that is shared by human beings but there are individual differences in abilities to meet these needs. Of all needs common to man, the "need to love and be loved and need to feel that we are worthwhile to ourselves and others" [142] are the two needs that are most encountered in therapy. Glasser points out that at all times people must be involved in an intimate relationship with other people and that two people must share genuine reciprocal feelings for each other—in other words, an honest caring. Other characteristics or principles of his approach reflect his deviation from the classical model. In reality therapy no use is made of historical material; in fact, it is discouraged and considered unimportant. Glasser feels that the past is irrelevant since it cannot be used to meet current needs. Additionally, no importance is placed on unconscious mental processes since they are unnecessary in the fulfillment of needs [142]. Glasser does not deny that these things exist; they just do not serve any useful purpose in his therapy procedure.

The term "responsibility" is germane to Glasser's approach. He states that responsibility is "the ability to fulfill one's needs and to do so in a way that does not deprive others of the ability to fulfill their needs" [142]. A person reflecting responsibility is one who meets his needs, who feels worthwhile and loved. People who fail to meet their needs are those categorized as "irresponsible," and he uses this basic term as a substitute for all diagnostic categories of mental illness.

Application of Therapy

Glasser divides his therapeutic procedures into three phases, which he identifies as (1) "involvement"—the therapist-client relationship, (2) "rejection of unreality"—the therapist's rejection of his client's irresponsible behavior but acceptance of the client as a person, and (3) the "teaching phase"—where the client finds more acceptable ways (reality) to meet needs.

Glasser feels that involvement may be the most critical stage of therapy since a prerequisite for success is an honest human relationship where a feeling of caring exists. Glasser's condition for successful therapy is quite similar to that of Rogers' premise of "unconditional positive regard," with the exception that the reality therapist makes conscious moral judgments of irresponsible behavior. The therapist may at first find his client resisting this direct involvement because of past failures in intimate relationships. According to Glasser, the ability to break through this recalcitrant behavior may be in part due to the personal characteristics of the therapist.

Obviously, the therapist must be a responsible person since he uses himself as a model. He must be sensitive to his client's needs so that he can understand the irresponsible actions yet be unyielding to the client's manipulations as he acts in irresponsible ways. Glasser is one of the first therapists to openly state that a practitioner must get emotionally involved with his client and feel the pain and trauma that his client experiences. In fact, if there is no emotional involvement, therapy will not be successful[142]. Glasser's position is supported by other research [347, 350] that shows that the personal qualities of the therapist, and not exclusively his intellectual training, are at least part of the necessary conditions for successful therapy.

Once the involvement phase has been thoroughly established, the therapist strives to secure a reality base for his client. "The therapist begins to insist that the patient face the reality of his behavior"[142]. If the client regresses to irresponsible behaviors, the therapist confronts this by insisting that the client behave in a responsible way. Thus, Glasser stresses overt behavior (the "what" quality) rather than attitudes and emotions (the "why" quality) since needs will not be fulfilled by inaction. Reality therapists parallel some behavior modifiers in that changing behavior (learning) will bring about change in attitudes (insight) rather than insight leading to behavior change, which is the position of many affectively oriented therapists. Glasser also draws from learning theorists in his use of praise (reinforcement) and disapproval (punishment). Since the therapist is a person of value to the client, he functions as an important reinforcing agent in the client's environment. Responsible behavior is reinforced and irresponsible behavior is negatively reinforced or punished.

Therapy sessions may deal with any topic that is of interest to the client, although the therapist will try to relate discussions to the behavior of the client and his value system. Special emphasis is placed on right and wrong[142]. These "rap" sessions build the client's trust in the therapist and allow the client to identify the therapist as a person of worth and to feel that he, the client, is also valued; this, in turn, develops his own self-worth. Like any other therapeutic encounter, sessions may be filled with pain, trauma, and emotion. Since the therapist is in an involved state, he experiences this emotion with his client. However, if the content of the interview reflects irresponsibility, he confronts his client and does not allow him to escape or utilize irresponsible excuses for his behavior such as blaming society, parents, etc. The therapist's emphasis is *what* are you doing and what are *you* going to do about it?[142] Glasser feels that it does little good to ask "why" because merely knowing why will not change the behavior.

The final stage of therapy involves relearning. This can only take place after the client recognizes his irresponsible behavior. Glasser points out that there is no real change in the therapy relationship since relearning is integrated into the total experience[142]. It is at this point that Glasser's approach resembles the cognitive therapist's model, since relearning involves teaching responsible behaviors. The stage of relearning is a slow and sometimes painful process and yet, when completed, the client behaves in a responsible way, which in turn allows him to fulfill his needs. When this is achieved, therapy is terminated. Glasser notes that clients return for brief periods for help in learning new behaviors.

In summary, reality therapy differs from conventional therapy in the following ways:

1. The concept of mental illness is not accepted since it allows irresponsibility in the behavior of the client. He does not have to take responsibility for his behavior because he is "sick."
2. The effect of past experience is rejected and stress is placed on the present and future. Concentration on the past inhibits relearning.
3. At all times the therapist is himself in the therapeutic relationship, not a transference figure.
4. Unconscious motives are not acceptable excuses for irresponsible behavior.
5. The morality of behavior, particularly right and wrong, is stressed. Unlike other therapists, reality-oriented practitioners face this issue head on and allow their own value systems to influence their clients. Most other therapeutic approaches would not support this moralistic position.

6. Reality therapists "teach" their clients better ways of meeting their needs. The therapists' involvement is direct and exacting in the behaviors they want their clients to adopt. This seems to take much freedom of decision from the client and puts the therapist into a position of knowing what is best for his client. This is totally opposite from the position of phenomenologists and other affectively oriented therapists.

It seems artificial to dissect a therapeutic approach like reality therapy since the techniques are so interwoven into the therapy relationship. Glasser states, "breaking it into small segments is as misleading as plucking a piece of a jigsaw puzzle from a box. . . . primary importance must be given to the whole process during which the patient gradually changes his behavior from irresponsible to responsible" [142]. Reality therapy seems to work well for William Glasser and his associates. He has reported fantastic success rates of 90 percent and better with delinquent girls at Ventura, although no good objective research is currently available in the literature. With the formation of the Institute for Reality Therapy and the new Education Training Center (which came into being after Glasser published *Schools Without Failure**) research should be forthcoming. It has been reported that the Education Training Center has processed 90,000 educators in the reality approach.

It is obvious that Glasser's interests take him beyond the confines of a therapy practice. His criticisms of public education and his subsequent successful involvement in programs for schools reflect his increasing influence on public opinion. Glasser's recent work, *The Identity Crisis*,† is an ambitious effort to utilize reality theory as an explanation of current human behavior. There is little doubt that Dr. Glasser has become an important force in the area of mental health.

SENSITIVITY TRAINING

Sensitivity training, a method of creating behavioral and attitudinal changes, is receiving a mixed reception. Some insist that it represents the best approach to good interpersonal understanding whereas others condemn it as a dangerous pastime reflecting current social immorality. Some psychologists believe it is professionally unsound whereas others consider it an important adjunct to their practice. This divided opinion has not interfered with its current popularity. It has literally exploded onto the

*Glasser, W. *Schools without failure.* New York: Harper & Row, 1969.
†Glasser, W. *The identity crisis.* New York: Harper & Row, 1972.

field of mental health and has become a favorite topic of the media. Many magazines, newspapers, and even the movie industry (with the film "Bob and Carol and Ted and Alice") have at times selected isolated events and extreme splinter groups to depict this training. Promoters have accentuated the sensational and sensual aspects of sensitivity training and this image has not aided its acceptance in professional circles. We use the term sensitivity training since it appears to have general acceptance, recognizing, nevertheless, that other terms such as encounter and T groups are equally applicable. The kinds of methods that should be used in sensitivity training are among the most controversial subjects in the profession of psychology. Yet, with all the criticisms, warnings, and charges, the sensitivity training field shows continual growth both in the number of participants and in the involvement of professional trainers.

The astonishing development of this form of training is difficult to explain since it lacks historical precedent. The origins of group experience cannot claim a founding father or point to an historical figure of stature. It appears to have evolved from several movements: progressive education, human relations, management training, and probably most important, the efforts of Kurt Lewin and his students [143]. Lewin's work in the area of social needs and problems was basic to the group encounter or sensitivity movement.

If one must point to a particular event in the birth of sensitivity training, it has to be the founding of the National Training Laboratory (NTL) in 1947. This laboratory was established by Lewin's students for the purpose of understanding the behavior dynamics of group processes.

> This is accomplished with the help of a trainer, who creates an atmosphere in which the motivations for typical human behavior... are brought to the surface.... An individual participant can observe both his behavior and that of others in the group, discover sources of different kinds of behavior and identify the effect on the group. [51]

From meager beginnings, NTL has expanded its training program to include two major centers—one at Bethel, Maine, and the other at Cedar City, Utah—and additionally has developed an international outreach program that sends teams into communities. This has permitted thousands of people to take part in the NTL program.

The clientele of this organization is varied and includes many professional and lay groups. It is not unusual to have representatives of the business world, members of the "God Squad" from various religious denominations, educators representing administration, staff, and faculty of colleges and public schools, medical personnel, etc. NTL also provides workshops for "in house" groups that represent a single industry, firm, or profession. The NTL has gained professional and public acceptance and is now considered by some factions of the group movement as the conservative old guard of sensitivity training.

Another impetus in the rise of popularity of sensitivity groups has been a parallel growth in group therapy. The work of W. R. Bion in England during and since World War II seems to have been one of the earlier beginnings of group therapy. According to Goldberg [143], Bion developed group methods to help individuals deal with intragroup tensions. Another major contributor to the field of group therapy was J. L. Moreno with his development of psychodrama, which has become an accepted treatment modality in mental health. Psychodrama allows a client to "act out" his feelings and emotions by creating life-like situations in a type of stage setting. Sensitivity groups have utilized many of Moreno's techniques in their own group interactions.

Currently, almost every major therapeutic approach has developed some type of group therapy to parallel individual methods. Although the group therapy approach started as a less than acceptable substitute for individual therapy and was permitted to continue because of financial and staff expediencies, it is now recognized as possessing unique therapeutic characteristics that may have benefits and advantages not found in individual therapy. No doubt the wide acceptance of group therapy has aided the popularity of sensitivity training.

Therapy versus Training

Although many therapists feel that encounter or sensitivity training is, in fact, a form of "group therapy for normals" [228], there do appear to be some distinctions. These differences sometimes become blurred because both sensitivity training and group therapy have borrowed techniques from each other and many therapists are also sensitivity trainers. The difference becomes even less distinct when both sensitivity training and group therapy stress the working out of personal problems and the replacement of inappropriate behaviors. There seems to be a difference in the type of problems manifested by the participants in the two processes. Those in therapeutic groups usually demonstrate a psychological disorder while the members in sensitivity training theoretically are normal in behavioral patterns. Emphasis in sensitivity training is on the expansion of normal experience and learning while group therapy stresses rehabilitation and the removal of the emotional dysfunction. Lakin [228] points out that there is also a difference in basic interaction since sensitivity training is group-oriented while group therapy is directed toward the individual member.

Categories of Groups

Current movements in sensitivity training are extremely diverse and difficult to categorize. As mentioned earlier, the NTL has become the conservative "old guard" while other more exotic forms have been characterized as the "in" groups. The Esalen movement is probably the best known of the more radical approaches. William Schutz [322] (their major spokesman) described in his book, *Joy*, the various group techniques used at Esalen for the improvement of interpersonal skills. The Esalen Institute, located at Big Sur, California, has received much criticism because of some of its more exotic techniques. Such activities as group nude bathing and meditation are not typical of the more traditional methods used by therapists or sensitivity trainers, yet the popularity of Esalen has led to the establishment of training centers across the United States. Like NTL, the Esalen community utilizes training teams for an outreach program. In reality, much of the criticism directed against Esalen should probably more correctly be focused on pseudo-Esalen procedures that have imitated their style but do not have the professional staff and the sophisticated learning centers to evaluate group processes and techniques.

As was mentioned in an earlier chapter, Carl Rogers has recently turned his attention and given prestige to sensitivity training. Rogers [313] has termed his procedure "Basic Encounter Group" and has adapted many of his therapy techniques to this process. As could be expected, his emphasis is on the climate of the group and the psychological growth of the members. He feels that if the proper group atmosphere is created and members become intensely involved with each other, reflecting real caring and acceptance, they will be less inhibited and will experience and grow. Incongruence in the self is minimized and individuals in the group are said to gain effective skills in interpersonal relations. Although criticized by Goldberg and others as bringing nothing new to sensitivity training, Rogers does provide prestige, skills, and knowledge to a neophyte movement. Also, his concern for objective research will hopefully carry over to sensitivity training. The lack of acceptable research in process, outcome, and theory has been a major weakness and Rogers' influence may help to alert the sensitivity practitioners to this need.

Need for Training

Reasons for the demand for sensitivity training are as diverse as the movement itself. In some ways it may be a reaction to a very cold, impersonal, materialistic society. Sociologists point to the evolution of an ego-centered environment where there has been a breakdown of traditional family and social structures. Thus, many people may be joining sensitivity groups for intimate contact with other human beings. Other experts have placed considerable emphasis on the fulfillment of individual needs.

Eric Berne[46] has recorded the elaborate, complex roles and games that are used by individuals in their daily transactions. These games may keep people from fulfilling needs that could be fulfilled if adequate communication could be established. Rogers writes about understanding the self and exploring communication that impedes growth, while other trainers emphasize sensitivity training as a method used by man in his struggle for self-actualization.

There is little doubt that some seek the group experience in the hope of solving serious emotional problems even though groups are purportedly designed for normals. Some psychologists point out the danger of admitting disturbed individuals into a T group. In his practice, Cameron, one of the authors of this book, has found that if these people join a group, they become quickly dissatisfied with sensitivity training because it does not meet their needs. This usually becomes evident early in the group process and the trainer can make an appropriate referral. The curiosity seeker, who would also be a misfit in a training group, quickly loses interest because a properly run sensitivity group requires a great deal of effort from each member.

Group Characteristics

Group sizes vary although the most common number is from six to 20. There are no hard and fast rules since trainers such as Jack Gibb[54] facilitate "community" groups that may number into the hundreds. Thus, group size is limited only by the general purpose of the group and the preference of the group leader.

Group composition is also affected by the purpose of the group. For example, a particular firm may want to improve communications among various levels of management personnel. This creates a homogeneous group as far as personnel participating and goals to be accomplished. Some groups may be specifically designed to improve marital relations or racial understanding, while others may combine diverse members such as school personnel and students. The most common group is one that is diverse in purpose and demographically heterogeneous when such things as age, sex, occupation, etc. are taken into account.

The length of time required for successful interaction is affected by the purpose and composition of the group and the availability of the group leader. No specific pattern has been shown to be superior although no significant research has tested this variable. Groups may be a one-time experience, which last from a few hours, to a three-day period. Workshops such as those sponsored by NTL and Esalen may continue for several weeks. Some groups meet once or twice a week for a specified number of weeks while other weekly groups may be ongoing with no specified time limit.

Group Procedure

The following outlines a group procedure sometimes used by Cameron when conducting sensitivity training. This is by no means offered as typical of all groups since no one pattern has been established.

Step I: Screening

Prospective group members are interviewed individually by the leader or co-leader in order to judge the interest, sincerity, and general reason for wanting the experience. Some demographic information is also collected for possible research. The use of a co-leader is at the discretion of the group facilitator. Cameron has found that co-leaders often provide a dimension to the group that is advantageous. Sometimes a co-leader is chosen because of a special need of the group—for example, exploration of male-female roles seems to work better with male-female co-leaders and interracial groups are usually more successful when there are black and white co-leaders.

Prospective group members may also be asked to complete a personality measure(s) in order to:

1. Screen out those who are emotionally disturbed or have severe adjustment problems and would benefit more from individual or group therapy.
2. Provide feedback for individuals in the group as to changes in personality characteristics.
3. Facilitate future research.

Step II: Orientation

Group members come together for the first time in a conventional setting—for example, a classroom, conference room, or a large office. The group leader(s) present some general information about group process, some historical background, and what the members can and cannot expect from the group experience. Cameron requires that a contract be signed by each member to insure that some initial responsibility has been accepted. It includes specific ground rules and emphasizes the involvement that is required by each member. The contract helps to establish the process as a serious undertaking and not a parlor game or an informal "rap" session. A sample contract can be found in Appendix C.

Each group member is asked to list and discuss the goals he hopes to achieve since it is felt that establishing goals is a necessary condition for group commitment. These written goals are reevaluated and sometimes revised during the group process.

Step III: Group Encounter

Finally, the group members encounter each other and begin the training or experience phase. The success of the experience centers on the honest interaction of group members.

Specific techniques used during interaction vary depending on the training of the facilitator and what processes are taking place. Leaders or facilitators may stress environmental exploration, body relaxation, non verbal and verbal communication, while some may concentrate on verbal interchange, utilizing such techniques as role playing, role reversal, alter ego, confrontation, etc. Some group leaders provide a very structured environment, taking the role of the "expert," while others remain quite removed or become just another member of the group. Unfortunately, research is lacking in the comparison of techniques and subsequent rates of success. Many group leaders would argue that there are no certain techniques good for all groups and there must be variations depending on the clientele, purpose and goals, and the interaction. Cameron suspects that, as in most therapy, the group leader himself may be more important than specific techniques.

Step IV: Evaluation and Follow-up

At the termination of the group, members evaluate the effectiveness of all aspects of the group (including facilitators) in terms of goals and purposes. Post-testing may be required for feedback and research and a time-elapse follow-up is carried out when possible.

Conclusion

When a movement such as sensitivity training explodes onto the mental health field, the tendency to meet the demand quickly outstrips the processes of evaluation and theory-building. Many professionals in the mental health field have voiced grave concerns about sensitivity training as have certain lay organizations and concerned citizens. The range of criticisms is as diffuse as the movement itself. For example, the John Birch Society has branded sensitivity training as a way of eroding society and spreading Communism [3]. A number of psychologists have warned that sensitivity training is psychologically dangerous or, at the very least, a "rip off" [245, 334]. The main criticisms seem to fall in three areas: training of leaders or facilitators, lack of theory, and paucity of research.

Currently there are no established standards for trainers. Many have acceptable academic degrees and/or clinical experience but this does not automatically qualify them for leading group sensitivity training. Trainers usually learn their group skills through practice and workshops as well as from their previous clinical or counseling experience. However, there are a number of trainers who are unqualified but continue to practice because there are no legal or ethical restrictions. Since so many people are involved and this movement certainly falls within the bounds of mental health, the need for establishing necessary training requirements as well as licensing procedures is paramount. Until requirements are agreed upon, it is recommended that people seeking a sensitivity experience only join groups that are sponsored by a reputable agency, whether it be a group organization such as NTL, a local mental health center, or a university counseling service.

The claims of danger in sensitivity training can be traced to accounts of people who have allegedly committed suicide, have had psychotic breaks, or have become severely disturbed [245]. Some critics have also reported the possibility of permanent psychological damage resulting from the effects of the training.

The need for research is painfully apparent. There are too many people being affected by this experience to ignore the consequences, good or bad. Clinical psychologists and counselors are trained scientists and specialists in the field of mental health, and many are practicing sensitivity training. It would seem that the time is now for leadership to be exercised. As Max Birnbaum[51] points out "this promising innovation may be killed before its unique properties have a fair chance to demonstrate their work."

SUMMARY

This chapter presents a number of new and different therapeutic procedures as well as one method that has been referred to as a form of preventive mental health or therapy for the normal. Most of these positions represent deviations from more traditional approaches and are eclectic. Time and performance will determine their value.

CHAPTER 11

Psychological Tests in Vocational and Educational Guidance

Those who wish to know how the psychologist obtains his clinical impressions may also be interested in the related areas of vocational guidance and rehabilitation. Many mental hospitals, vocational rehabilitation centers, community mental health centers, and public schools employ vocational and educational counselors to assist clients in their search for a suitable occupation. To be a self-supporting contributing member of society is the goal in the vocational rehabilitation of a client or of a student who is about to embark on the world of work. The importance of a sound vocational guidance program is a matter in which mental health workers have legitimate interests, yet many have little knowledge or training.

THEORIES OF VOCATIONAL GUIDANCE

How does the vocational counselor arrive at his conclusions regarding his client's job fitness or his vocational aptitude? In reality, the vocational specialist cannot give total attention to a vocational problem without taking into consideration a variety of other factors. It has become obvious that the selection of a vocation is very much a part of the total life style of a client and, therefore, cannot be viewed as an isolated facet of behavior.

Several theories have been proposed to explain vocational selection. Probably the most quoted developmental approach is that presented by Donald Super. He has divided his theory into life stages:

1. Growth stage (birth–14 years)—includes growth of the self concept, which develops through role playing and fantasy. (4–10 years)—

personal likes and dislikes are important in determining aspirations and activities. Child becomes aware of his abilities and the basic requirements of jobs.

2. Exploration stage (15–24 years)—some occupational exploration, tentative choices are tested, a beginning job may be attempted or professional training started.
3. Establishment stage (25–44 years)—selection of an appropriate field, some possible shifting, career pattern stabilized with maximum effort.
4. Maintenance stage (45–64 years)—the status quo, little shifting, continuation along established lines.
5. Decline stage (65–)—work activity declines and new roles are developed to meet waning capacities. Occupation may completely cease with retirement [358].

Much of Super's theory is still untested by empirical research; however, it does indicate that the process of selecting a vocation is an intricate and long-term developmental procedure.

Another popular theory proposed by Ginzberg *et al.* [139] has been characterized as an interdisciplinary approach since it combines the thinking of a psychiatrist, psychologist, sociologist, and economist. These behavioral scientists originally felt that the process of occupational choice began in early adolescence (age 11) and continued into the early twenties but now have recognized that this may continue as long as the person is active in the world of work. Ginzberg has also altered this early position to account for some women who do not select a vocation until their middle or late thirties. The developmental aspects of the theory takes into account three stages: (1) fantasy choices, (2) tentative choices, and (3) crystallization and specialization. Fantasy usually occurs prior to age 11 and is described as the simple identification with the work of an admired adult. Ginzberg describes tentative choices as those made during the ages of 11–18 years when the client investigates vocational alternatives, exploring some and eliminating others. Crystallization takes place when the person reaches a "compromise" between his strengths and desires and the reality of the vocational field. The authors of this theory first thought that occupational decisions were generally irreversible because of the rigid structure of the educational system, but Ginzberg reports [138] that they have been forced to reconsider this. Research has shown that although most men do not alter their vocation after crystallization, some do make dramatic changes; at times, these decisions are made long after the person has reached his early twenties.

Ginzberg has continued his investigations and the reformulation of his original premises. In the updating of his theory, the reopening of the client's stage of crystallization is now accepted, but initially it was felt that the reopening of a crystallization reflected an immature or premature decision. Another change points out the effect of society on the choice of an occupation [140]. This is particularly critical in the occupational choice of minority and ethnic groups. In his reformulation, Ginzberg recognized that the selection of a vocation is only a part of a person's life style. He has collected data that show that when someone selects a vocation it is not just an act in the pursuit of a career, but a decision that will give direction to his total life [138].

It is obvious from these two theoretical positions that the role of the vocational counselor requires much more than just a narrow focus on available occupations. Since vocations are now recognized as an integral part of the total development of the individual, the vocational specialist must not only possess information about occupations and the current employment situation, but, additionally, he must be aware of the complex pressures of society and specifically the environment of his client. The counselor must also have an understanding of the personality dynamics that will affect his client's vocational decision.

SIX INTERRELATED FACTORS

One of the authors, Kahn, has developed a system that can aid mental health workers in understanding the integration of the primary vocational factors. He feels that there are six essential considerations in vocational guidance: (1) interest, (2) aptitude, (3) personality, (4) training opportunities, (5) availability of funds and time for training, and (6) employment opportunities. Good vocational guidance cannot take place if any one of these six factors does not relate harmoniously to the others. For example, if a person is interested in becoming a veterinarian, has the aptitude, personality, and sufficient money, and has found employment opportunities, he may still encounter the problem of the availability of training. At one time there were very few schools of veterinary medicine in certain areas of the United States and there are foreign countries where these schools do not exist. In some fields, training opportunities may be so limited that a client, in planning his future, may wish to explore other occupational opportunities as alternatives to his first choice. In another situation, a client may have everything required for a specific occupation, including high interest, superior aptitude, plenty of opportunity for training, as well as employment opportunity, but still lack the personal qualities required to get along with fellow workers and with an employer. In this case, personality factors affect job selection and the vocational counselor may have to utilize clinical skills or an appropriate referral source to help his client understand and accept the limitations that his personality imposes on his life style. The following explains the factors of each of the six considerations for vocational guidance.

1. Interest

The number of occupational choices currently available to an individual is staggering. The *Dictionary of Occupational Titles* (DOT) lists over 75,000 operational vocations [373]. There is virtually no way that a person can gain experience or acquire even a general knowledge of such complexity. The vocational counselor must provide the necessary guidance in this selection process and one of the most useful methods is an understanding of his client's interests.

The impetus for interest inventories seems to have come from a graduate seminar conducted at the Carnegie Institute of Technology in 1919–1920 [103]. Although Thorndike and others had designed interest measures prior to this (1912), it appears that the results of the Institute provided the ideas and models that were to become the guide for standard measures used today. The most significant participant in the Carnegie seminar was E. K. Strong.

The Strong Vocational Interest Blank (*SVIB*) [346]

Strong observed that people in the same profession shared many of the same interests and those of different professions shared other interests. He identified a professional group, submitted to this reference sample thousands of questions, calculated their responses, and then compared these to a heterogeneous group that represented people-in-general. By selecting questions homogeneous to each occupational group, he constructed an inventory for the measurement of vocational interests. An innovation of the SVIB was the utilization of criterion scoring similar to that used on the Minnesota Multiphasic Personality Inventory (MMPI), the California Psychological Inventory (CPI), and other objective personality measures. By using contrasting groups (e.g., men-at-large and physicians), Strong could measure the relationship of responses of the two groups and thus ascertain the usefulness of a test question. Therefore, when a person takes the SVIB his responses are compared to the answer patterns of the criterion group and people-in-general. The first inventory was designed for males and later a parallel form was devised for females. The 1966 revision has 54 occupational scores on the men's form and 32 on the women's.

Scores are reported on a well-designed profile sheet, which the vocational counselor and client can utilize to study and discuss the vocational patterns that reflect both general areas and specific occupations. The counselor's copy of the profile also includes some nonoccupational scales. Examples of some of these are Academic Achievement (AACH), which contrasts the interests of those who do well in school with those who have mediocre records, Diversity of Interest (DIV), which reflects the variety of interests among professions, and the Masculinity Femininity Scale (MFII), which contrasts the interests of men and women in the same profession [67].

The inventory has certain limitations. "The SVIB cannot tell anyone where he can succeed, it is not a test of aptitude or intelligence" [67]. Although there is a relationship between interests and abilities, there is no guarantee that they exist; therefore, it is possible to show a high interest in a certain occupation but not possess the capacity to meet the demands of the vocation. The SVIB seems to be designed primarily for professional occupations and is not a particularly good measure for trade and technical positions. Other inventories, such as the Minnesota Vocational Interest Blank (MVIB), Psychological Corporation, 1965, and the Kuder Preference Record [226], may be more appropriate for this population. The minimum age for the SVIB is reported to be 16 although the reliability of interest inventories between the ages of 16 and 20 is not impressive.

The advantages of the SVIB are numerous. Extensive research studies over a period of 40 years have led to several improvements, revisions, and the establishment of good validity and reliability as well as the addition of a great deal to the general knowledge in the area of interests. The test design is such that new occupations can be added and obsolete ones dropped. In all, the SVIB is an excellent measure of interests for clients over 16 who are contemplating a vocation in professional fields.

Kuder Interest Inventories [226]

The Kuder Inventories might be considered the "other" major interest tests. The basic premise differs from the Strong in that it measures a small number of broad vocational areas (such as outdoor, computational, mechanical, etc.) rather than specific occupations. (An exception to this is the Kuder OIS published in 1966.) There are a number of forms of the Kuder Inventories[226] available to the vocational counselor: form C, which is primarily for secondary school students, yields scores in ten general areas and also provides a verification scale; form E is a simplified form of C constructed for young children; and the OIS is for high school and entering college students and resembles the Strong in composition and interpretation.

Items on the Kuder Preference Records (C and E)[225] were prejudged as representative of one of the content areas; thus, choices are quite obvious and directly related to the general scales. Form C of the Kuder is usually given at the 9th grade level and form E is designed for those with sixth grade reading ability. One of the interesting innovations of the Kuder Preference series is that the tests are designed for self-scoring and profiling. Therefore, the client can score this test, change raw scores to percentiles on a preset profile grid, and then make a bar graph of the results. This visual graph is simple to read and interpret. Kuder states that these inventories are not designed for occupational choice but to provide general background information[225].

The Kuder Occupational Interest Survey (OIS)[223] is a criterion-scored inventory designed for the prediction of specific occupations and college majors. Using the same content materials as the Kuder Preference form, it makes direct occupational comparisons with the use of criterion groups. While the preference records are designed for younger children, the OIS is normed on high school juniors and seniors and entering college students. Like the Strong, the Kuder OIS uses people in the occupation as a criterion group; however, the OIS does a direct comparison and eliminates the people-in-general category. Many scales on the Strong and Kuder OIS overlap, but, as Zytowski[412] has pointed out, the derivation of the scales are not the same and there may be little relationship. One interesting aspect of the Kuder OIS is that there is one form for both men and women; although generally divided into male and female occupations, it reports scores for females in occupations that are predominantly male but still have possible employment opportunities for women.

The Kuder Preference scales appear to be useful in the measurement of general areas of interest, particularly for younger clients or persons with poor reading ability. It should be kept in mind that responses are obvious and can be easily faked; generalization from the broad areas to specific occupations would be extremely tenuous. The Kuder OIS provides information on specific occupations and college majors. The scoring of the OIS must be done by computer, thus doing away with the convenience and simplicity of the hand-score methods of the Kuder Preference Record. Although resembling the SVIB, there are some obvious differences and these can only be evaluated by research. The OIS is still considered by some to be in an experimental stage while the SVIB has an extensive research background.

Pictorial Inventories

Many persons do not respond well to true and false or multiple-choice questionnaires. When there is time for individual attention, other devices are available. One of these is known as the Vocational Apperception Test (VAT)[16]. It consists of a set of 18 drawings of persons working in various vocational tasks in typical surroundings. Ten of the cards are designed for women and eight for men. The pictures include representations of teachers, office workers, physicians, engineers, lawyers, salesmen, dieticians, social workers, laboratory technicians, and others. The originators of this test state that it has the advantages of a projective technique in that free association with the cards may elicit tension areas and show the interrelationship of tensions and interests.

Another method designed to assist in the identification of vocational interest areas was constructed by one of the authors and is described in order to illustrate the visual rather than the verbal method of vocational testing. It consists of cards with photographs portraying typical vocational activities covering ten different vocational interest areas. Simple levels of the occupation are shown at one corner and the more complex levels associated with occupational tasks of increasing difficulty that require much formal training are shown at the opposite corner. Additionally, photographs illustrating concrete and abstract areas of every vocational category are shown on separate corners of the card. Thus, the card on medicine shows routine tasks in ascending order of difficulty—changing bedpans, making beds, washing laboratory equipment, taking blood samples, working with a microscope, and taking X-rays. Laboratory work, in which there is no contact with the patients, is shown in a different section of the card from tasks in which a patient relationship is involved. Photographs of work in radiology, pathology, and bacteriology are on one corner; psychiatry and the non-laboratory occupations are on the opposite corner. Nursing activities are portrayed near the center of the card. Another section shows people at work with medical statistics, or medical illustrations. The client is given the opportunity to select the card he prefers and asked to point to the sections on the cards that appeal to him most. An eleventh card is used, which shows pictures of all the vocations and different levels arranged in random order to be used as a validity check on the client's earlier choices. Sufficient variation of location is introduced so that one could be relatively sure that those who consistently selected high, low, or middle ranges for preferred job levels have ambitions that correspond to these levels.

Interest tests and devices that have been described are only some of the different methods that help the vocational counselor in determining interest areas. Hobbies, vocational interests, preferred reading material, as well as best-liked school subjects offer important clues useful to the counselor. Field trips or excursions to factories, shops, offices, and laboratories (which give opportunity for personal observation of people at work in various occupations) should not be overlooked as sources for establishing interests.

The counselor must check all the reasons for job preference given by an individual to determine if he is dealing with real or spurious interests. Spurious interest or pseudo-interests are based only on interest in financial gain, desire for respectability, or status that a particular profession offers. If a person would "like to like" an area of vocational activity, rather than actually liking it, he has pseudo-interests in this occupation. For example, a client's favorite person may be a lawyer and, because he admires him, the client would like to become a lawyer, too. Actually, the client may have low verbal interests, dislike speaking in public, and not care for any of the elements that go into the making of a law career. Law interest is, for the client, only a way of showing his admiration for this person. This pseudo-interest in law can thrust him into an unsuitable career.

2. Aptitude

In a previous chapter we described "aptitude" as the capacity to learn or perform—in other words, the potential of the individual. (See discussion of aptitudes in Chapter 2.) The vocational counselor uses aptitude tests as another measuring device in helping his client to select the occupation that best fits his total life style. Aptitude is closely related to other factors in vocational selection. Potential skills do not have much significance if the subject lacks interest in the career field or if aptitude is high but employment training is not available. Aptitude, as well as any of the other six factors, should not be considered as an isolated entity.

Probably the most direct method in judging a client's aptitude is to use aptitude tests. These have the advantage of being objective and rapid, and of yielding scores that permit the analysis of tested traits. They also permit the comparison of any one person's performance scores with the scores of previously tested groups.

There are several levels and kinds of aptitude tests at the disposal of the counselor. He may choose a scholastic aptitude measure, although these have a definite overlap with intelligence tests. An example of a scholastic aptitude test is the School and College Ability Test (SCAT)[106] which gives a general prediction of verbal and mathematical potential. Levels are available from upper elementary grades through two years of college. The client may also be given a type of scholastic aptitude test that is used for screening candidates for advanced education and training. Many students seeking higher education are painfully aware of the series of tests used for college entrance, graduate school, and other professional training facilities. The most common measures used for selection of undergraduates is the Scholastic Aptitude Test (SAT)[84] given by the College Entrance Examination Board and the ACT[5] given by the American College Testing Program. Test content is similar but organization of materials and scoring systems differ. The ACT supplies standard scores in the areas of English, mathematics, social studies, and natural sciences; the SAT also uses a standard form method but it limits test results to two areas—verbal and quantitative. General and specialized area tests are used for screening students for graduate programs and other professional schools. The Graduate Record Examinations (GRE)[105] and the Miller Analogies Test (MAT)[264] are the two most used in this area. Specific aptitude tests have been designed for medical, nursing, law, trade schools, technical programs, and many other types of training.

Aptitude tests are also available for the prediction of success in specific vocations. These may be designed to measure general areas (mechanical, clerical, musical, artistic) or they may be constructed for a specific occupation. Mechanical and performance tests usually employ some measure of motor function or manual dexterity. Examples of these are the Crawford Small Parts Dexterity Test[91] and the Purdue Pegboard[296]. Tests used to predict aptitude in art and music are usually designed for both visual and auditory distinction. The Seashore Measures of Musical Talents[323] and the Meir Art Judgment Test[259] are two examples of those specialized aptitude measures.

There have been efforts to build general aptitude batteries that would combine the exploration of the scholastic and vocational areas. One of the most widely used tests, particularly with high school students, is the

Differential Aptitude Tests (DAT)[40]. This measure includes eight subtests that range from verbal to mechanical reasoning. The DAT has been widely used as a predictor of school performance and vocations.

Another example of a multiple exam is the General Aptitude Test Battery (GATB)[374]. This test was the result of an ambitious effort on the part of the United States Employment Service to develop a measurement that could be utilized in the public employment services. It is comprised of 12 tests that cover a wide range of aptitudes including both motor and verbal factors. The GATB would seem more valuable for vocational counselors working with a population seeking direct employment rather than training since the test design is vocationally oriented and has been validated on occupations rather than academic performance. The test is available through the employment services and can be administered through special arrangement in high schools, employment agencies, and other types of institutions.

At the present stage of their development, the use of psychological aptitude tests in forming career decisions seems justified when they are used as guides that indicate direction, but not when they are interpreted as indicators that are absolutely correct. This is equally true of the entire battery of vocational tests. Results of such tests should be evaluated within the context of the whole person, his culture, his personality, and many other important factors that are not amenable to testing at the present time.

3. Personality

Numerous investigations have disclosed that more people are discharged from their jobs because of personality problems than because of their inability to perform required tasks[205]. The factor of personality may be the most elusive link in the vocational chain. As was pointed out in Chapter 2, the measurement of personality is difficult. Objective measures are often too clinically oriented to be helpful in vocational guidance. Often they also ignore cultural factors. Projective tests, though desirable, may not be practical for the vocational counselor since the administration may be difficult and time consuming, and results may require a more highly trained evaluator. Often this leaves the vocational counselor with only the limited resources of observations and interviews. It is possible that he can structure an interview method that will tap many personality variables important in vocational choice. Optimally however, the counselor should also be a qualified psychologist or have such a psychologist available as a resource person. It is always desirable to utilize personality tests to corroborate subjective impressions in assessing the personality of a person seeking vocational counseling. There are a number of tests that claim to measure traits of the "normal" personality.

California Psychological Inventory (*CPI*)[151]

The CPI has already been mentioned in conjunction with the MMPI. It is considered by many as a similar standard for testing "normal" persons. No doubt this is because of the number of common items found on both scales and the general design of the instruments. The CPI yields 18 discrete scales grouped into four general clusters. Examples of some of the scales are dominance, well-being, sociability, intellectual efficiency, and flexibility. The technical aspects of the test are probably the test's best qualities; however, questions are raised as to the usefulness of the CPI[367]. Scales have shown some overlap and this may lead to confusion in interpretation. One of the authors, Cameron, has found the CPI useful as a measure in a battery of tests to help a client consider a vocation within the context of personality characteristics that would affect job satisfaction and performance.

Sixteen Personality Factor Questionnaire (16 *PF*)[77]

The 16 PF is another test commonly applied as a measure of normal personality. The test is purported to be a "measure of adult personality for business and industry, education, vocational guidance, clinical diagnosis, and research"[78]. It is stated that "the 16 PF provides useful job and clinical profiles to guide both the vocational counselor and clinician"[78].

The test measures 16 general personality factors by describing each factor with the use of dichotomous polar adjectives with each set of adjectives on a 10-point continuum. Scores are derived by standard score method (Sten Score) and are plotted on a profile sheet. Examples of factors are: easily upset-calm, trusting-suspicious, and self-assured-apprehensive. A computer-scoring and interpretation service provided by the Institute for Personality and Ability Testing (IPAT) has greatly expanded information available with this test. Besides the 16 factors, the computer profile reports a precise personality description, clinical observations, treatment conditions, and vocational observations with occupational comparisons and occupational fitness projections. Like the CPI, the

16 PF is also criticized for a lack of independence among its scales as well as some methods used in establishing reliability. The test is currently receiving increased publicity [76] and, through the efforts of its author, R. B. Cattell, and IPAT, the 16 PF may become a more widely used measure in personality assessment.

Edwards Personal Preference Schedule (EPPS) [107]

The EPPS is another test that is utilized in vocational counseling. Although originally designed to measure the personality-needs system of Murray, this function is now questionable. Some of the 15 traits purportedly measured are such things as achievement, dominance, aggression, and succorance. Much criticism has been leveled at the EPPS for its paucity of validity data and lack of concern for the improvement of the test. It has remained virtually unchanged since its inception despite strong criticisms [216]. Another area of concern is the utilization of ipsative scores, which have clouded much of the independent research carried out on the instrument [17]. However, Edwards has received approval for his effort to control the misleading effect of social desirability through his method of construction of test questions [59]. Some critics feel that until adequate research is completed and subsequent improvements made, the use of the test is quite limited.

Projective Techniques

Projective measures should not be overlooked for personality assessment. An adequate discussion of these can be found throughout the book and need not be repeated at this time. However, we will use one not previously mentioned in this book to illustrate how such tests can be useful to the counselor and how they are constructed. The Group Personality Projective Test will serve as an example.

Group Personality Projective Test (GPPT) [74]

Since its publication in 1958, the GPPT has been used increasingly every year. This test offers projective information by using objective methods to obtain scores. The test consists of a booklet that has 90 simple cartoons and questions relating to each cartoon. For example, in question 58 (see Fig. 11.1) two individuals are pictured in the form of stick figures that could represent any type of person, male or female. One is labeled *A*, the other

Fig. 11.1 Test illustration from the Group Personality Projective Technique.

one *B*. *A* is shown holding a lamp. The question associated with this picture is:

What are the persons in the picture doing?
1. *A* and *B* are fixing up their home.
2. *A* is trying to sell a lamp to *B*.
3. *A* is trying to decide which one of the lamps he wants to buy.
4. *A* is the mother of *B* and is giving him a gift.
5. *B* does not know *A* and does not trust him.

The manual describes a factor-analytic evaluation, which yields scores in the following areas: Happiness, Depression, Nurturance, Withdrawal, Neuroticism, Affiliation, Succorance, and Tension. Test clusters may be combined to derive an evaluation of Social Insight, Leadership, Ego Strength, and Cooperation. The test was designed by Cassel and Kahn[75] and its validation norms are found in the manual. An IBM-type answer sheet is provided for the client, which can be either hand- or machine-scored. The test can be given individually or to groups.

4. and 5. Training Opportunities and Availability of Funds and Time for Training

The job market has become more selective with the increase of automation and the corresponding decrease in jobs for non-skilled and semi-skilled workers. The need for highly skilled workers places added strains on training facilities. Expansion of these facilities seldom keeps pace with the demand for increased education. As time goes on, training in the field in which an individual has demonstrated interest and aptitude may become more difficult to acquire. In the United States, in certain fields such as medicine, law, and dentistry, applicants experience an agonizing competitive selection process and many times must leave their local community or state in order to attend an appropriate school. There are also new vocations for which training programs are not yet available. This situation exists in foreign countries that are in a stage of new development calling for skills and knowledge that cannot be imparted by institutions of learning in the country itself. Students in such a country must take part or all of their training where adequate facilities exist.

There are situations with which the vocational counselor must deal realistically. If scholarships are available, he must ascertain the individual's eligibility. A client may demonstrate exceptionally high interest, aptitude, and the proper personality for a given profession, but if he lacks the means and finances to obtain the training, a reappraisal of his vocational objective may be necessary. This is particularly true for those clients with family obligations and debts, or when ill health or disabilities make it difficult for him to earn extra money. However, many persons have obtained training in spite of what appeared to be insurmountable obstacles. Whether or not he considers the obstacles in his way as insuperable, the client should weigh the factors of training opportunities and means of support as realistically as he must face the limitations of his capacity and direction of his interests.

6. Employment Opportunities

Employment represents one of the terminal goals of vocational guidance. It is unfortunate that vocational counselors sometimes lose sight of this goal in their preoccupation with requirement procedures when they view employment opportunities as static. They study the findings of national or private surveys on industrial expansions and resulting employment opportunities, but fail to realize that predictions may be incorrect because of factors not considered when the predictions were made. A

Table 11.1 Summary of vocational guidance factors.

Factors	Six Areas of Consideration					
	I Interests	II Aptitudes	III Personality	IV Training Opportunities	V Funds and Time Availability	VI Employment Opportunity
A Origin	1. Acquired by identification or observation. 2. Results of inborn skills. 3. Because of earning potential.	1. Inborn traits and skills.	1. Constitutional factors and environmental conditioning.	1. On the job apprenticeship. 2. School or university.	1. Parents. 2. Self-employment. 3. Stipends and scholarships.	1. Government service. 2. Private economy. 3. Self-employment.
B How to identify or reveal the presence of areas	1. Interest tests. 2. Hobbies 3. Favorite school subjects. 4. Tasks liked in past work experience.	1. Intelligence tests. 2. Aptitude tests. 3. School grades. 4. Past work performance.	1. Personality tests. 2. Case history. 3. Interview. 4. Reports from teachers or past employers.	1. School catalogs. 2. Newspaper advertisements. 3. Union or government information agencies.	1. Analysis of the sources of funds for studying.	1. Union or government informational services. 2. Personal contacts. 3. Survey of economic conditions.
C Disqualifying elements negating positive findings	1. Evidence that interests are pseudo-interests or transient.	1. Insufficient health or strength for tasks. 2. Personal appearance, size, weight.	1. Neurosis. 2. Psychosis. 3. Emotional immaturity.	1. Absence of, or distance to training facilities.	1. Obligation to support family or self.	1. Racial or ethnic discrimination affecting applicant. 2. Age, too young or too old for the job.

D Factors affecting vocational predictions	1. Change of interests with time or experience. 2. Changes in salary or earning potential.	1. Incorrect assessment of aptitudes. 2. Maturation of new aptitudes. 3. Health changes.	1. Incorrect assessment of personality. 2. Changes due to situational stress or disease. 3. Maturation or environmental factors not anticipated.	1. New schools or training facilities. 2. Closing of schools or training facilities. 3. Changes in admission requirements. 4. Changes in training requirements.	1. Death or illness of person supplying support. 2. Loss of scholarship. 3. Loss of funds for other reasons.	1. New industries, inventions or processing methods, automation. 2. Movement of industries or population shifts. 3. Major disasters, including wars or preparation for wars. 4. Revolutions in government or political upheavals. 5. Depressions, recessions, or inflationary periods. 6. Labor-management conditions, strikes, or restrictive practices, legislation, licensing, new laws of certification.

number of years ago, many vocational counseling centers in the United States were informed that opportunities for the employment of engineers were limited. Young men were dissuaded by vocational counselors from training for engineering professions at that time because of the information supplied by these surveys. The advent of increased military preparation together with the invention of new processes and unexpected demand for consumer goods reversed the employment trend a few years later. An unprecedented number of engineers was then required and there was much competitive bidding for their services. Some of the unanticipated shortages could be prevented if vocational counselors interpret reports on future employment needs more cautiously.

The summary of vocational guidance factors, Table 11.1, presents six general factors affecting vocational prediction of employment opportunities. In addition to these, there are specific limitations that apply more to one country or type of employment than to others. These include personal connections with employment resources, politics, and other complex factors that may be socio-economic, regional, national, or cultural. No one can say in advance how prominent a role these limitations or advantages will play in a given case.

THE COUNSELING RESPONSIBILITY

The responsibilities of vocational counseling are not always taken seriously. Some school administrators insist that every student must be counseled without realizing that poor counseling based on insufficient data is worse than none. There are schools where a teacher, relatively untrained in counseling methods, is given the title of "counselor" and assigned to help students make far-reaching educational and vocational decisions. In some cases, students enter occupations selected by the untrained counselor who devoted only a few minutes to the perusal of the student's personality test, interest inventory scores, school grades, or training record. Some school authorities take pride in the fact that their students are given guidance, even though these methods are questionable and superficial. Much damage can be done by mass-produced guidance programs, even if the counselors are technically trained to acceptable levels of competence.

On the basis of several years of personal experience in the field of vocational guidance, the authors suggest the following principles:

1. Persons should be encouraged rather than forced to seek vocational

guidance. Students should apply for vocational counseling on their own initiative, at the advice of their teachers, parents, or supervisors, without coercion.

2. Vocational counselors must be qualified psychologists who are able to detect the presence of emotional disturbance if it is masked as vocational dissatisfaction or as an educational problem.
3. Facilities for referring students to mental health clinics must be available and students must be referred to these clinics when emotional disorders are recognized as underlying vocational or educational problems.
4. A counselor must never be assigned a definite number of clients to be processed within a given period. Sufficient time must be provided so that he can do a thorough job in each case. The matter of how much time is required with each client must be left to the counselor's own judgment.
5. The counselor must use only approved psychological tests and techniques, and must use enough of them to avoid reaching conclusions based on insufficient evidence. If a question or personality difficulty arises, he must know how to use or obtain the use of projective techniques. The counselor should be given a role in the selection of the tests he uses.
6. The counselor must be aware of the limitations of vocational guidance and must respect the basic right of every person to make his own decisions regarding his future. Instead of telling the client what do do, he should present the facts, explain their significance, mention their limitations, and then permit the client to make his own decisions.
7. The counselor should have at his disposal library facilities and other sources of information to which the client may be referred. He should maintain contacts with persons in various professions, occupations, and labor unions so that he may keep abreast of new developments having a bearing on employment conditions and opportunities. Time should be allotted the counselor for keeping up to date with the current literature on guidance and techniques of counseling.
8. The counselor must not be required to follow a mechanical format in reporting findings, nor should he be asked to report on matters not related to the counseling situation. He should not make statements that he cannot support with evidence. The length and content of the report should be left to the judgment of the counselor.

QUALIFICATIONS OF PSYCHOLOGISTS AND COUNSELORS

At the present time there is an increasing emphasis at many universities to provide counselors who are fully trained at the Ph.D. level and who have adequate experience in the interpretation of the projective and objective tests now in clinical use. We see this as an important trend, since vocational and educational counselors are, perhaps more than any other group of people working in the helping services, in a position to identify and refer for treatment young people having potentially serious emotional problems. With the increasing complexity of vocational choices and the newly recognized role that vocational satisfaction plays in the important field of community mental health, the responsibilities of vocational and educational counselors have vastly increased and, accordingly, it seems necessary that the type and amount of training that qualifies persons as guidance counselors be increased proportionately.

In order to promote adequate training and experience for specialists in counseling and guidance and the other specialties in mental health, as well as in clinical psychology, an American Board of Examiners in Professional Psychology has been established. Clinical psychologists and counselors who qualify may apply to take specialty examinations in these or other service areas within psychology. After passing rigorous examinations, a psychologist is entitled to indicate that he has been awarded a diploma as a specialist by the Board. He may then list himself as a diplomate within this specialty. This move was encouraged by the American Psychological Association to assist clients seeking psychological services in locating professional specialists within their community. Additionally, to safeguard the public, most states now have certification or licensing requirements for psychologists and counselors who do clinical work or mental health counseling. These are awarded only after appropriate examinations have been passed indicating that the practitioner has the professional skills and the training necessary to meet the standards of the examination board.

SUMMARY

The desire to fit each man to a proper niche in a nation's economy is a normal accompaniment of increasing industrialization and specialization. Insuring the "right job for the right man" represents a challenge that in some ways may conflict with a client's right to decide his own vocation that best fits his life style or to embark on a career that need not necessarily reflect the counselor's recommendations. Poorly staffed mass counseling programs that are operated in a routine and mechanical manner may be worse than no counseling at all. These programs can only succeed if individual testing is employed and a sufficient number of trained counselors are available to give each client as much attention as he requires. Emphasis on counseling should not be limited to a client's future vocational goals. Instead, the evaluation should be focused on the client himself as a human being and his vocational potentialities should be considered as only one aspect of his total life plan.

CHAPTER 12

Clinical Psychology, Medicine, Education, and Law

Within a short period of time, certain disciplines have been clustered together to contribute, each in its own unique way, to the understanding of human behavior in health and states of dysfunction. Many within the consortium of behavioral sciences deal with clinical applications. Others, in addition, concern themselves with developing methods and techniques to enhance diagnostic acuity, measure the progress and determine the resolution of pathological states. Some specialties concern themselves with the various steps that lead to the final pathway. The science of psychology belongs within this realm and through its clinical specialty contributes meaningfully to patient care and understanding. The field of psychology is broad and its clinical application is no less so.

On the 26th of May, 1952, a paper delivered at the Psychological Medical Society in Paris was to have remarkable effect on the behavioral sciences. The article, "The Therapeutic Use of a Phenothiazene with Selective Central Action"[97], ushered in what some have called the "Age of Psychopharmacology." Through the observations of Delay, Deniker, Heil, and others, new doors were opened to the investigation of mental disease. Volumes of observations, development of new concepts, theories of interaction of these new drugs and enzyme systems poured forth at meteoric rates, all of which brought psychiatry abreast of the exploding advances being made in the fields of surgery, organ transplants, and other aspects of medicine.

MEDICINE NEEDS OTHER SPECIALTIES

In the infancy of medicine it was not difficult to acquire all the available knowledge and techniques necessary to diagnose and prescribe a course of treatment for a patient. Whether the diseased state was explained as a confusion of humors or infestation of demons, the physician could carry out with clarity an approved and accepted regimen. As individuals freed themselves from superstition and critically observed the human in health and disease, a body of factual knowledge concerning abnormal states was developed. With the addition of new techniques in diagnosis and improved treatment, it became increasingly difficult for any one individual to remain proficient in all phases of medicine. Because of this, specialization became a necessity. With specialization came more knowledge and the perfection of techniques and treatment, which required years of study and practice before an individual became fully qualified. Specialties themselves have divided and subdivided. This is not peculiar to medicine; it is found in all modern sciences. Yet even with its high degree of specialization, medicine is not a self-contained science but must and does rely on other specialties and fields for assistance. Clinical psychology is one of these.

Medical studies focus on the organic aspects of the human body with detail on cellular and tissue structure—their changes in various disease states and aging processes. In many instances, it has been our experience that while the physician is well-versed in the physiology and pathology of the human, he is at times perplexed at the symptomatology that cannot be measured with his diagnostic instruments and procedures. It is impossible for him to conceive of any approach to this conglomeration of cells and tissues other than the organic. Unfortunately, most medical curricula have given too little attention to the emotional and psychological growth and development of the human. As a result, many physicians are ill-equipped to fathom the discomforts and disease states that can and do arise from faulty emotional and psychological growth. They have not been given sufficient understanding and knowledge to comprehend the defensive procedures and maneuvers the organism uses to keep an emotional homeostasis. They can perceive, follow, and discuss the pathological physiology, the changes that accompany organic disease states, and with fair accuracy predict further changes and reparative processes in the field of organic medicine. To the physician, psychological and psychophysiological changes do not appear to be orderly, rational, and understandable. In spite of the indivisibility of the human organism, we are prone (because of our organic training) to regard the patient as a collection of organs, anatomically arranged, with little appreciation of the individual before us—his needs, hopes, fears, and their influence on his pathological state.

The Value of Clinical Insights

In many instances, even the slightest inkling that the symptoms may be of a non-organic nature will either result in the patient being labeled "neurotic" and sent on his way or his rapidly being referred to a psychiatrist. Sooner or later a psychiatric report, which may also include a psychological protocol, will find its way to the referring physician. Upon receiving the consultation report from the psychiatrist, he may accept the report as he would any consultation from another M.D. In reading over the psychological protocols and the findings of the clinical psychologist, he may be perplexed at the information and, if he is inquisitive, question how one could logically arrive at definitive points about an individual from blocks, pictures, ink spots, and other seemingly childish paraphernalia. Yet, with his professional achievements, his education, training, and specialized techniques, the clinical psychologist (as any other specialist) can render valuable insights into the status of patients. His capabilities run the gamut of assisting in the determination of origin, diagnosis, and prognosis of disease states as well as aiding in the measurement of the severity of an illness. He can give his impression of the defensive strength of an individual as well as detect the weaknesses in the protective armor and estimate how these can withstand the probing of therapy. He can evaluate the therapeutic procedure and the clinical gains in therapy, and relay this information to the therapist.

The concept of a team of individuals being necessary to the understanding of illnesses and suffering is not a new aspect of medicine. In a group or hospital setting, the individual patient, while under the care of one physician, is followed directly or indirectly by many specialists who cooperate in the evaluation of the changes occurring. If disease states were always consistent with their prodromal signs, course, and termination, and if each disease had uniqueness so that it could, at a moment's observation, be differentiated from all other disease states, the services of specialists would not be needed. This is not the case and herein lies the fascination of medicine; the knowledge and experiences of a group of individuals is necessary to assist in the diagnosis and treatment of patients. If the physician depended merely on a case history and physical examination to arrive at a diagnosis, many diseases might be recorded inaccurately or merely as ill-defined states. The use of diagnostic aids and specialized techniques has become an ingrained and indispensable part of the practice of medicine.

In some cases these special procedures are performed by M.D.s. In other instances, specialists who are not M.D.s are called upon to assist in the ministration of the patient. The bacteriologist and biochemist perform an important and definitive function and materially assist in the practice of medicine. The clinical psychologist, like these other non-medical specialists, deserves an honored place in a profession dedicated to the understanding of abnormal emotional states. The clinical psychologist in a clinic or hospital setting is allied most closely with the psychiatric department, but because he is an important member of this group it should not be construed that his whole function is merely one of assisting in this branch of medicine. Actually, he can function in a much wider range. With our modern concept that the patient cannot be divided into a psyche and soma, that the individual responds as a whole to insult whether it be of a physical or emotional nature, the psychologist can render aid to other branches of medicine offering a more complete understanding of the total problem confronting the physician.

To the neurologist and neurosurgeon, the psychological battery of tests is often an important diagnostic aid in confirming suspicions of a growth within the cranial cavity. At times, physical findings, specialized X-ray studies, and electroencephalograms may be within normal limits or so equivocal as to be considered of little significance. Yet, in the psychological tests, indications may give substantial support to a diagnosis of tumor or degenerative disease. Also, these tests are capable of localizing the site of a lesion. On occasion, we have been called in to evaluate patients who had previously been diagnosed as "hysterical"; when seen psychiatrically, there was a marked suspicion of organic brain disease. Psychological testing further substantiated this position and the lesion was proven upon surgery. The neurologist and neurosurgeon do not utilize a psychological examination only to aid in diagnosis and localization but also ask for assistance in estimating the amount of damage a patient may have sustained by trauma or surgery. An accurate estimate of loss due to intellectual impairment is difficult to make by observation alone. Correct estimates are important for medical-legal considerations, compensation, and planning for the individual's future. To say that damage is present is as vague as saying that an individual has a temperature. Without a thermometer to measure the degree of temperature, the seriousness of the disease may not be detected. Psychological tests can determine the percentage of loss of intellectual and abstract function with reasonable accuracy.

Clinical Psychology and Pediatrics

On a large and busy pediatric service, the clinical psychologist serves a much needed support function. With the establishment of well-baby clinics and their widespread use, problems of delay in mental growth and development and deviant behavior can be detected at an early age. With psychological evaluation even of the very young, a great deal of information can be obtained. Seeming backwardness or mental defectiveness as reported by the family may, on testing, prove to be emotional blocking. With proper handling and assistance, these children can be led toward normal development. Since an estimate of the level of mental ability can be obtained on very young infants, it is advisable in cases of adoption to evaluate infants psychologically before final papers are signed. The pre-adoption examination should never be considered complete until a psychological evaluation including testing is done.

The Value of Psychological Testing

The clinical interview is a major tool utilized to assist the psychiatrist in developing his concept of what is wrong with the patient. However, a clinical interview does not necessarily lead to the immediate understanding of the origin of the events that have caused a specific symptomatology. For the most part, the patient is a poor observer of events that have precipitated his illness. His disease may be of such a nature that it is impossible for him to relate his difficulties. He might be able to actively defend himself by his use of words, giving answers or denials that do not convey his true feelings. He might consciously neglect to convey sufficient information to aid the physician in arriving at a working diagnosis and an understanding of the dynamics that have caused the deviant behavior. Often it takes much time and effort before an individual feels free to relate his feelings. It requires considerable experience in interview techniques before this method can be used to gain an understanding of the dynamics that make up the personality.

The psychological test is structured differently from the clinical interview, and the techniques used in this type of an examination are not the same as a face-to-face conversation. Test materials usually represent a new situation with which the patient is unfamiliar and they are, therefore, not as apt to elicit stereotyped defenses. The patient can project himself into the test, revealing his personality even though he may be guarded and resistive. He will meet these new stimuli in a manner characteristic of the way he reacts to untried and untested experiences. In some instances, a faster and more complete picture of the individual's personality becomes evident. With the information gleaned from the psychological test, the physician can have available a clearer concept of the dynamics involved. Often this facilitates a more rapid entry into the problem areas of the patient.

Psychological testing should not be conceived of as a mere laboratory procedure in a class with routine blood and urine tests. It should be viewed as a specialized procedure like the visualization of the interior of the body by radiographic techniques or the observation on tissues reported by the clinical pathologist. Both of these specialists can shed light on morbid states—their severity, origin, and treatment potentials. The clinical psychologist can use his specialized techniques to visualize a little more clearly and rapidly the faulty areas of development and the malignant tendencies in the personality of the patient.

The best appraisal from a psychologist is obtained if a consultation is of a positive nature. It should not be expressed as a vague hope that something might be found to make a diagnosis. The referring physician should have a definite reason for his referral and should prepare his patient for psychological testing as he would for any other medical or diagnostic procedure. The consultation request should cover the pertinent and significant points in the patient's history and it should mention the specific areas of the psychiatrist's interest. It is insufficient to state merely: "request psychometric testing." The psychologist must be given enough information to know which of the many different kinds of tests and techniques are most appropriate for the problem at hand.

In medicine, then, the physician calls upon the clinical psychologist to assist in formulating the diagnosis, uncovering the dynamics, and assessing the severity of the illness, ego strength, and the presence of destructive behavior or suicidal intent. By using objective measurements, he helps determine amount of loss suffered by patients with organic lesions of the brain. He assists in the evaluation of the physically handicapped by probing for aptitudes and disclosing vocational interest patterns. He assists materially in the study of emotionally ill children. His tests and techniques are basic in the evaluation of new therapeutic methods and to all aspects of psychiatric research.

Thus far in this chapter we have dealt with clinical psychologists and their relationship with medicine. Often in educational settings, the school psychologist has the primary responsibility for assisting teachers and principals in understanding the emotionally and intellectually handicapped as well as the exceptionally gifted child. He examines children referred to him by teachers, counselors, and the school principal. He makes recommendations, assists in planning programs for the exceptional child by advising teachers of the personality and educational problems that his tests have revealed, and makes referrals to other specialists when necessary. He can explain the probable origin and the severity of the difficulty so that teachers can carry out their functions more effectively.

CLINICAL PSYCHOLOGY AND LAW

The law, both as a profession and as an arm of society, has been troubled in its efforts to deal with the problem of mental disease and deviant behavior. From both the philosophical and conscience viewpoints, the law has endeavored by its rules to deal with these problems as effectively and honestly as possible. There have been many attempts by learned scholars to define rules that are acceptable to assist the law in dealing with criminal responsibility, competency, hospitalization, and patients' rights. The law, at times, has reluctantly turned toward psychiatry for assistance. Psychologists, by and large, have been excluded or merely utilized to serve as consultants to psychiatrists and have had little stature before the courts in the actual decision-making process or the determination of competency. In many jurisdictions, the clinical psychologist, in spite of his training and occupational experience, has not been permitted to answer the ultimate question of the effect of mental disease and/or behavioral patterns as they affect responsibility. There have been some interesting cases and judicial decisions concerning the position of the clinical psychologist and the use of his testimony. In a brief filed by the American Psychological Association pursuant to Jenkins versus the United States, the court held that the psychologist is an established scientist and professional. Psychologists are highly trained experts in their profession and thus are able to express expert opinions in the field of mental disease and mental defect. By reason of his professional competency, the court reasoned that the psychologist could be qualified to assist the court in establishing legal competency and responsibility and thus assist the law in its ministrations of justice. While this decision is not universal, it does point in the direction of possible decisions by other jurisdictions.

In the preceding chapters, we hope that the reader will have gained an understanding of the specific application, usefulness, and limitations of some of the tools, methods, and techniques of diagnosis and evaluation that psychologists use. We hope that an acquaintance with these will enable the reader to make full use of this interesting specialty—clinical psychology.

SUMMARY

The relationship between medicine and clinical psychology was discussed. The psychologist was described as a specialist who can materially assist the physician in arriving at a diagnosis, establishing the etiology and prognosis of an emotional illness. The psychological test differs from a psychiatric interview and makes its own unique contribution to the clinical evaluation. The skills of the psychologist can also be utilized in the fields of education and law.

CHAPTER 13

Case Illustrations

The authors have selected five cases and adapted them for use as illustrations. Names and background material have been changed to insure that the clients involved will not be recognized. These reports are not presented as typical of what is found in all psychological practice. They were selected specifically to complement the content materials of this book and to offer a sample of reporting results.

CASE ONE: MALE, AGE 18

Reason for Referral

An evaluation of the personality is desired in order to better understand this young man and his problems of adjustment.

Summary of Social History

The client's father has been divorced and remarried. John is the son of the first wife. There have been some problems in the son-father relationship.

Tests Administered

1. Quick Test
2. Goldstein-Scheerer Color Form Sorting Test
3. Bender Motor Gestalt Test
4. Incomplete Sentence Blank[205]

5. Draw-A-Person-Test
6. Rorschach Test
7. Kahn Test of Symbol Arrangement
8. California Psychological Inventory

Test Evaluations

Quick Test

On this test John obtained an IQ score of 106. This placed him in the upper 30 percent of the general population as far as intelligence is concerned. It should be noted, however, that this test is not a wide-range one, being limited only to certain aspects of verbal functions. It is not a broad measure of the general intelligence. To obtain a more accurate picture of John's real intelligence, a Wechsler Adult Intelligence Scale should be administered.

Goldstein-Scheerer Color Form Sorting Test

The test was performed entirely within normal limits. The sequence of shape to color is characteristic of persons who are striving to obtain emotional control and who tend to intellectualize.

Bender Motor Gestalt Test

This test elicited good eye-motor coordination. The drawings had excellent fidelity to the original figures. The striving for accuracy might suggest a mild obsessive compulsive tendency. Excellent control was used in the performance of this test.

Incomplete Sentence Blank

The test revealed that this young man has a deep feeling of sensitivity toward other people. More than anything else he wants to be loved and give love. He still suffers from emotional trauma stemming from the divorce of his parents. He regrets that he is "not more responsible." He states that during childhood he was "not good to people." He feels that he needs "to become a man." His future is seen as bright. He pictures himself as being "very slow at times." His concern in becoming a man represents an area of considerable anxiety.

Draw-A-Person-Test

In general, the drawings represent a personality that can be described as normal. A number of characteristics, however, are noteworthy. Among these are signs of a somewhat compulsive element within the personality. Greater than average dependency needs were projected. Signs of inner tensions were present. An effort toward masculine striving was also noted. Characteristics in the female drawing suggest that the client's experiences with females were not usually pleasant and a fear of female figures was implied by specific signs on this test.

Rorschach Test

On this test John gave responses that are associated with those who suffer from a fear of being overwhelmed and destroyed. It was also seen that his fear was a cause of considerable anxiety to him. Since the nature of the anxiety seems to be of the free-floating type, John may not be aware of the cause of his anxiety. Free-floating anxiety is evoked when a client finds it necessary to disguise the origins of his fear.

Other signs on this test suggest that John does not feel that he is a whole person. He projects the feeling that there is something missing in his life. In a previous test he stated that he needed "love." Perhaps he also needs a direction, a purpose in life, and a feeling of self-worth. The test elicited a number of signs associated with emotional immaturity. A sense of loneliness and a need to belong to something that will give him strength and confidence were indicated by specific Rorschach responses. A mild hysterical element within the personality pattern was identified. Problems of masculine self-identification were projected.

The Rorschach test pattern is not an abnormal one and the characteristics elicited by the test are not unusual in terms of the problems that many young people have in today's world. A number of signs pointed to the possibility of future growth. A capacity for good interpersonal relationships was indicated by the human movement.

Kahn Test of Symbol Arrangement

This test elicited some emotional depression and a sense of caution, stemming perhaps from a feeling of threat and hostility that is in part self-directed. The depression could stem from the self-directed hostility. John responds to what he himself interprets as emotional trauma, which he feels he has experienced in life. This makes him somewhat suspicious of people's motives. There were signs present on this test that suggest that John has a strong status drive and a need to succeed in order to prove himself.

On the Sorting task of the KTSA, John placed all the transparent objects and the blue heart in the HATE category. This suggests that he harbors considerable hostility toward those who may have contributed to unhappy experiences in his past life. The phallic symbol was associated with LIVING and this is entirely to be expected among young men who are attempting to achieve a positive masculine image. The object that often represents the self was placed in SMALL, suggesting that John suffers from feelings of inferiority. A poor identification with the father figure was projected and no objects were sorted into the FATHER-MAN-BOY category. Instead, four objects were sorted into the MURDER-WAR-KILL category. This suggests that John feels that he has been emotionally hurt very deeply and that life can be very threatening. The female symbols were associated with FAILURE-SADNESS-LOSS and this may perhaps be explained by the fact that through the divorce and the poor health of the mother the normal interaction between mother and son was aborted, leaving John with some resulting emotional scars. The phallic symbol was associated with ESCAPE-RUN AWAY. It seems that although John wishes to be a man, he has a deep dread of the need to prove himself successful in this area. In other words, he may fear failure, or regret deeply that there is such a thing as masculinity that must be demonstrated in order to be recognized. It is social pressure rather than internal motivation that makes him wish to prove his masculinity.

The symbol pattern of 105-XYCFZB was within the limits of normal expectation.

California Psychological Inventory

The overall profile reflects an average-to-poor adjustment pattern. Area one, dealing with self-concept, is within normal limits although the client perceives himself as "worse" than what he actually reports. Area two, which indicates social responsibility, is depressed, thus reflecting a lack of responsibility, some trauma in interpersonal relations, and a lack of intimate contact and perceived acceptance by others. His intellectual qualities appear normal although intellectual efficiency is below average, thus suggesting a concern about other problems. Area four shows the client to be somewhat rigid and controlled and possibly oversensitive to the reaction of others.

Summary and Conclusions

Essentially we are dealing with a normal person who has problems that stem in part from an adolescent turmoil to which many young men are subject today. John's compulsive characteristics should not be viewed as a liability since in many endeavors they can become an asset if properly controlled and directed. Successful scientists and physicians often must have a compulsive element within their personalities in order that they may be successful at their work.

The test reveals that John requires reassurance of his own worth. He craves affection as a means of convincing himself that he is important. Too much censure and criticism will not help him since he is already highly self-critical. He has to build up self-confidence and this can best be accomplished by giving John a feeling of being accepted and by some evidence that John can interpret as a sign of success. Praise for his good qualities may accomplish more than criticism for his shortcomings. It is believed that if John can experience a year or two of successful achievement and feel that he is being accepted as a person, a beneficial growth of his personality may take place. Having goals and purpose in life would play an important role in such a therapeutic experience.

CASE TWO: MALE, AGE 41

Reason for Referral

This foreign-born chemical engineer suffers from insomnia, migraine headaches, tiredness, irritability, and tensions. He left______and worked in______. Changing jobs brought him to______, where he feels isolated and is unable to make friends. He states that he becomes excited when things don't go well and finds himself aware of increased blood pressure.

Summary of Social History

The client is married to a woman with whom he lived for several years before their marriage. He does not describe any problems with her except that he cannot accept the friends she is making. They are non-intellectuals. His parents are in good health in______. He reports excellent relations with both of his parents. He has two older brothers and thinks very well of both of them. He has a son, 10 years old, and a daughter, 7 years of age, and expresses concern about his children. In spite of the fact that the client states that he thinks very highly of his wife and describes her many good qualities, he also states that she was not the best choice for him and he knew this from the beginning.

Tests Administered

1. Incomplete Sentence Blank
2. Quick Test
3. Goldstein-Scheerer Color Form Sorting Test
4. Bender Motor Gestalt Test
5. Draw-A-Person-Test
6. Kahn Test of Symbol Arrangement
7. Rorschach Test
8. Minnesota Multiphasic Personality Inventory

Test Evaluations

Incomplete Sentence Blank

On this test the client used some unusual verbalizations. For example, "A mother is abnegated for their children." He also stated that his greatest worry is the future of his children. This, combined with other responses, suggests that the client may be in a state of competition for his wife's attention and sees his children (especially his son) as rivals. The "concern" may camouflage unconscious hostility stemming from this rivalry.

Quick Test

On this test the client's IQ of 116 places him in the upper 15 percent of the general population. When the fact that the client is bilingual is taken into account, the IQ score is impressive, since it was obtained largely by means of vocabulary-picture identification.

Goldstein-Scheerer Color Form Sorting Test

No abnormality was seen in the client's test responses. However, the color-over-form selection yields the impression that the client is basically motivated by his emotions, using his intellect secondarily.

Bender Motor Gestalt Test

The test performance was within normal limits. However, it is significant that the figure sometimes suggestive of male-female interaction was drawn with a distortion in which accuracy was sacrificed. A lack of capacity to interact realistically with females could explain this distortion. Greater than average psychic pressure and exaggerated affect was noted by the manner in which the figures were drawn.

Draw-A-Person-Test

The impression from this test is that the client has projected a self-image in which he feels compelled to over-conform and to present an acceptable front to the world. It represents an exaggerated need by the client to give the impression that he is a "good" person and does everything right. A strong obsessive-compulsive element within the personality emerged on this test. In addition to this there are signs suggestive of greater than average dependency needs that are not currently being met.

The female figure suggests the client sees hostility and rigidity in his male-female interactions. The summary will cover a possible explanation of this reaction on the part of the client.

Kahn Test of Symbol Arrangement

The Arrangement Time is consistent with the presence of psychic pressure and the directional performance of the arrangements suggests unevenness in intellectual activities. It is noted that the first Arrangement was performed in a "mixed" manner and other Arrangements were Center and Left-Right performances. Mixed performance on the first Arrangement is suggestive of a person who is threatened by new experiences and tends to get "mixed up" when he confronts things that are unfamiliar to him. This impression is strengthened by the fact that the reason for performance given by the client was "random." Random Arrangement suggests a lack of motivation or a fear of challenges. This usually stems from a lack of self-confidence when it occurs among otherwise intellectually qualified persons.

The client's exceedingly high Z score on this test is consistent with stereotyped thinking and difficulty in interpersonal relationships. Although intellectual and creative superiority is indicated by Z, there is an accompanying unrealistic orientation toward life when Z responses are excessive and Y responses are few. The Sorting task performance suggests that the client is ambitious, status seeking, and has a tremendous need for recognition and approval. Other signs derived from the Sorting performance suggest that this client tends to be cynical, overcritical, suspicious, and lacks capacity for rapport. The symbol pattern was 130-ZFDCBEA. The absence of Y responses is consistent with lack of a practical orientation toward the demands of everyday life. The combination of FD scores is characteristic of a hysterical orientation and the high C score suggests a compulsive trend.

On the second Sorting task, a feminine identification was projected by the client. Love was equated with sex and this is typical of persons who are unable to separate these two kinds of emotions. This type of performance is often associated with males who suffer from the residuals of difficult son-mother relationships during their adolescence.

Rorschach Test

Three factors were represented in the test results. These were: (1) a hysterical personality pattern, (2) a suspiciousness that had schizoid coloration with paranoid implications, and (3) a hypomanic trend within the personality, held in check by obsessive-compulsive ego defenses. This combination of ego defenses is incompatible since the hysterical personality is emotionally oriented while the obsessive-compulsive front is intellectual, creating a conflict in regard to whether emotional drives experienced by the client should be expressed or repressed. If repressed, the client will find the building up of psychic pressure intolerable; if expressed, the client will be wracked by the resulting guilt feelings.

The Rorschach test pattern is clinically significant in revealing a deep social anxiety. There is an awareness and sensitivity to people and a concomitant anxiety in dealing with them. The large number of human detail responses (Hd) is typical of persons who are directly involved with people but who feel unable to cope with ordinary day-to-day situations. Other test signs suggest obsessive-compulsive, suspicious, and paranoid ideation. The client is in the grip of strong feelings of inferiority. Ideas of influence were detected in the Rorschach revealing the presence of some near-pathological personality trends.

Minnesota Multiphasic Personality Inventory

Validity scales are moderately evaluated with K approaching 70. This may reflect extreme defensiveness and the repression of emotional problems. The general pattern is bimodal although there is some scattering. Scales reflect moderate peaks with four above 70. The client appears rigid and worrisome, possibly moralistic, and may have a poor family relationship. He may suffer from several physical complaints and these may function as a way of gaining attention and releasing anxiety. Social relationships are probably very poor and the client may feel very alone and unwanted. He appears to be a person struggling with emotional problems that could become more severe and incapacitating if left untreated.

Summary and Conclusions

We are dealing here with a borderline adjusted individual who is presently fending off paranoid ideation which he finds unacceptable and which could eventually lead to a full-blown schizophrenic process unless it is treated. The client is in an emotional panic, at war with himself, and leaning very heavily on incompatible ego-defenses to avoid further personality disintegration.

The Draw-A-Person-Test, among others, suggests that the client has never been able to resolve his conflict-ridden son-mother relationship. In childhood he was given acceptance largely on how well he performed and, therefore, was never able to achieve emotional independence. Because of his own unresolved conflicts, he is deeply threatened by his son's present relationship with his wife. Obviously it reactivates his own difficult son-mother relationship and causes him considerable anxiety and, essentially, sibling rivalry toward his son.

The client can be helped only if he is permitted to express all the bitterness he feels (but represses) regarding his childhood where performance was rated over acceptance. Since this client, in childhood and youth, was only intellectually accepted on the basis of his performance, he felt himself emotionally rejected as an individual. He learned to repress emotions recognizing that these could be dangerous. He has hidden from himself the traumatic parent-child relationships through which he suffered, calling these relationships "good." He converts his feelings of hostility for not being accepted into guilt. He regards his wife as a non-performer and uses the same harsh evaluation of her that his parents used of him. It is predicted that gaining insights will be painful for this client since he is too guilt-ridden by his underlying hostility to be able to accept them easily. Also, he is well defended with denials and an unrealistic self-image. Unless such insights are explored with the client and unless he learns to accept himself, the condition from which he suffers is inclined to worsen.

CASE THREE: MALE, AGE 6

Reason for Referral

This child has difficulty identifying with other children of his own age. He responds to adults as an adult and expects them to treat him as one. He has considerable problems in school and does not adjust well to new social situations within his classroom. He has difficulty taking orders and refuses to accept criticism from his teachers. The child is described as restless and attention-seeking, with feelings of inferiority. He frequently cries over minor annoyances. Psychological testing is requested in order to understand the underlying personality dynamics.

Summary of Social History

Jeff's mother has been married three times. He is the son of the first husband. Other husbands have adopted him. Each of the fathers has treated Jeff differently and there has been a constant shift of behavior. The wife's family has overcompensated for the deprivations the child has suffered and this in turn has added to the lack of stability the child experiences. The child now seems to be hypersensitive, tense, and disobedient.

Tests Administered

1. Wechsler Intelligence Scale for Children
2. Rorschach Test
3. Bender Motor Gestalt Test
4. Goldstein-Scheerer Color Form Sorting Test
5. Draw-A-Person-Test
6. Kahn Test of Symbol Arrangement

Test Evaluations

Wechsler Intelligence Scale for Children

The client's mental age was that of a child of seven years of age. Since Jeff is six years and five months old, testing suggests that he is somewhat above average as far as intelligence is concerned. This rules out the possibility that his school difficulties stem from a lack of understanding or intelligence.

Rorschach Test

In many respects the Rorschach responses are typical of those expected from a seven-year-old child. Some of the concepts elicited are precocious. Considerable hyperactivity was noted in the response pattern. The responses suggest that Jeff has a very active imagination and excellent powers of observation.

The test was abnormal only from the point of view that there was much more than the average amount of guilt projected. Other responses given by this child suggest that he is attempting to cope with feelings of inferiority and rejection.

Bender Motor Gestalt Test

On this test Jeff did poorly. Other children of his age are more successful in controlling their psychomotor activities. Jeff's test performance is consistent with behavior of children who have too much emotional drive and too little cortical control. Such children tend to be restless and over-active.

Goldstein-Scheerer Color Form Sorting Test

Jeff's ability to perform well on this test makes it unlikely that diffuse brain damage or extensive neurological disease is responsible for his hyperactive behavior.

Draw-A-Person-Test

On this test Jeff projected his feelings that people can be dangerous and threatening. Also there are indications on this test that he feels helpless and unable to grasp what is demanded of him by people in authority. The absence of hands and the prominence of feet are often signs associated with the desire to run away because one can't do anything about a situation. This drawing suggests that the boy suffers from intense dysphoria. The drawing of the female suggests that he considers women to be threatening and fear-provoking. Jeff drew the male figure without teeth, explaining that "the teeth fell out." In the female figure, the teeth are very much in evidence. In a discussion of this, Jeff denied ever seeing or knowing anyone with false teeth. The punitive aspect associated with "teeth" may be related to a discipline-enforcing father followed by an indulging one and then again one who attempts to reestablish discipline. Consequently, Jeff said that the "male figure is going to have new teeth." In effect, he is saying that males will again gain the power to give him a directional focus and impose discipline.

Kahn Test of Symbol Arrangement

Most noticeable on this test was the fact that Jeff kept moving the objects around in the sorting task. He could not make up his mind on how to relate to the concept MOTHER-WOMAN-GIRL. Finally, many of the objects were placed in the ESCAPE-RUN AWAY category. Jeff liked the object best that represented a gun. Several responses revealed this boy's striving for masculinity and power. Signs of guilt and frustration were also noted on this test. The symbol pattern of 80-XDZFEC is consistent with Jeff's age and suggests average intelligence. The absence of Y responses suggests a lack of ability to cope with the everyday realities of life.

Summary and Conclusions

One cannot expect to easily solve the problems that stem from this boy's behavior. Jeff's background has predisposed him to becoming a behavior problem in the classroom. It will be difficult to teach Jeff how to get along with other children and to be less of a problem in school. Involvement in games and especially in sports may be of considerable help in providing outlets for Jeff's restlessness.

Whereas Jeff may relate to adults better than to children, he is actually more immature than the average child of his age. The behavior that he has adopted represents a defense against his feelings of failure. An attempt should be made to enroll Jeff in some type of activity in which he could interact noncompetitively with other boys of his age.

The pressures placed on teachers today are such that it might be difficult for his teacher to give Jeff special attention but if she could give him some tasks or assignments that involve responsibility, it would tend to build up Jeff's self-confidence. Psychological testing suggests that there is nothing seriously wrong with Jeff and that his disruptive behavior is a reaction to past experiences that have given him feelings of guilt and inferiority. This reaction need not be lasting. There are elements of strength in this child's personality and the long range outlook for satisfactory adjustment may be favorable if Jeff can experience some stabilized home life in the near future.

CASE FOUR: FEMALE, AGE 50

Reason for Referral

The client is quite upset because of her sense of defeat due to her failure in influencing a foster child. Psychological testing is requested for further clarification of the relationship between herself and this foster child. It is also desired to find out the cause and depth of the sense of failure the client experiences due to her lack of ability to influence this child.

Summary of Social History

This 50-year-old female has had a history of almost unbelievable trauma. First her parents were divorced and she was raised by her stepfather and grandparents. Then she had polio, which affected the use of her legs. Nevertheless, she became valedictorian of her high school class and finished college. While in college she was elected popularity queen. She was married at the age of 19 and then her husband died on St. Valentine's Day, which is also the same day her stepfather died. She was pregnant after her husband's death and gave birth to a son who was extremely brilliant and had an excellent future. He was killed in an automobile crash. The client adopted a girl named Margery as a foster child but has not been successful in this effort. Lack of success is presently the cause of great concern to her.

Tests Administered

1. Incomplete Sentence Blank
2. Quick Test
3. Bender Motor Gestalt Test
4. Goldstein-Scheerer Color Form Sorting Test
5. Draw-A-Person-Test
6. Rorschach Test
7. Kahn Test of Symbol Arrangement
8. Minnesota Multiphasic Personality Inventory

Test Evaluations

Incomplete Sentence Blank

On the Incomplete Sentence Blank, the client indicated the great extent she has invested her emotions in the welfare of Margery and how much success means to her self-image in this respect. There were signs of self-rejection on the test. Also, the client indicated a sense of infallibility. This is seen as a reaction formation to many traumatic experiences she has suffered. She has, in a sense, immunized herself against future loss by adopting the self-concept of omnipotence. The client consistently described herself as emotionally stable.

Quick Test

On the Quick Test the client obtained an IQ of 118, which places her in the upper 12 percent of the general population as far as intelligence is concerned. This appears to be consistent with her success in college. Actually, however, a higher IQ would have been anticipated. Some of the success she has gained may have been derived from teachers' admiration of her courage in handling some of the difficulties that resulted from her polio.

Bender Motor Gestalt Test

The Bender was performed within normal limits although there were a number of distortions present. These were suggestive of psychological rather than neurological origins. The tendency to distort reality was noted. However, this was not the type of reality distortion associated with psychosis; rather, it was seen as a defense mechanism. It was believed that the client required a considerable share of such defenses in order to have handled the traumas and tragedies of her life.

Goldstein-Scheerer Color Form Sorting Test

On this test there was a failure to shift from shape to color. This is prevalent among persons who suffer some type of organic brain pathology. It may also appear on individuals who tend to perseverate because of extreme rigidity in their personality.

Draw-A-Person-Test

On the Figure Drawing Test both the female and male figure were drawn in a childish manner. Signs of emotional rigidity were projected and this is consistent with the findings on previous testing. Signs of emotional tensions were elicited.

Rorschach Test

On the Rorschach the response pattern suggests that client's father or father-substitute was visualized by her as a passive, weak man against whom she had considerable unconscious hostility. The client blocked completely on the so-called "reality card." Throughout her life she has found it necessary to immunize herself against the realities that were too difficult to bear, such as the loss of both son and husband and her own experience of having been crippled by polio in her early youth. The Rorschach suggested that there is a conflict present—the client's faith, devotion, conformity, and morality on the one hand, and impulses to reject social convention and to rebel against authority on the other hand. Fears of aging and deterioration were elicited by the test.

Kahn Test of Symbol Arrangement

On the KTSA there were signs that suggested that the client adopted rigidity of personality as a defense against inner conflicts. Signs of depression were also noted. There was a tendency on the part of the client to overestimate her ability to recall. The test shows that the client turned to religion as a means to gain stability and hope in view of her tragic life. On the Sorting task, the performance was typical of individuals who tend to withdraw and who have feelings of inability to work out problems effectively. This is in direct contradiction to the client's own statement on the Incomplete Sentence Blank that "she has never failed in what she attempted to do." In other words, we can see that underneath the self-assuredness there is a deep feeling of insecurity. This is further confirmed by the client's sorting the symbol she called "ambition" in the SMALL category. The male and female sexual symbols were both associated with DEAD. On the second sorting most of the objects were sorted into the SECURITY-COMFORT-PEACE category. Fear of aging and death were projected on this test. The symbol pattern of 119-YCXDEBZ reveals a lack of inner freedom and the presence of emotional rigidity.

Minnesota Multiphasic Personality Inventory

Validity scales are within normal range with the exception of K, which shows moderate elevation, indicating some defensiveness. The overall profile reflects general elevation, with five peaks above 70. The slope of the profile is downward from left to right with the exception of scale 0. The client appears to be somewhat depressed, worried, and pessimistic. She also shows some concern over bodily functions and health. The client may be somewhat passive-aggressive, possibly directed toward parents although overt behavior may not reflect this. She seems unsure of herself in social settings and in her ability to relate to people.

Summary and Conclusions

It appears from the psychological testing that the role of Margery's behavior represents a kind of self-test for the client. She feels that she must obtain the self-image of being able to do all things in spite of severe handicaps and obstacles. She used this self-concept to overcome the many disadvantages associated with her illnesses and past experiences. In order to be consistent with the concept that nothing can get her down, she must succeed in controlling Margery's behavior. The client is presently confined to a wheelchair and she is trying to live her life over again in Margery. This is unsatisfactory from the point of view of both of these persons. She fails to realize that Margery must live her own life and has had an environment that differs greatly from her own. Instead of placing all sense of self-worth and happiness in Margery's successful adaptation, the client should attempt to gain other types of satisfactions. Of course, this is extremely difficult in view of her present confinement to a wheelchair or a bed. It is maladaptive for her emotionally to have so much of herself invested in Margery. The more that the client feels that she is handicapped, the more she is determined to manipulate the environment around her. This she was able to do during her childhood years. She must learn that she is not now able to manipulate people as she was when she was a child. Instead she must make peace with the world as she finds it at present. This includes accepting as best she can the type of person that Margery is. She should realize that even if Margery is mixing with the wrong type of people there is little that can be done about it by her. Instead, Margery should be referred for counseling and guidance. In this way, the client could help her most. It would be desirable for the client to obtain outside interests in which she could contribute to some service organization and develop a sense of self-importance that does not rely solely on Margery's behavior.

CASE FIVE: FEMALE, AGE 49

Reason for Referral

The client is depressed and claims that she has hallucinations. She states that she is in poor physical condition. Request psychodynamics, ego strength, and rule out psychosis.

Summary of Social History

The client has had an extremely frustrating and disappointing life. After two unsuccessful marriages, she is living alone at this time. She has financial problems and has no close friends.

Tests Administered

1. Incomplete Sentence Blank
2. Wechsler Adult Intelligence Test
3. Draw-A-Person-Test
4. Goldstein-Scheerer Color Form Sorting Test

5. Bender Motor Gestalt Test
6. Rorschach Test
7. Kahn Test of Symbol Arrangement
8. Minnesota Multiphasic Personality Test

Test Evaluations

Incomplete Sentence Blank

Evasiveness was the chief characteristic elicited by this test. Pat sayings replaced meaningful statements. The client admitted that "sexual relations are annoying." The majority of the responses were flippant and superficial.

Wechsler Adult Intelligence Test

On this test the client obtained an IQ of 98, which places her in the average category of the general population as far as intelligence is concerned.

Draw-A-Person-Test

This test shows the results of the client's art training. It is significant that the male was drawn first, suggesting that the client has perhaps never entirely made peace in accepting her own sexual role. In contrast to the female, the male drawing was devoid of features and resembled a stick-figure. The implication is that males do not count in this client's life. This could stem from the frustrations and disappointments the client has had in her two marriages and also the trauma of the rape attack described in the client's history.

Goldstein-Scheerer Color Form Sorting Test

This test was performed within normal limits, suggesting an absence of diffuse organic brain pathology.

Bender Motor Gestalt Test

The test revealed a number of distortions and exhibited some bizarre features. However, these distortions were not typical of those expected in the presence of organic brain disease. Instead, the darkness and shading of the lines suggest intense hostility coupled with depression. A tendency toward grandiosity was also observed by some of the exaggerations associated with the reproductions.

Rorschach Test

The pattern elicited on the Rorschach test is typical of females who are or have been involved in a relationship with a threatening and seemingly brutal male. Commonly, such women are depressed and have developed both paranoid reactions toward their husbands (and possibly all males) and intense anxiety about sexual relations. Typically, the sexual difficulties are derived from apprehension about the husband's abuse and it is not uncommon for these women to insist that intercourse be discontinued.

Additional signs on this test support the presence of a paranoid element that permits the personality to take flights into an unreal fantasy world. Responses that are indicative of paralyzing anxiety were elicited.

Kahn Test of Symbol Arrangement

The slanting on this test was largely confined to the male and female symbols, suggesting that the basic traumatic relationships from which this client suffers may stem from difficulties between herself and male figures that had important roles in her life. Signs of depression were elicited but it was also seen that the client attempted to cover these up and to present a facade as if nothing really mattered. The phallic symbol reminded the client of her first marriage when she was 14 years of age. The sorting task revealed the presence of considerable conflict. Authority and male symbols, which had first been placed in LARGE, were later switched to HATE. The symbols designating ambitions and love were associated with SMALL. This is typical among persons who have a feeling of affective deprivation and believe that there is little hope of ever living a life where there will be genuine affection. In the second sorting, the self-image was associated with ESCAPE-RUN AWAY. The symbol pattern of 73-YXCDBAZ is compatible with the impression of a schizophrenic core in a neurotic condition.

Minnesota Multiphasic Personality Inventory

Validity scales are within the normal range with a slight elevation on the F scale suggesting a possible poor attitude toward test-taking. The profile reflects moderate elevation with a bimodal distribution. The right side of the profile shows the highest elevation. The client appears to be resentful and suspicious and sometimes these types of feelings may be accompanied by bizarre thought patterns. She may be hostile and dissatisfied with her family relations—blaming them for her problems. There may be a tendency to worry excessively and be concerned about physical health. Prognosis of her response to treatment is guarded.

Summary and Conclusions

The client suffers from feelings of bitterness and disillusionment. She attempts to handle these feelings by using a number of defenses. One of these is to be flippant and superficial in her affectual responses; the other is to use denial and ritualizations.

Some of her fantasy life represents a form of compensation for the many deprivations that she has suffered. Occasionally, her fantasy life becomes vivid to the point of a loosening of reality and it is then that transitory paranoid schizophrenic episodes may take place. Because of her ritualizations and her compensations, this disillusioned person will be difficult to treat. The testing clearly reveals that she still craves interaction with other people but is afraid to permit herself to be outgoing because of fear of getting hurt. The recommended form of therapy for this patient may be situational—that is, a change in environmental conditions in which she may become part of a larger group that will give her acceptance. Without this, it is likely that the client will tend to withdraw ever more deeply within a shell and develop additional and prominent schizoid behavioral characteristics.

Bibliography

1. Albee, G. W. A declaration of independence for psychology. In B. Lubin and E. E. Levitt (Eds.), *The clinical psychologist.* Chicago: Aldine, 1967.
2. Albee, G. W. Emerging concepts of mental illness and models of treatment: A psychological point of view. *American Journal of Psychiatry,* 1969, **125**, 870–876.
3. Allen, G. Hate therapy. *American Opinion,* 1968, **11**(1), 84.
4. Allison, J., Blatt, S. J., and Zimet, C. *The interpretations of psychological tests.* New York: Harper & Row, 1968.
5. American College Testing Program. *ACT.* Iowa City, Iowa: American College Testing Program, 1967.
6. American Medical Association. Report of Committee on Mental Health. *Journal of the American Medical Association,* 1954, **156**(1), 72.
7. American Psychiatric Association. *Diagnostic and statistical manual: Mental disorders* (DSM-I). Washington, D.C.: American Psychiatric Association, 1952.
8. American Psychiatric Association. *Diagnostic and statistical manual of mental disorders* (DSM-II). (2nd ed.) Washington, D.C.: American Psychiatric Association, 1968.
9. American Psychological Association, Committee on Relations with Psychiatry. 1958 Annual Report. *American Psychologist,* 1958, **13**, 761–763.
10. American Psychological Association, Education and Training Board. APA approved doctoral programs in clinical and in counseling psychology: 1969. *American Psychologist,* 1970, **25**, 1049–1050.
11. American Psychological Association. Ethical standards for psychologists. *American Psychologist,* 1963, **18**, 56–60.
12. American Psychological Association. *Standards for educational and psychological tests and manuals.* Washington, D.C.: American Psychological Association, 1966.
13. Ames, L. B., Learned, J., Metraux, R., and Walker, R. *Child Rorschach responses: Developmental trends from two to ten years.* New York: Hoeber, 1952.
14. Ammons, R. B., and Ammons, H. *The Full Range Picture Vocabulary Test.* Missoula, Mont.: Psychological Test Specialists, 1948.
15. Ammons, R. B., and Ammons, H. *Quick Test.* Missoula, Mont.: Psychological Test Specialists, 1962.

16. Ammons, R. B., Butler, M., and Herzig, S. A. *Vocational Apperception Test.* Louisville: Southern Universities Press, 1949.
17. Anastasi, A. *Psychological testing.* (3rd ed.) New York: Macmillan, 1968.
18. Anderson, D. E., and Morton, F. A comparison of the Peabody Picture Vocabulary Test with the Wechsler Intelligence Scale for Children. *Journal of Educational Research*, 1968, **62**, 114–116.
19. Anderson, L. A., and Clack, G. S. Interscorer reliability and the KTSA. *Canadian Psychologist*, 1966, **7**, 213–215.
20. Arthur, A. Z. Diagnostic testing and the new alternatives. *Psychological Bulletin*, 1969, 372–376.
21. Arthur, G. *Arthur Point Scale of Performance Tests, Form I.* Chicago: Stoelting, 1943.
22. Arthur, G. *Arthur Point Scale of Performance Tests, Form II.* New York: Psychological Corporation, 1947.
23. Ayllon, T., and Azrin, N. H. *A motivating environment for therapy and rehabilitation.* New York: Appleton-Century-Crofts, 1968.
24. Ayllon, T., and Azrin, N. H. *The token economy.* Des Moines, Iowa: Meredith, 1968.
25. Back, K. W. *Beyond words: The story of sensitivity training and the encounter movement.* New York: Russel Sage Foundation, 1972.
26. Baer, D. M. Some remedial uses of the reinforcement contingency. In J. M. Shlien (Ed.), *Research in psychotherapy*, Vol. 3. Washington, D.C.: American Psychological Association, 1968.
27. Bahn, A. K. An outline of community mental health research. *Community Mental Health Journal*, 1965, **1**, 23–28.
28. Balance, W. D. G., Hirschfield, P. P., and Bringmann, W. G. Mental illness: Myth, metaphor, or model. *Professional Psychology*, 1970, **1**, 133–138.
29. Bandura, A. *Principles of behavior modification.* New York: Holt, Rinehart and Winston, 1969.
30. Barclay, A., and Carolan, P. A comparative study of the Wechsler Intelligence Scale for Children and the Stanford-Binet Intelligence Scale, Form L-M. *Journal of Consulting Psychology*, 1966, **30**(6), 563.
31. Bard, M. Relevancy in clinical training. *Professional Psychology*, 1970, **1**, 263–264.
32. Barrett, J. H. *Gerontological psychology.* Springfield, Ill.: Charles C. Thomas, 1972.
33. Bayley, N. On the growth of intelligence. *American Psychologist*, 1955, **10**, 805–818.
34. Beck, S. J. The Rorschach Test as applied to a feeble-minded group. *Archives of Psychology*, 1932, **136**, 84.
35. Beers, C. W. *A mind that found itself.* New York: Longmans, Green, 1908.
36. Bell, J. E. *Projective techniques: A dynamic approach to the study of personality.* New York: Longmans, Green, 1948.
37. Bellak, L., and Bellak, S. *Children's Apperception Test.* (rev. ed.) New York: C.P.S. Co., 1949–50.
38. Bender, L. A visual motor gestalt test and its clinical use. *Research Monographs of the American Orthopsychiatric Association*, 1938, No. 3.
39. Bender, L. *Motor Gestalt Test.* Beverly Hills, Calif.: Western Psychological Services, 1938–1964.
40. Bennett, G. K., Seashore, H. G., and Wesman, A. G. *Differential Aptitude Tests.* New York: Psychological Corporation, 1965.
41. Bennett, G. K., Seashore, H. G., and Wesman, A. G. *Manual for the Differential Aptitude Tests.* (4th ed.) New York: Psychological Corporation, 1968.

42. Benton, A. L. *The Revised Visual Retention Test. Clinical and experimental applications.* Ames, Iowa: The State University of Iowa, 1955.
43. Berenda, C. W. Is clinical psychology a science? *American Psychologist*, 1957, **12**, 725–729.
44. Bergin, A. E. Some implications of psychotherapy research for therapeutic practice. *Journal of Abnormal Psychology*, 1966, **71**, 235–246.
45. Berne, E. *Transactional analysis in psychotherapy.* New York: Grove Press, 1961.
46. Berne, E. *Games people play.* New York: Grove Press, 1964.
47. Berne, E. *Principles of group treatment.* New York: Oxford University Press, 1966.
48. Berne, E. *A layman's guide to psychiatry and psychoanalysis.* New York: Simon & Schuster, 1968. London: Andre Deutsch, 1969.
49. Berne, E. *What do you say after you say hello?* New York: Grove Press, 1972.
50. Bindrim, P. A. Report on a nude marathon. *Psychotherapy: Theory, Research, and Practice*, 1968, **5**, 180–188.
51. Birnbaum, M. Sense (and nonsense) about sensitivity training. *Saturday Review*, 1969, **52**, 82–83, 96–98.
52. Bloom, B. L. The evaluation of primary prevention programs. In L. M. Roberts, N. S. Greenfield, and M. H. Miller (Eds.), *Comprehensive mental health.* Madison: University of Wisconsin Press, 1968.
53. Blum, G. S. *The Blacky Pictures: A technique for the exploration of personality dynamics.* New York: Psychological Corporation, 1950.
54. Bradford, L. P., Gibb, J. R., and Benne, K. D. (Eds.) *T group theory and laboratory methods: Innovation in re-evaluation.* New York: Wiley, 1964.
55. Bradway, K. P., Thompson, C. W., and Cravens, R. B. Preschool IQ's after twenty five years. *Journal of Educational Psychology*, 1958, **49**, 278–281.
56. Breger, L., and McGaugh, J. L. Critique and reformulation of "learning theory" approaches to psychotherapy and neurosis. *Psychological Bulletin*, 1965, **63**, 338–358.
57. Brittain, M. A comparative study of the use of the Wechsler Intelligence Scale for Children and the Stanford-Binet Intelligence Scale (Form L-M) with eight-year-old children. *British Journal of Educational Psychology*, 1968, **38**, 103–104.
58. Brown, D. G. Behavior analysis and modification in counseling and psychotherapy: A review of reviews. In H. C. Rickard (Ed.), *Behavioral intervention in human problems.* New York: Pergamon Press, 1971.
59. Brown, F. G. *Principles of educational and psychological testing.* Hinsdale, Ill.: Dryden, 1970.
60. Buck, J. N. *House-Tree-Person Projective Technique.* Witchita, Kan.: Western Psychological Services, 1964.
61. Buhler, C., and Kelly, G. *The World Test: A measurement of emotional disturbance.* New York: Psychological Corporation, 1941.
62. Burgemeister, B., Blum, L. H., and Lorge, I. *Columbia Mental Maturity Scale* (rev. ed.) New York: Psychological Corporation, 1959.
63. Buros, O. K. (Ed.) *The seventh mental measurements yearbook.* Highland Park, N.J.: Gryphon Press, 1972.
64. Cahoon, D. D. Symptom substitution and the behavior therapies: A reappraisal. *Psychological Bulletin*, 1968, **69**(3), 149–156.
65. California Test Bureau. *Guide to interpretation of the California Test of Mental Maturity Series.* (1963 rev.) Monterey, Calif.: The Bureau, 1964.
66. California Test Bureau. *Technical report on California Test of Mental Maturity Series.* (1963 rev.) Monterey, Calif.: The Bureau, 1965.

67. Campbell, D. P. *Strong Vocational Interest Blank Manual:1969 Supplement.* Stanford, Calif.: Stanford University Press, 1969.
68. Campbell, D. T., and Stanley, J. C. Experimental designs for research on teaching. In N. L. Gage (Ed.), *Handbook of research on teaching.* Chicago: Rand McNally, 1963.
69. Campbell, J. P., and Dunnette, M. D. Effectiveness of T-group experiences in managerial training and development. *Psychological Bulletin,* 1968, **70**, 73–104.
70. Campos, L. P. Other projective techniques. In A. I. Rabin (Ed.), *Projective techniques in personality assessment.* New York: Springer, 1968.
71. Caplan, G. *The theory and practice of mental health consultation.* New York: Basic Books, 1970.
72. Carse, W. T. Further validation of the Kahn Intelligence Tests. *Educational and Psychological Measurement,* 1967, **27**, 1055–1060.
73. Cashdan, S. *Abnormal psychology.* Englewood Cliffs, N.J.: Prentice-Hall, 1972.
74. Cassel, R. N., and Kahn, T. C. Group Personality Projective Test (GPPT). Missoula, Mont.: Psychological Test Specialists, 1958.
75. Cassel, R. N., and Kahn, T. C. Group Personality Projective Test Manual. *Psychological Reports,* Monograph Supplement L-V8, 1961, **8**, 23–41.
76. Cattell, R. B. Personality pinned down. *Psychology Today,* 1973, **7**(2), 40–46.
77. Cattell, R. B. *Sixteen Personality Factor Questionnaire.* Champaign, Ill.: Institute for Personality and Ability Testing, 1967–1968.
78. Cattell, R. B. *Sixteen Personality Factor Brochure.* Champaign, Ill.: Institute for Personality and Ability Testing, 1973.
79. Cattell, R. B. *The Culture Fair Intelligence Test.* Champaign: Ill.: Institute for Personality and Ability Testing, 1969.
80. Charles, D. C. Ability and accomplishment of persons earlier judged mentally deficient. *Genetic Psychology Monographs,* 1953, **47**, 3–71.
81. Clack, G. S., Guerin, A. J., and Latham, W. R. Scorer reliability of the KTSA. *Journal of Clinical Psychology,* 1966, **22**, 91–93.
82. Clawson, A. *The Bender Visual Motor Gestalt Test for children.* Wichita, Kan.: Western Psychological Services, 1970.
83. Cohen, H. T. Educational therapy: The design of learning environments. In J. M. Shlien (Ed.), *Research in psychotherapy.* Washington, D.C.: American Psychological Association, 1968.
84. College Entrance Examination Board. *Scholastic Aptitude Test* (SAT). Princeton, N.J.: College Entrance Examination Board, 1966.
85. Cooke, G. The efficacy of two desensitization procedures: An analogue study. *Behavior Research and Therapy,* 1966, **4**, 17–24.
86. Cooper, G. L. Coping with life stresses after sensitivity training. *Psychological Reports,* 1972, **3**(2), 602.
87. Cooperative Test Division. *Technical report: School and college ability tests.* Princeton, N.J.: Educational Testing Service, 1963.
88. Cowen, E. L., and Zax, M. The mental health field today: Issues and problems. In E. L. Cowen, E. A. Gardner, and M. Zax (Eds.), *Emergent approaches to mental health problems.* New York: Appleton-Century-Crofts, 1967.
89. Craddick, R. A., and L'Abate, L. *The Kahn Test of Symbol Arrangement (KTSA): A second critical review.* Atlanta, Ga.: The International Society for the Study of Symbols, 1972.
90. Craddick, R. A., and Stern, M. R. Note on the scorer reliability of the Kahn Test of Symbol Arrangement. *Journal of Clinical Psychology,* 1965, **21**, 197.

91. Crawford, J. *Crawford Small Parts Dexterity Test.* New York: Psychological Corporation, 1973.
92. Cronbach, L. J. *Essentials of psychological testing.* (3rd ed.) New York: Harper & Row, 1970.
93. Dahlstrom, W. G., and Welsh, G. S. *An MMPI handbook: A guide to use in clinical practice and research.* Minneapolis: University of Minnesota Press, 1960.
94. Datel, W. E., and Gengerelli, J. A. Reliability of Rorschach interpretations. *Journal of Projective Techniques*, 1955, **19**, 372–381.
95. Davis, L. J. The internal consistency of the WISC with the mentally retarded. *American Journal of Mental Deficiency*, 1966, **70**, 714–716.
96. Deich, R. F. Usefulness of the Kahn Intelligence tests in assessing the intelligence of retardates. *Perceptual and Motor Skills*, 1972, **34**, 161–162.
97. Delay, J., Deniker, P., and Heil, J. M. Utilisation en therapeutique d'une phenothiazine á action centrale elective. *Annales Medico Psychologiques*, June 1953, **110**, 112–117.
98. Doerken, H., and Kral, A. V. The psychological differentiation of organic brain lesions and their localization by means of the Rorschach Test. Paper read at the 107th Annual Meeting of the American Psychiatric Association, Cincinnati, 1951. *American Journal of Psychiatry*, 1952, 108.
99. Doley, M. F. The reinforcement menu: Finding effective reinforcers. In J. D. Krumboltz and C. E. Thoresen (Eds.), *Behavioral counseling: Cases and techniques.* New York: Holt, Rinehart and Winston, 1969.
100. Dollard, J., and Miller, N. E. *Personality and psychotherapy.* New York: McGraw-Hill, 1950.
101. Dreger, R. M. Objective tests and computer processing of personality test data. In I. A. Berg and L. A. Pennington (Eds.), *An introduction to clinical psychology.* (3rd ed.) New York: Ronald Press, 1966.
102. Dreikurs, R. Individual psychology: The Adlerian point of view. In J. M. Wepman and R. W. Jeine (Eds.), *Concepts of personality.* Chicago: Aldine, 1963.
103. DuBois, P. H. *History of psychological testing.* Boston: Allyn & Bacon, 1970.
104. Dunn, L. M. *Peabody Picture Vocabulary Test.* Circle Pines, Minn.: American Guidance Service, 1970.
105. Educational Testing Service. *Graduate Record Examinations* (GRE). Princeton, N.J.: Educational Testing Service, 1970.
106. Educational Testing Service. *School and College Ability Test* (SCAT). Princeton, N.J.: Educational Testing Service, 1970.
107. Edwards, A. L. *Edwards Personal Preference Schedule.* New York: Psychological Corporation, 1953.
108. Egan, G. *Encounter: Group processes for interpersonal growth.* Belmont, Calif.: Brooks-Cole, 1970.
109. Eisenson, J. *Examining for aphasia and related disturbances.* (rev. ed.) New York: Psychological Corporation, 1954.
110. Ellis, A. Rational psychotherapy. *Journal of General Psychology*, 1958, **59**, 35–49.
111. Ellis, A. *Reason and emotion in psychotherapy.* New York: Lyle Stuart, 1962.
112. Ellis, A. A weekend of rational encounter. *Rational Living*, 1970, **4**(2), 1–8.
113. Ellis, A. The no cop-out therapy. *Psychology Today*, 1973, **7**(2), 56–62.
114. Eysenck, H. J. The effects of psychotherapy: An evaluation. *Journal of Consulting Psychology*, 1952, **16**, 319–324.
115. Eysenck, H. J. Review of C. R. Rogers and R. F. Dymond. "Psychotherapy and personality change." *British Journal of Psychology*, 1955, **46**, 237–238.

116. Eysenck, H. J. Learning theory and behavior therapy. *Journal of Mental Science*, 1959, **195**, 61–75.
117. Eysenck, H. J. (Ed.) *Behavior therapy and the neuroses.* New York: Pergamon Press, 1960.
118. Eysenck, H. J. The effects of psychotherapy. *International Journal of Psychiatry*, 1965, **1**, 99–178.
119. Fagan, J., and Shepherd, I. L. (Eds.) *Gestalt therapy now.* Palo Alto, Calif.: Science and Behavior Books, 1970.
120. Fiedler, F. E. Comparison of therapeutic relationships in psychoanalytic, nondirective and Adlerian therapy. *Journal of Consulting Psychology*, 1951, **14**, 436, 445.
121. Fils, D. H. Comparative performance of schizophrenics and normals on a new projective test of object-symbol arrangement. Paper read at the Western Psychological Association, San Jose, April 1951. *American Psychologist*, 1951, **6**, 501. (Abstract)
122. Fink, H. H., and Kahn, T. C. A comparison of normal and emotionally ill children on the Kahn Test of Symbol Arrangement. *Journal of Educational Research*, 1959, **53**, 35–56.
123. Fiske, D. W., Luborsky, L., Parloff, M. B., Hunt, H. F., Orne, M. T., Reiser, M. F., and Tuma, A. H. Planning of research on effectiveness of psychotherapy. *American Psychologist*, 1970, **25**, 727–737.
124. Fowler, R. D. Automated interpretation of personality test data. In J. N. Butcher (Ed.), *MMPI: Research developments and clinical applications.* New York: McGraw-Hill, 1969.
125. Frank, G. H. Psychiatric diagnosis: A review of research. *Journal of General Psychology*, 1969, **81**, 157–176.
126. Frankl, V. E. *Man's search for meaning.* Translated by I. Lasch. New York: Washington Square Press, 1963.
127. Franks, C. M. (Ed.) *Behavior therapy: Appraisal and status.* New York: McGraw-Hill, 1969.
128. Freud, S. *New Introductory lectures on psychoanalysis.* New York: Norton, 1933.
129. Freud, S. *An outline of psychoanalysis.* Vol. 23. London: Hogarth Press, 1935.
130. Freud, S. *The problem of anxiety.* New York: Norton, 1936.
131. Freud, S. *A general introduction to psychoanalysis.* New York: Washington Square Press, 1960.
132. Fromm-Reichmann, F. *Principles of intensive psychotherapy.* Chicago: Phoenix Books, University of Chicago Press, 1950.
133. Garfield, S. L. Clinical psychology and the search for identity. *American Psychologist*, 1966, **21**, 353–362.
134. Garvey, W., and Hegrenes, S. R. Desensitization techniques in the treatment of school phobia. *American Journal of Orthopsychiatry*, 1966, **36**, 147–152.
135. Gazda, G. M. (Ed.) *Basic approaches to group psychotherapy and group counseling.* Springfield, Ill.: Charles C. Thomas, 1968.
136. Gazda, G. M. (Ed.) *Innovations to group psychotherapy.* Springfield, Ill.: Charles C. Thomas, 1968.
137. Gibb, J. R. The effects of human relations training. In A. E. Bergin and S. L. Garfield (Eds.), *Handbook of psychotherapy and behavior change.* New York: Wiley, 1970.
138. Ginzberg, E., and Herma, J. L. *Talent and performance.* New York: Columbia University Press, 1964.

139. Ginzberg, E., Ginzberg, S. W., Axelrod, S., and Herma, J. L. *Occupational choice: An approach to a general theory.* (3rd ed.) New York: Columbia University Press, 1963.
140. Ginzberg, E. *et al. The middle class Negro in a white man's world.* New York: Columbia University Press, 1967.
141. Glasser, A. J., and Zimmerman, I. L. *Clinical interpretation of the Wechsler Intelligence Scale for Children.* New York: Grune and Stratton, 1967.
142. Glasser, W. *Reality therapy: A new approach to psychiatry.* New York: Harper & Row, 1965.
143. Goldberg, C. *Encounter: Group sensitivity training experience.* New York: Science House, 1970.
144. Goldenberg, H. *Contemporary clinical psychology.* Monterey, Calif.: Brooks/Cole, 1973.
145. Goldenson, R. M. *The encyclopedia of human behavior: Psychology, psychiatry, and mental health.* Vol. 2. Garden City, N.Y.: Doubleday, 1970.
146. Goldstein, K. *Human nature in the light of psychopathology.* Boston: Harvard University Press, 1940.
147. Goldstein, K., and Scheerer, M. Abstract and concrete behavior and experimental study with special tests. *Psychological Monograph*, 1941, **43**, 1–151.
148. Golembiewski, R., and Blumberg, A. (Eds.) *Sensitivity training and the laboratory approach.* Itasca, Ill.: F. E. Peacock, 1970.
149. Goodenough, F. L. *Mental testing: Its history, principles, and applications.* New York: Rinehart, 1949.
150. Goodenough, F. L., and Harris, D. B. *Goodenough-Harris Drawing Test.* New York: Harcourt Brace Jovanovich, 1963.
151. Gough, H. G. *California Psychological Inventory.* Palo Alto, Calif.: Consulting Psychologist Press, 1956.
152. Gough, H. G. Some reflections on the meaning of psychodiagnosis. *American Psychologist*, 1971, **26**, 160–167.
153. Grassi, J. R. *The Grassi Block Substitution Test for Measuring Brain Pathology.* Springfield, Ill.: Charles C. Thomas, 1953.
154. Gross, M. L. *The brain watchers.* New York: Random House, 1962.
155. Grosser, C., Henry, W. E., and Kelly, J. G. *Nonprofessionals in the human services.* San Francisco: Jossey-Bass, 1969.
156. Guedre, C. A., and Reed, C. F. *An Introduction to the Minnesota Multiphasic Personality Inventory—a handbook.* Downey, Ill.: Veterans Administration Hospital, 1954.
157. Guertin, W. H. *et al.* Research with the Wechsler Intelligence Scales for adults: 1960–1965. *Psychological Bulletin*, 1966, **66**, 385–409.
158. Guilford, J. P. *The nature of human intelligence.* New York: McGraw-Hill, 1967.
159. Guirdham, A. The Rorschach Test in epileptics. *Journal of Mental Science*, 1935.
160. Gutbrodt, E. J., Lyman, R. C., and Jerry, M. B. Suicide attempts and suicide in psychiatric patients, a risk assessment with psychological techniques. Proc. 78th Ann. Conven., APA, 1970, **5**, 559–560.
161. Hall, C., and Lindzey, G. *Theories of personality.* New York: Wiley, 1957.
162. Hall, M. H. Carl Rogers speaks out on groups and the lack of a human science. *Psychology Today*, 1967, 19–21, 62–66.
163. Hammer, E. F. Projective drawings. In A. I. Rabin (Ed.), *Projective techniques in personality assessment.* New York: Springer, 1968.

164. Hammer, M., and Kaplan, A. M. Theoretical considerations in the practice of psychotherapy with children. In M. Hammer and A. M. Kaplan (Eds.), *The practice of psychotherapy with children.* Homewood, Ill.: Dorsey Press, 1967.
165. Harper, R. A. *Psychoanalysis and psychotherapy: 36 systems.* Englewood Cliffs, N.J.: Prentice-Hall, 1959.
166. Harris, A. J. *Harris Tests of Lateral Dominance.* New York: Psychological Corporation, 1947.
167. Harris, T. *I'm O.K., You're O.K.: A practical guide to transactional analysis.* New York: Harper & Row, 1967.
168. Harrison, R. Thematic apperceptive methods. In B. B. Wolman (Ed.), *Handbook of clinical psychology.* New York: McGraw-Hill, 1965.
169. Harrower-Erickson, M. R. Personality changes accompanying cerebral lesions: Rorschach studies of patients with cerebral tumors. *Archives of Neurological Psychiatry,* 1940, **43**, 1081–1107.
170. Hartwell, S., Walton, R. E., Andrew, G., and Hutt, M. *The Michigan Picture Test.* Chicago: Science Research Associates, 1955.
171. Hathaway, S. R. MMPI: Professional use by professional people. *American Psychologist,* 1964, **19**, 204–210.
172. Hathaway, S. R., and McKinley, J. C. *Minnesota Multiphasic Personality Inventory.* (rev. ed.) New York: Psychological Corporation, 1951.
173. Hathaway, S. R., and McKinley, J. C. *Minnesota Multiphasic Personality Inventory.* New York: Psychological Corporation, 1967.
174. Hathaway, S. R., and Meehl, P. E. *An atlas for the clinical use of the MMPI.* Minneapolis: University of Minnesota Press, 1951.
175. Heine, R. W. *Psychotherapy.* Englewood Cliffs, N.J.: Prentice-Hall, 1971.
176. Henry, W. E. *The analysis of fantasy.* New York: Wiley, 1956.
177. Hernstein, R. *IQ The Atlantic,* Sept. 1969, **228**(3), 63–64.
178. Hersche, C. The discontent explosion in mental health. *American Psychologist,* 1968, **23**, 497–506.
179. Hersche, C. From mental health to social action: Clinical psychology in historical perspective. *American Psychologist,* 1969, **24**, 909–915.
180. Hewett, P., and Massey, J. O. *Clinical clues from the WISC with special sections on testing black and Spanish-speaking children.* Palo Alto, Calif.: Consulting Psychologists Press, 1969.
181. Hill, L. K., Latham, W. R., and Theiner, E. C. Diagnostic agreement of variously trained psychologists using the KTSA. *Journal of Clinical Psychology,* 1963, **19**, 74–77.
182. Himelstein, P. Research with the Stanford-Binet, Form L-M. *Psychological Bulletin,* 1966, **65**, 156–164.
183. Hoch, E. L. *Experimental contributions to clinical psychology.* Belmont, Calif.: Brooks/Cole, 1971.
184. Hoch, E. L., Ross, A. O., and Winder, C. L. (Eds.) *Professional preparation of the clinical psychologists.* Washington, D.C.: American Psychological Association, 1966.
185. Holt, R. R. Diagnostic status and future prospects. *Journal of Nervous and Mental Disease,* 1967, **144**, 444–465.
186. Holt, R. R. The evaluation of personality assessment. In I. L. Janis, G. F. Mahl, J. Kagan, and R. R. Holt (Eds.), *Personality: Dynamics, development and assessment.* New York: Harcourt Brace Jovanovich, 1969.
187. Homme, L. *How to use contingency contracting in the classroom.* Champaign, Ill.: Research Press, 1969.

188. Hoppock, R. *Occupation information.* New York: McGraw-Hill, 1963.
189. Howard, J. *Please touch: A guided tour of the human potential movement.* New York: McGraw-Hill, 1970.
190. Hunt, H. F. *The Hunt-Minnesota Test for Organic Brain Damage.* Minneapolis: University of Minnesota Press, 1943.
191. Jacobson, E. *Progressive relaxation.* Chicago: University of Chicago Press, 1938.
192. Jensen, A. How much can we boost IQ and scholastic achievement? *Harvard Educational Review*, 1969, **39**, 1–123.
193. Jones, C. D. *Hominology—Psychiatry's Newest Frontier.* Springfield, Ill.: Charles C. Thomas, 1974.
194. Jones, M. C. A laboratory study of fear: The case of Peter. *Journal of Genetic Psychology*, 1924, **31**, 308–315.
195. Jung, C. G. *Collected works.* New York: Pantheon, 1953.
196. Kahn, T. C. Cross-validation of the organic brain pathology scale for a test of symbol arrangement. *Journal of Consulting Psychology*, 1955, **19**, 130.
197. Kahn, T. C. *Kahn Test of Symbol Arrangement.* Missoula, Mont.: Psychological Test Specialists, 1957.
198. Kahn, T. C. Kahn Test of Symbol Arrangement, Clinical Manual. *Perceptual and Motor Skills*, Monograph Supplement No. 1. Missoula, Mont.: Psychological Test Specialists, 1957.
199. Kahn, T. C. *Kahn Intelligence Test.* Missoula, Mont.: Psychological Test Specialists, 1960.
200. Kahn, T. C. Signs of creativity on the Kahn Test of Symbol Arrangement. *Perceptual Motor Skills*, 1968, **26**, 1065–1066.
201. Kahn, T. C. *An introduction to hominology: The study of the whole man.* (2nd ed.) Springfield, Ill.: Charles C. Thomas, 1972.
202. Kahn, T. C. Hominology—a new therapeutic dimension. *Journal of Contemporary Psychotherapy*, 1972, **4**(2), 67–73.
203. Kahn, T. C. *Kahn Aphasia Test, Experimental.* Unpublished.
204. Kahn, T. C., and Fink, H. H. Comparison of normal with emotionally disturbed children by the Kahn Test of Symbol Arrangement. Paper read at the American Psychological Association, New York, 1957.
205. Kahn, T. C., and Giffen, M. B. *Psychological techniques in diagnosis and evaluation.* Oxford: Pergamon Press, 1960.
206. Kalis, B. L. Crisis theory: Its relevance for community psychology and directions for development. In D. Adelson and B. L. Kalis (Eds.), *Community psychology and mental health.* Scranton, Pa.: Chandler, 1970.
207. Kanfer, F. H., and Phillips, J. S. *Learning foundations of behavior therapy.* New York: Wiley, 1970.
208. Kanfer, F. H., and Saslow, B. Behavioral diagnosis. In C. M. Franks (Ed.), *Behavior therapy: Appraisal and status.* New York: McGraw-Hill, 1969.
209. Kaplan, S. R. Therapy groups and training groups: Similarities and differences. *The International Journal of Group Psychotherapy*, 1967, **17**, 473–504.
210. Kelly, A. Role construct repertory test and basic theory. In B. A. Maher (Ed.), *Progress in experimental personality research.* New York: Academic Press, 1965.
211. Kelly, G. A. *The psychology of personal constructs.* New York: Norton, 1955, 2 vols.
212. Kemp, C. G. *Foundations of group counseling.* New York: McGraw-Hill, 1970.
213. Kipper, D. A. Diagnosis of psychotic patients with the Kahn Test of Symbol Arrangement. *British Journal of Social and Clinical Psychology*, 1967, **6**, 70–71.

214. Kipper, D. A. Identifying habitual criminals by means of the Kahn Test of Symbol Arrangement. *Journal of Consulting and Clinical Psychology*, 1971, **37**, 151–154.
215. Klein, M. H., Dittmann, A. T., Parloff, M. B., and Gill, M. M. Behavioral therapy: Observations and reflections. *Journal of Consulting and Clinical Psychology*, 1969, **33**, 259–266.
216. Kleinmuntz, B. *Personality measurement: An introduction.* Homewood, Ill.: Dorsey, 1967.
217. Klopfer, B. Rorschach signs of nonpsychotic organics-idiopathic epileptics. Adapted from lectures by Bruno Klopfer, University of California, 1949.
218. Klopfer, B., and Kelley, D. M. *The Rorschach technique.* New York: World Book, 1946.
219. Koppitz, E. M. *The Bender Gestalt Test for young children.* New York: Grune & Stratton, 1971.
220. Kreigman, L. S., and Kreigman, G. The Pate Report: A new psychodynamic and therapeutic evaluative procedure using the KTSA. *Psychiatric Quarterly*, 1965, **39**, 646–674.
221. Kroske, W. H., Fretwell, L. N., and Cupp, M. E. Comparison of the Kahn Intelligence Tests: The Stanford-Binet and the WAIS for familial retardates. *Perceptual and Motor Skills*, 1965, **21**, 428.
222. Krumboltz, J. D., and Thoresen, C. E. (Eds.) *Behavioral counseling: Cases and techniques.* New York: Holt, Rinehart and Winston, 1969.
223. Kuder, G. F. *Kuder Occupational Interest Survey.* Chicago: Science Research Associates, 1966.
224. Kuder, G. F. *Kuder Occupational Interest Survey General Manual.* Chicago: Science Research Associates, 1966.
225. Kuder, G. F. *Kuder Preference Record: Vocational—Forms C, and E Administrators Manual.* Chicago: Science Research Associates, 1960.
226. Kuder, G. F. *Kuder Interest Inventories.* Chicago: Science Research Associates, 1971.
227. Lakin, M. Some ethical issues in sensitivity training. *American Psychologist*, 1969, **24**, 923–928.
228. Lakin, M. *Interpersonal encounter: Theory and practice in sensitivity training.* New York: McGraw-Hill, 1972.
229. Lazarus, A. A. The results of behavior therapy in one hundred and twenty-six cases of severe neurosis. *Behavior Research Therapy*, 1963, **1**, 69–79.
230. Lazarus, A. A. Classical and operant factors in the treatment of school phobia. *Journal of Abnormal Psychology*, 1965, **70**, 225.
231. Leiter, R. G. *Leiter International Performance Scale.* (rev. manual) Washington, D.C.: Psychological Service Center Press, 1948.
232. Leiter, R. G., and Arthur, G. *The Leiter International Performance Scale.* Chicago: Stoelting, 1972.
233. Littell, W. M. The Wechsler Intelligence Scale for Children: Review of a decade of research. *Psychological Bulletin*, 1960, **57**, 132–156.
234. Little, K. B., and Schneidman, E. S. The validity of thematic projective technique interpretations. *Journal of Personality*, 1955, **23**, 285–294.
235. Lomranz, J., Lakin, M., and Schiffman, H. Variants of sensitivity training and encounter: Diversity of fragmentation. *Journal of Applied Behavioral Science*, 1972, **8** (4), 399–420.
236. London, P. *The modes and morals of psychotherapy.* New York: Holt, Rinehart and Winston, 1964.

237. Lorge, I., Thorndike, R. L., and Hagen, E. *Lorge-Thorndike Intelligence Tests.* (Multi-Level ed.) Boston: Houghton Mifflin, 1966.
238. Lovaas, O. I. Some studies on the treatment of childhood schizophrenia. In J. M. Shlein (Ed.), *Research in psychotherapy.* Washington, D.C.: American Psychological Association, 1968.
239. Lovell, V. R. The human use of personality tests: A dissenting view. *American Psychologist*, 1967, **22**, 383–393.
240. Lowenfeld, M. *The Lowenfeld Mosaic Test.* London: Newman, Neame, 1954.
241. Lowenfeld, M. The nature and use of the Lowenfeld World Technique in work with children and adults. *Journal of Psychology*, 1955, **30**, 325–331.
242. Lubin, B., Wallis, R. R., and Paine, C. Patterns of psychological test usage in the United States: 1935–1969. *Professional Psychology*, 1971, **2**, 70–74.
243. Lundin, R. W. *Personality: A behavioral analysis.* London: Macmillan—Collier-Macmillan, 1969.
244. Machover, K. *Personality projection in the drawing of the human figure.* Springfield, Ill.: Charles C. Thomas, 1949.
245. Maliver, B. *The encounter game.* New York: Stein & Day, 1973.
246. Mann, E. T. The symbolic process of recidivist and non-recidivist children as assessed by the Kahn Test of Symbol Arrangement. *Journal of Projective Techniques and Personality Assessment*, 1967, **31**, 40–46.
247. Mann, E. T. Use of the KTSA as a technique for assessing intelligence and psychodynamics in drug addicts. *International Journal of Symbology*, 1969, **1**(2), 57–66.
248. Mariner, A. S. A critical look at professional education in the mental health field. *American Psychologist*, 1967, **22**, 271–281.
249. Marmor, J. (Ed.) *Modern psychoanalysis.* New York: Basic Books, 1968.
250. Martin, D. G. *Introduction to psychotherapy.* Belmont, Calif.: Brooks/Cole, 1971.
251. Maslow, A. H. *Toward a psychology of being.* Princeton, N.J.: Van Nostrand, 1962.
252. Maslow, A. H. Self-actualization and beyond. In J. F. T. Bugental (Ed.), *Challenges of humanistic psychology.* New York: McGraw-Hill, 1967.
253. Matarazzo, J. D. *Wechsler's measurement and appraisal of adult intelligence.* (5th ed.) Baltimore: Williams & Wilkins, 1972.
254. May, R. (Ed.) *Existential psychology.* (2nd ed.) New York: Random House, 1969.
255. McFate, M., and Orr, F. Through adolescence with the Rorschach. *Rorschach Research Exchange and Journal of Projective Techniques*, 1949, **13**, No. 3.
256. McLeod, H. N. The use of the Kahn Test of Symbol Arrangement as an aid to diagnosis with psychiatric patients. *Ontario Hospital Psychological Bulletin*, 1961, **7**, 10–20.
257. Meehl, P. E. *Clinical versus statistical prediction.* Minneapolis: University of Minnesota Press, 1954.
258. Megargee, Edwin I. (Ed.) *Research in clinical assessment.* New York: Harper & Row, 1966.
259. Meir, N. C. *Meir Art Judgment Test.* Iowa City, Iowa: Bureau of Educational Research and Service, University of Iowa, 1942.
260. Menninger, K. *Theory of psychoanalytic technique.* New York: Harper & Row, 1958.
261. Menninger, K. *The vital balance: The life process in mental health and illness.* New York: Viking Press, 1963.
262. Mikulas, E. L. *Behavior modification: An overview.* New York: Harper & Row, 1972.
263. Miles, W. R. *A-B-C Vision Test for Ocular Dominance.* New York: Psychological Corporation, 1946.

264. Miller, W. S. *Miller Analogies Test.* New York: Psychological Corporation, 1970.
265. Mogel, S., and Satz, P. Abbreviation of the WAIS for clinical use: An attempt at validation. *Journal of Clinical Psychology*, 1966, **19**, 298–300.
266. Moreno, J. L. *Psychodrama.* New York: Beacon House, 1946.
267. Moreno, J. L. (Ed.) *The international handbook of group psychotherapy.* New York: Philosophical Library, 1966.
268. Moreno, J. L., and Moreno, Z. *Psychodrama.* New York: Beacon House, 1959.
269. Murphy, M. Esalen: Where it's at. *Psychology Today*, December 1967, 34–41.
270. Murphy, P. D., Bolinger, R. W., and Ferriman, M. R. Screening neuropsychiatric patients by means of the Kahn Test of Symbol Arrangement. *Behavioral Science*, 1958, **3**(4), 344–346.
271. Murphy, P. D., Ferriman, M. R., and Bolinger, R. W. The Kahn Test of Symbol Arrangement as an aid to psychodiagnosis. *Journal of Consulting Psychology*, 1957, **21**(6), 503–505.
272. Murray, H. A. *Thematic Apperception Test.* New York: Psychological Corporation, 1973.
273. Murray, H. A. *et al. Thematic Apperception Test Manual.* Cambridge: Harvard University Press, 1943.
274. Nakanishi, N., and Lee, H. H. A psycho-cultural study of KTSA symbolization among Chinese students. *Bulletin on Literature in Sociology of Osaka University*, 1966, **2**, 119–150.
275. O'Banion, T., and O'Connell, A. *The shared journey: An introduction to encounter.* Englewood Cliffs, N.J.: Prentice-Hall, 1970.
276. Ohlsen, M. *Group counseling.* New York: Holt, Rinehart and Winston, 1970.
277. Onimaru, M., and Matsumoto, K. On a new type personality test—the KTSA. *Mental Health*, 1969, **18**, 13–17.
278. Onimaru, M., and Saito, H. A study on the standardization of the objective scores in the KTSA. *Japanese Journal of Clinical Psychology*, 1970, **9**, 61–72.
279. Otis, A. S., and Lennon, R. T. *Otis–Lennon Mental Ability Test.* New York: Harcourt Brace Jovanovich, 1969.
280. Patterson, C. H. *Theories of counseling and psychotherapy.* (2nd ed.) New York: Harper & Row, 1973.
281. Paul, G. L. *Insight vs. desensitization in psychotherapy: An experiment in anxiety reduction.* Stanford, Calif.: Stanford University Press, 1966.
282. Paul, G. L. Insight versus desensitization in psychotherapy two years after termination. *Journal of Consulting Psychology*, 1967, **31**, 333–348.
283. Paul, G. L., and Shannon, D. T. Treatment of anxiety through systematic desensitization in therapy groups. *Journal of Abnormal Psychology*, 1966, **71**, 124–135.
284. Pavlov, I. P. *Conditioned reflexes.* London: Oxford University Press, 1927.
285. Peacher, W. G. Review of the Harris Tests of Lateral Dominance. In O. K. Buros (Ed.), *The fourth mental measurements yearbook.* Highland Park, N.J.: Gryphon Press, 1953.
286. Pearson, J. S., and Swenson, W. M. *A users guide to the Mayo Clinic Automated MMPI program.* New York: Psychological Corporation, 1967.
287. Peck, H. (Ed.) Encounter and T-groups: The current use of the group for personal growth and development. *International Journal of Group Psychotherapy*, July 1970.
288. Perls, F. S. *Gestalt therapy verbatim.* Lafayette, Calif.: Real People Press, 1969.
289. Perls, F. S. Four lectures. In J. Fagan and I. L. Shepherd (Eds.), *Gestalt therapy now.* Palo Alto, Calif.: Science and Behavior Books, 1970.

290. Perls, F., Hefferline, R., and Goodman, P. *Gestalt therapy*. New York: Dell, 1965.
291. Peterson, D. R. *The clinical study of social behavior*. New York: Appleton-Century-Crofts, 1968.
292. Phillips, L., and Smith, J. G. *Rorschach interpretation: Advanced technique*. New York: Grune & Stratton, 1953.
293. Pinneau, S. R. Pinneau revised IQ tables. In L. M. Terman and M. A. Merrill (Eds.), *Stanford-Binet Intelligence Scale Manual*. (rev. ed.) Boston: Houghton Mifflin, 1960.
294. Piotrowski, Z. On the Rorschach Method and its application in organic disturbances of the central nervous system. *Rorschach Research Exchange*, 1936–1937, **1**, 23–40.
295. Potthorst, K. E. To renew vitality and provide a challenge in training: The California School of Professional Psychology. *Professional Psychology*, 1970, **1**, 123–130.
296. Purdue Research Foundation. *Purdue Pegboard*. Chicago: Science Research Associates, 1971.
297. Quereshi, M. Y. The internal consistence of the WISC scores for ages 5 to 16. *Journal of Clinical Psychology*, 1968, **24**, 79–85.
298. Raimy, V. C. (Ed.) *Training in clinical psychology*. New York: Prentice-Hall, 1950.
299. Rakstis, T. Sensitivity training: Fad, fraud, or new frontier? *Today's Health*, January 1970, 20–25, 86–87.
300. Rank, O. *Will therapy and truth and reality*. New York: Knopf, 1945.
301. Rapaport, D., Gill, M., and Schafer, R. *Diagnostic Psychological Testing*. Vol. I. Chicago: The Yearbook Publishers, 1946.
302. Rapaport, D., Gill, M., and Schafer, R. *Diagnostic Psychological Testing*. Vol. II. Chicago: The Yearbook Publishers, 1947.
303. Raven, J. C. *Progressive Matrices*. New York: Psychological Corporation, 1962.
304. Reilly, S. Dr. Glasser: Without failure. *Human Behavior*, 1973, 17–23.
305. Robb, G. P., Bernardoni, L. C., and Johnson, R. W. *Assessment of individual mental ability*. Scranton: Intext Educational Publishers, 1972.
306. Rogers, C. R. *Counseling and psychotherapy*. Boston: Houghton Mifflin, 1942.
307. Rogers, C. R. *Client-centered therapy*. Boston: Houghton Mifflin, 1951.
308. Rogers, C. R. The necessary and sufficient conditions of therapeutic personality change. *Journal of Consulting Psychology*, 1957, **21**, 95–103.
309. Rogers, C. R. A theory of therapy, personality and interpersonal relationships, as developed in the client-centered framework. In S. Koch (Ed.), *Psychology: A study of a science*, Vol. 3. New York: McGraw-Hill, 1959.
310. Rogers, C. R. *On becoming a person*. Boston: Houghton Mifflin, 1961.
311. Rogers, C. R. The process of the basic encounter group. In J. F. T. Bugental (Ed.), *Challenges of humanistic psychology*. New York: McGraw-Hill, 1967.
312. Rogers, C. R. The group comes of age. *Psychology Today*, December 1969, 27–31, 58–61.
313. Rogers, C. R. *On encounter groups*. New York: Harper & Row, 1970.
314. Rogers, C. R., and Dymond, R. *Psychotherapy and personality change*. Chicago: University of Chicago Press, 1954.
315. Rogers, C. R., Gendlin, E. T., Kiesler, D. J., and Traux, C. B. *The therapeutic relationship and its impact: A study of psychotherapy with schizophrenics*. Madison: The University of Wisconsin Press, 1967.
316. Rorschach, H. *Psychodiagnostics, a diagnostic test based on perception*. New York: Grune & Stratton, 1942.
317. Rorschach, H. *Rorschach Technique*. New York: Psychological Corporation, 1966.

318. Ross, R., and Moreledge, J. Comparison of the WISC and WAIS at chronological age 16. *Journal of Consulting Psychology*, 1967, **31**, 331–332.
319. Rotter, J. B. *Clinical psychology*. (2nd ed.) Englewood Cliffs, N.J.: Prentice-Hall, 1971.
320. Salzinger, K. On the operant conditioning of complex behavior. In J. M. Shlein (Ed.), *Research in psychotherapy*. Washington, D.C.: American Psychological Association, 1968.
321. Sattler, E. Analysis of Functions of the 1960 Stanford-Binet Intelligence Scale, Form L-M. *Journal of Clinical Psychology*, 1965, **21**, 173–179.
322. Schutz, W. C. *Joy: Expanding human awareness*. New York: Grove Press, 1967.
323. Seashore, C. E. *et al. Seashore measures of Musical Talents*. (rev. ed.) New York: Psychological Corporation, 1960.
324. Shaw, D. J. Estimating WAIS from progressive matrices scores. *Journal of Clinical Psychology*, 1967, **23**, 184–185.
325. Shearn, C. R., and Warren, S. L. Performance of hospitalized male alcoholics on the Kahn Test of Symbol Arrangement. *Perceptual Motor Skills*, 1967, **25**, 705–710.
326. Shemberg, K., and Keeley, S. Psychodiagnostic training in the academic setting: Past and present. *Journal of Consulting and Clinical Psychology*, 1970, **84**, 205–211.
327. Sherman, A. R. *Behavior modification: Theory and practice*. Monterey, Calif.: Brooks/Cole, 1973.
328. Shertzer, B., and Stone, S. C. *Fundamentals of counseling*. Boston: Houghton Mifflin, 1968.
329. Shipley, W. C. A self-administering scale for measuring intellectual impairment and deterioration. *Journal of Psychology*, 1940, **9**, 371–377.
330. Shneidman, E. S. *The Make-A-Picture Story Test*. New York: Psychological Corporation, 1949.
331. Shneidman, E. S. *Manual for The Make-A-Picture Story Test*. New York: Psychological Corporation, 1952.
332. Shneidman, E. S. Manual for the Make-A-Picture Story Test. *Projective Techniques Monograph, No. 2*. New York: The Society for Projective Techniques and Rorschach Institute, 1952.
333. Shoben, E. J., Jr. Psychotherapy as a problem in learning theory. *Psychological Bulletin*, 1949, **46**, 366–392.
334. Shostrom, E. L. Group therapy: Let the buyer beware. *Psychology Today*, May 1969.
335. Siegel, M. Use and misuse of group technology in education, industry, and counseling practice. *Group Process*, 1970–1971, **3**(2), 5–6.
336. Silvers, D., and Wirls, C. J. A determination of the symbolic meanings of the Kahn Test of Symbol Arrangement objects. *Journal of Projective Technique and Personality Assessment*, 1970, **34**, 401–408.
337. Silverstein, A. B. A further evaluation of the Stanford-Binet. *American Journal of Mental Deficiency*, 1966, **70**, 928–929.
338. Silverstein, A. B. Validity of WISC short forms at three age levels. *Journal of Consulting Psychology*, 1967, **31**, 635–636.
339. Skinner, B. F. *Walden two*. New York: Macmillan, 1948.
340. Skinner, B. F. *Science and human behavior*. New York: Macmillan, 1953.
341. Sohl, J. *The lemon eaters*. New York: Simon & Schuster, 1967.
342. Stefflre, B., and Grant, W. H. *Theories of counseling*. (2nd ed.) New York: McGraw-Hill, 1972.
343. Sternbach, R. A., Abroms, G. M., and Rice, D. G. Clinical responsibility and the psychologist. *Psychiatry*, 1969, **32**, 165–173.

344. Stoller, F. H. The long weekend. *Psychology Today*, December 1967, 28–33.
345. Stoller, F. H. Marathon group therapy. In G. M. Gazda (Ed.), *Innovations to group psychotherapy*. Springfield, Ill.: Charles C. Thomas, 1968.
346. Strong, E. K. *Strong Vocational Interest Blank*. Stanford, Calif.: Stanford University Press, 1966.
347. Strupp, H. H. Psychotherapeutic technique, professional affiliation, and experience level. *Journal of Consulting Psychology*, 1955, **19**, 97–102.
348. Strupp, H. H. A multidimensional comparison of therapist activity in analytic and client-centered therapy. *Journal of Consulting Psychology*, 1957, **21**, 301–308.
349. Strupp, H. H. Nature of psychotherapist's contribution to treatment process. *Archive of General Psychiatry*, 1960, **3**, 219–231.
350. Strupp, H. H. *Psychotherapists in action*. New York: Grune & Stratton, 1960.
351. Strupp, H. H. The outcome problem in psychotherapy revisited. *Psychotherapy*, 1963, I, 1–13.
352. Strupp, H. H. Psychoanalytic therapy of the individual. In J. Marmor (Ed.), *Modern psychoanalysis*. New York: Basic Books, 1968.
353. Strupp, H. H. *Psychotherapy and the modification of abnormal behavior*. New York: McGraw-Hill, 1971.
354. Sullivan, E. T., Clark, W. W., and Tiegs, E. W. *California Test of Mental Maturity*. Monterey, Calif.: California Test Bureau, 1963.
355. Sullivan, H. S. *Conceptions of modern psychiatry*. Washington, D.C.: William Alanson White Psychiatric Foundation, 1947.
356. Sullivan, H. S. *The interpersonal theory of psychiatry*. New York: Norton, 1953.
357. Sundberg, N. D. The practice of psychological testing in clinical services in the United States. *American Psychologist*, 1961, **16**, 79–83.
358. Super, D. E., Crites, J. O., Hummel, R. C., Moser, H. P., Overstreet, P., and Warnath, C. F. *Vocational development: A framework for research*. New York: Bureau of Publications, Teachers College, Columbia University, 1957.
359. Swanson, D. W., Brown, E. M., and Beuret, L. J. A family with five schizophrenic children. *Diseases of the Nervous System*, 1969, **30**(3), 189–193.
360. Symonds, P. M. *Adolescent fantasy: An investigation of the picture story method of personality study*. New York: Columbia University Press, 1949.
361. Szasz, T. C. Behavior therapy and psychoanalysis. *Medical Opinion and Review*, 1967, **3**(6), 24–29.
362. Terman, L. M. *The measurement of intelligence*. Boston: Houghton Mifflin, 1916.
363. Terman, L. M., and Merrill, M. A. (Eds.) *Measuring intelligence*. Boston: Houghton Mifflin, 1937.
364. Terman, L. M., and Merrill, M. A. (Eds.) *Stanford-Binet Intelligence Scale*. Boston: Houghton Mifflin, 1960.
365. Theiner, E. C., and Giffen, M. B. A comparison of abstract thought process among three cultures. *Comprehensive Psychiatry*, 1964, **5**, 54–63.
366. Theiner, E. C., Hill, L. K., Latham, W. R., and McCarty, W. D. Validation study of the Kahn Test of Symbol Arrangement. *Journal of Clinical Psychology*, 1962, **18**, 454–457.
367. Thorndike, R. L. Review of the California Psychological Inventory. In O. K. Buros (Ed.), *The fifth mental measurements yearbook*. Highland Park, N.J.: Gryphon Press, 1969.
368. Thorne, F. C. Critique of recent developments in personality counseling theory. *Journal of Clinical Psychology*, 1957, **13**, 234–244.

369. Tinker, M. A. Review of the A-B-C Vision Test for Ocular Dominance. In O. K. Buros (Ed.), *The fourth mental measurements yearbook.* Highland Park, N.J.: Gryphon Press, 1953.

370. Traux, C. B., and Carkhuff, R. R. *Toward effective counseling and psychotherapy: Training and practice.* Chicago: Aldine, 1967.

371. Turner, R. K., Mathews, A., and Rachman, S. The stability of the WISC in a psychiatric group. *British Journal of Educational Psychology,* 1967, **37**, 194–200.

372. Ullmann, L. P., and Krasner, L. *A psychological approach to abnormal behavior.* Englewood Cliffs, N.J.: Prentice-Hall, 1969.

373. United States Department of Labor. *Dictionary of occupational titles.* (3rd ed.) Washington, D.C.: United States Government Printing Office, 1965.

374. United States Employment Service. *General Aptitude Test Battery.* Washington, D.C.: United States Employment Service, 1970.

375. Van Hoose, W. H., and Pietrofesa, J. J. (Eds.), *Counseling and guidance in the twentieth century.* Boston: Houghton Mifflin, 1970.

376. Van Kaam, A. Counseling and psychotherapy from the viewpoint of existential psychology. In D. S. Arbuckle (Ed.), *Counseling and psychotherapy: An overview.* New York: McGraw-Hill, 1967.

377. Volsky, T., Magoon, T. M., Norman, W. T., and Hoyt, D. P. *The outcome of counseling and psychotherapy: Theory and research.* Minneapolis: University of Minnesota Press, 1965.

378. Wagner, R. F. Levels of symbolization in adolescent adjustment patterns. *International Journal of Symbology,* 1969, **1**(1), 67–74.

379. Wagner, R. F. Form symbolization in normal readers and based on a modified pattern recognition theory. *International Journal of Symbology,* 1970, **1**(3), 51–56.

380. Wagner, R. F. Symbolization deficits in dyslexic conditions. *Academic Therapy,* 1971, **6**, 359–365.

381. Wallen, R. Gestalt therapy and Gestalt psychology. In J. Fagan and I. L. Shepherd (Eds.), *Gestalt therapy now.* Palo Alto, Calif.: Science and Behavior Books, 1970.

382. Ward, C. H., Beck, A. T., Mendelson, M., Mock, J. E., and Erbaugh, J. K. The psychiatric nomenclature, reasons for diagnostic disagreement. *Archives of General Psychiatry,* 1962, **7**, 198–205.

383. Wechsler, D. *The measurement of adult intelligence.* (3rd ed.) Baltimore: Williams & Wilkins, 1944.

384. Wechsler, D. Intelligence: Definition, theory and the IQ. In R. Cancro (Ed.), *Intelligence: Genetic and Environmental Influences.* New York: Grune and Stratton, 1971.

385. Wechsler, D. *Wechsler Intelligence Scale for Children.* New York: Psychological Corporation, 1949.

386. Wechsler, D. *Wechsler Adult Intelligence Scale.* New York: Psychological Corporation, 1955.

387. Wechsler, D. *The measurement and appraisal of adult intelligence.* (4th ed.) Baltimore: Williams & Wilkins, 1958.

388. Wechsler, D. *Wechsler Preschool and Primary Scale of Intelligence.* New York: Psychological Corporation, 1967.

389. Wells, F. L., and Ruesch, J. *Mental Examiners' Handbook.* (rev. ed.) New York: Psychological Corporation, 1945.

390. Wertheimer, M. Studies in the theory of Gestalt psychology. *Psychologische Forschung,* 1923, **4**, 300.

391. White, P. O., and McLeod, H. M. A multiple discriminant analysis comparing psychotic, neurotic, and character disorder patients on the Kahn Test of Symbol Arrangement. *Ontario Psychological Association Quarterly*, 1963, **26**(3), 2–5.
392. White, R. W. *The abnormal personality.* New York: Ronald Press, 1964.
393. Williamson, E. G. *How to counsel students: A manual of techniques for clinical counselors.* New York: McGraw-Hill, 1939.
394. Williamson, E. G. Discipline and counseling. *Education*, 1954, **74**, 512–518.
395. Williamson, E. G. The fusion of discipline and counseling in the educational process. *Personnel and Guidance Journal*, 1955, **34**, 74–79.
396. Williamson, E. G. Value orientation in counseling. *Personnel and Guidance Journal*, 1958, **37**, 520–528.
397. Williamson, E. G. Some issues underlying counseling theory and practice. In W. E. Dugan (Ed.), *Counseling points of view.* Minneapolis: University of Minnesota Press, 1959.
398. Williamson, E. G. The counselor as technique. *Personnel and Guidance Journal*, 1962, **41**, 108–111.
399. Williamson, E. G. The societal responsibilities of counselors. *Illinois Guidance and Personnel Association Newsletter*, 1963, Winter, 5–13.
400. Williamson, E. G. Vocational counseling: Trait-factor theory. In B. Stefflre (Ed.), *Theories of counseling.* New York: McGraw-Hill, 1965.
401. Williamson, E. G. Value options and the counseling relationship. *Personnel and Guidance Journal*, 1966, **44**, 617–623.
402. Williamson, E. G. Value commitments and counseling. *Teachers College Record*, 1967, **62**, 602–608.
403. Wolpe, J. *Psychotherapy by reciprocal inhibition.* Stanford, Calif.: Stanford University Press, 1958.
404. Wolpe, J. Behavior therapy in complex neurotic states. In J. M. Shlein (Ed.), *Research in psychotherapy.* Washington, D.C.: American Psychological Association, 1968.
405. Wolpe, J. *The practice of behavior therapy.* New York: Pergamon Press, 1969.
406. Wolpe, J., and Lazarus, A. A. *Behavior therapy techniques.* Oxford: Pergamon Press, 1966.
407. Yates, A. J. The validity of some psychological tests of brain damage. *Psychological Bulletin*, 1954, **51**, 359–379.
408. Yates, A. J. *Frustration and conflict.* New York: Wiley, 1962.
409. Yudin, Lee. An abbreviated form of the WISC for use with emotionally disturbed children. *Journal of Consulting Psychology*, 1966, **30**, 272–275.
410. Yule, W. *et al.* The WPPSI: An empirical evaluation with a British sample. *British Journal of Educational Psychology*, 1969, **39**, 1–13.
411. Zigler, E., and Phillips, L. Psychiatric diagnosis: A critique. *Journal of Abnormal and Social Psychology*, 1961, **63**, 607–618.
412. Zytowski, D. G. Relationships of equivalent scales on three interest inventories. *Personnel and Guidance Journal*, 1968, **47**, 44–49.

APPENDIX A

New Trends

In this appendix we present three articles that have implications for psychology's future. The first article deals with the exciting new direction that psychology is taking in consort with other sciences in which electronic properties of the human brain are probed and utilized by means of feedback mechanisms in order to make possible an entirely new kind of therapy. Another article describes the development of the Community Mental Health movement which, increasingly, is enlisting the services of clinical psychologists in various new ways. The third article, on hominology, represents one of several recent efforts by psychologists to develop techniques of assessment and therapy that involve the whole person concept and that represent an integration of various behavioral sciences to create a global approach to the problem of understanding human behavior.

THE USES OF BIO-FEEDBACK TRAINING IN CLINICAL PSYCHOLOGY

*Curt Stensrude, M.A.**

Throughout the history of man there has been a continuing search for means of achieving a peaceful state of mind that would permit calm reflection on the course and meaning of man's existence. As our society

*Staff psychologist—Southern Colorado Comprehensive Mental Health Center, Pueblo, Colorado. Formerly staff member of The Center for Behavior Therapy, Beverly Hills, California.

has become more complex and confusing, this has become increasingly difficult to achieve. Man has turned to various chemical means to reach this state of altered consciousness—for example, tranquilizers, alcohol, and various drugs, all of which have definite drawbacks. In addition, a number of meditative techniques, some very ancient, some quite new, are now being used. However, these techniques have a common shortcoming in that they do not provide an *immediate feedback* as to the progress the person is making.

Over the past several years, researchers have discovered that most people can exert far more control over their internal, mental, and physical processes than was once believed. A means has been developed whereby an individual can discover how he can best make progress toward the goal of a calm, peaceful state of mind and become more effective in his day-to-day activities. The practical application of these techniques is just beginning to be explored. With assistance from an electronic technique called "bio-feedback," many people can quickly learn to control processes once thought to be entirely involuntary, such as blood pressure, brainwaves, heart rate, skin temperature, and the constriction of blood vessels.

A "bio-feedback" device is simply an electronic gadget that reports physiological information back to the client. Until scientists developed bio-feedback, the dynamics of the relationships between a mental-emotional state and physiological functioning of the body had been considered inaccessible to scientific research. Today, by using electronic bio-feedback equipment, important scientific studies can be made that, heretofore, have been the private domain of philosophers and mystics. For centuries, Eastern religions have given instruction in the voluntary control of physiological processes that are involuntary according to Western scientific models. Yoga practitioners have given credible reports of individuals who have learned to control such basic processes as heart rate, respiration, and body temperature through meditation exercise.

In 1905 Johann Schultz began to study different techniques of hypnosis, which he combined with conscious self-regulation aspects of yoga. By 1910, he had developed a therapeutic system that he eventually named "autogenic" training. In the autogenic system, clients learn to relax their muscles and to regulate blood flow and heart rate by using verbal phrases such as "warm" and "relax." After 50 years, in spite of a large measure of success, autogenic training remains almost unknown in the United States. The autogenic system has not been formally accepted by American psychologists because it normally takes a great deal of time to master.

With the advent of bio-feedback, people have been able to control almost every part of the body for which appropriate feedback can be obtained. The partial list of these functions includes brainwaves, heart rate, blood pressure, muscle tension, body temperature, blood flow, galvanic skin response, insulin production, urine production, and stomach acidity (Barber *et al.*, 1971). Voluntary control of these functions has been obtained without bio-feedback through yoga, hypnosis, and autogenic training. However, bio-feedback offers an opportunity to gain such control easily, quickly, and more independently than by these other methods. Without bio-feedback devices, people have no way of knowing which training is effective. Most humans are not good at sensing their own degree of relaxation or body awareness.

PRACTICAL APPLICATIONS OF BIO-FEEDBACK TRAINING

Bio-feedback has been called the "happiness machine" and the solution to many of man's mental or physical ailments. It has even been used as a substitute for dangerous drugs. With these types of claims, it is not surprising that bio-feedback is one of the more controversial subjects in the behavioral sciences today. Some researchers even think that bio-feedback devices will eventually become as popular as home appliances. In reality, the potential of bio-feedback is just beginning to be known. Probably the most successful treatment techniques to date is in the control of *migraine headaches.*

At the Menninger Foundation in Topeka, Kansas, Sargent (1971) taped temperature sensors to the forehead and finger of migraine sufferers to train them to *abort* headaches by directing blood from their head to their hands. Most physicians now agree that the pain of migraine results from increased pressure within the blood vessels of the scalp. This vasodilation, or expansion of the vessels, is presumably caused by an increased flow of blood in the head. Until the recent discovery at Menninger, the only way to get the blood vessels in the scalp back to normal size was through the use of powerful drugs.

Unfortunately, the most effective of these drugs, called Sansert (methysergite), can have dangerous side effects. It is a chemical cousin of LSD, although it does not cause hallucinations. In addition, Sansert can only be taken consecutively for a three-month period, followed by a 30-day period of rest. This means that for at least 90 days of each year migraine sufferers have no way of preventing the headaches.

The subjects who participated in the Menninger research were told that their hands would feel warm and heavy, and they should try to make the needle of the temperature gauge move to the right—thus indicating that the hand was warming. One of the 12 clients who was improved by the training learned to increase the temperature in her hands by ten degrees Fahrenheit in a few minutes. Sargent believes that the increased blood flow to the hands probably alters its flow into the head, thus reducing or eliminating the vasodilation that causes the pain. Since the beginning of its work with migraine clients, the Menninger clinic has treated approximately 60 persons and nearly 80 percent have reported relief (Green *et al.*, 1969).

There is evidence that other forms of bio-feedback can also have direct benefits. This is particularly demonstrated in treating *tension headaches.* Without really knowing that their muscles are tensed, people may unconsciously be creating their own ailments. Psychologists Johann Stoyva and Thomas Budzinski, at the University of Colorado Medical School, taught clients with tension headaches to relax their forehead muscles. Using their method, clients lie down in a comfortable position with a small surface electrode taped to their forehead. They then listen to a tone on a pair of headphones. As the muscle contraction of the forehead increases (increased muscle tension), the pitch of the tone is raised. Clients are instructed to try to lower the tone. Within 20 minutes, the tone drops and they have halved the original muscle tension. A number of individuals who have suffered from severe tension headaches for many years reported that they were cured after daily practice. Clients can usually achieve the same muscle relaxation later without the bio-feedback device by recalling internal "cues" that they used to keep muscle activity low when the bio-feedback device was in operation. (Budzinski *et al.*, 1970).

Temperature feedback can also be used with dramatic results in *Raynaud's disease,* in which the vessels of the hand become severely constricted. In fact, in some cases the constriction may be so severe that gangrene of the hand can result. The treatment strategy follows the same method as for migraines. Once hand-warming techniques are mastered, the therapist periodically wires the client to the temperature meter to check that his ability to increase blood flow into his hand remains constant.

In experimental studies, scientists have found that clients (after ingesting tiny "stomach acid meters" attached to a wire) could control the level of acid in their stomachs. For ulcer and colitis victims, as well as the vast number of people who consume antacid tablets every day bio-feedback may offer some relief. Varying degrees of success using bio-feedback training have been achieved by teaching breathing relaxation to *asthmatic children*, as well as clients with severe *facial tics*.

It is interesting to note that there is a considerable amount of sleep research being done, but there is very little on *insomnia*. Insomnia is probably the most common of all sleep disorders. Jacobson reported success ranging from 80 to 85 percent in overcoming insomnia. (Jacobson, 1938). Support of bio-feedback possibilities are justified from the fact that the two most common symptoms resulting from insomnia are (1) an inability to relax and (2) an inability to "switch off" disturbing thoughts.

The president of the bio-feedback research society, Dr. Thomas B. Mulholland, is testing Alpha brainwave rhythms at a Veteran's Administration hospital in Massachusetts. Since the Alpha brainwave rhythm disappears when the eyes are in focus, Mulholland finds that it can be useful to evaluate visual attention with *brain-damaged individuals* or *children with perceptual problems*. The research indicates that these children benefited from two half-hour Alpha bio-feedback sessions per week for four weeks. Of the children in the group, one stopped stuttering, one insomniac was able to sleep, and one extremely hyperactive child slowed down to normal activity. No change was reported in the eight subjects of the control group. In several laboratories, bio-feedback monitoring is also being used in training *epileptic clients* to suppress abnormal brainwave spikes.

CHRONIC ANXIETY TREATED BY BIO-FEEDBACK MUSCLE RELAXATION TRAINING

An estimated five percent of the United States population is afflicted by *chronic anxiety*, which is a persistent state of apprehension accompanied by signs of physiological arousal. This painful and disabling state may persist for years. Tranquilizers constitute the most popular treatment for chronic anxiety; however, even the safest and most effective anti-anxiety agents expose clients to some risk of undesirable side effects.

In hopes of developing an effective therapy, many researchers have explored the use of feedback for induced muscle relaxation in states of chronic anxiety (Raskin *et al.*, 1973). The effects of daily muscle relaxation achieved through electromyographic feedback (EMG) training, have shown striking results. These have occurred when a client has learned to use relaxation techniques when stress occurs.

Bio-feedback training may have important applications in a number of areas. An example of this would be in the field of *psychoanalysis* or analytic therapy, where unconscious material could more easily be brought to a conscious state by having the client utilize deep muscle relaxation. Additionally, people susceptible to *hypnosis* have high Alpha durations and this would make bio-feedback training a valuable tool to the practitioner (London *et al.*, 1968).

Other areas in which bio-feedback monitoring might be used are in disorders of self-regulation. For example, people suffering from *obesity*, *alcoholism*, and *drug problems*, to a great degree, are suffering from high anxiety levels. These disorders are prime examples of the fact that as man becomes liberated from his environmental restraints the self-regulation problem increases. Therefore, self-control training in relaxation may alleviate anxiety and environmental stress.

Bio-feedback training in helping clients overcome tics and other neuromuscular disorders (stuttering, stammering) is just beginning to be utilized. Peper (1970) reports a case of a client with severe facial tics who tried EMG bio-feedback after an extensive period of psychoanalysis had failed to alleviate his symptoms. The training procedure utilized a portable EMG machine, which allowed the client to detect tension in his forehead muscle through clicks. The client's goal was to reduce the number of clicks, thereby relaxing the forehead muscle and reducing the number of tics. Another application of bio-feedback training to neuromuscular disorders is reported by Booker *et al.* (1969). It involved helping a young woman to *rehabilitate facial muscles* damaged in an automobile accident. The client had lost voluntary control of the muscles on the left side of her face and was unable to close or move her left eye. This was particularly upsetting to her because the muscular problems had destroyed her facial appearance, giving her a distorted look. By using an EMG bio-feedback approach, where the woman first learned to regulate one muscle and then several at a time, the client was able to regain total control of her facial muscles.

In the management of *phobias*, a good part of the anxiety involves the fear of fear itself. For example, if one knows he is going to be hurt, he will feel the pain more each time he is exposed to the stimulus. The phobia can be controlled and regulated utilizing bio-feedback procedures (EMG, GSR) and the behavior therapy technique called systematic desensitization. Systematic desensitization is a procedure in which the client is asked to visualize in his "mind's eye" a frightening situation or scene from a graded list of fears, ranging from least anxious to most anxious. The therapist then only has to watch the meter of the bio-feedback instrument to detect at what level the client is experiencing stress or anxiety. Therefore, he gets a much more objective measure of the actual level of a client's discomfort.

In the area of *sexual dysfunctions*, bio-feedback training could be helpful. It is well-recognized that many sexual problems are caused initially by mistraining by the parents and later are complicated by muscular and emotional anxiety. The procedure would, therefore, be as follows: train the individual in muscular relaxation and then teach him by visualization procedures how to cope with sexually frightening scenes.

The ability to voluntarily control any of the functions of the cardiovascular system would be considered a breakthrough in medicine. Interest in the possible application of bio-feedback in the control of *hypertension* (high blood pressure of unknown origin) is being conducted in a number of clinics throughout the country. At the time of this writing, only two published studies have appeared reporting heart-rate bio-feedback research.

In one of these studies, Engle investigated the ability of eight clients with heart problems to learn to eliminate irregularities of their heart beat through mental control. The clients, while lying comfortably in bed, were attached to a heart pacer that converted each heart beat into an electrical signal. These signals, in turn, were fed into an analyzer, which translated them into different colored lights on a panel. Watching this light panel, thc client was instructed to regulate his heart by slowing his heart beat when the red light flashed and increasing it when the green light appeared. The safe limits of heart beats were signaled by a steady yellow light. Using bio-feedback light signals, the client first learned to speed his heart beat, slow it, and then to maintain its rhythm within safe limits. Engle and Chism noted that after extensive training on the machines, the client was able to regulate his heart beat at home without any outside bio-feedback devices (Engle and Chism, 1967).

It has been suggested that bio-feedback training may have an important application in *cancerous tumors.* It may be possible that cancerous tumors can be controlled by restricting the blood flow to cancer cells (Smart, 1970).

THOUGHTS TO CONSIDER

There are a number of precautions that should be taken into account when using the bio-feedback approach. The clinician should *carefully evaluate* exactly how he administers feedback to his client in order that he can precisely determine and control what the client will and will not learn. In some of the more complex problems (e.g., anxiety) it is important to determine what function or pattern of responses occurs in each state of learning for a particular individual since persons differ in their biological responses.

Another factor that must be considered in bio-feedback training is the amount of time that can reasonably be invested by the therapist. Depending upon the particular function, dysfunction, and the client involved, training in bio-feedback may take many sessions. Schwartz (1972) states that motivating a client to devote sufficient time in the practice of feedback training is sometimes difficult. For this reason, it is essential to develop home bio-feedback devices that can be coupled with a weekly consultation with the therapist.

SUMMARY AND CONCLUSION

Bio-feedback training is clearly an important discovery that may prove to be of significant value to medical and psychological treatment. Every new disease, every mental state, every so-called involuntary behavior has the possibility of being brought under conscious control. The author would like to point out that even if direct voluntary control of bodily functions should prove to have little therapeutic value, bio-feedback as feedback per se could serve an important function. It signals to both therapist and client how the client is currently feeling and thinking. With the aid of this feedback method, the client may be able to alter his life style in such a way as to keep his internal state within control. Bio-feedback may be similar to other psychotherapies since they all attempt to provide corrective feedback.

BIBLIOGRAPHY

Barber, T. X. *et al. Bio-feedback and self control.* Chicago: Aldine-Atherton, 1971.

Booker, H., Rubow, R., and Coleman, P. Simplified feedback in neuromuscular retraining. *Archives of Physical Medicine and Rehabilitation*, 1969, **50**, 625.

Budzinski, T., Stoyva, J., and Adler, C. Feedback—induced muscle relaxation: Application to tension headache. *Journal of Behavior Therapy Experimental Psychiatry*, 1970, **1**, 205–211.

Engle, B., and Chism, R. Operant conditioning of heart rate speeding. *Psychophysiology*, 1967, **3**, 418–426.

Green, E., Walters, E., Green, A., and Murphy, G. Feedback techniques for deep relaxation. *Psychophysiology*, 1969, **6**, 371–377.

Jacobson, E. *Progressive relaxation.* (2nd ed.) Chicago: University of Chicago Press, 1938.
London, P., Hart, J., and Leibovitz. EEG. Alpha rhythms and susceptibility to hypnosis. *Nature,* 1968, **210**, 71–72.
Luthe, W., and Schutz, F. *Autogenic training.* New York: Grune & Stratton, 1965.
Peper, E. Reduction of efferent motor comments during alpha feedback as a precondition for changes in consciousness. *Kybernetik,* 1970, **7**, 107–112.
Raskin, M., Johnson, G., and Rondestvedt, W. Chronic anxiety treated by feedback-induced muscle relaxation. *Archives of General Psychiatry,* 1973, **28**, 263–267.
Sargent, J. D., Green, E. E., and Walters, E. D. Preliminary report on the use of autogenic feedback techniques in the treatment of migraine and tension headaches. Unpublished research report. Topeka, Kan.: Menninger Foundation, 1971.
Schwartz, F. Clinical applications of bio-feedback: Some theoretical issues. *In Behavior modification with the individual patient.* N.J.: Roche Laboratories, 1972.
Smart, Allan. Conscious control of physical and mental states. *Menninger Perspective,* April–May 1970.
Whatmore, G. B., and Kohl, D. R. Dysponesis: A neurophysiological factor in functional disorders. *Behavioral Science,* 1968, **13**, 102–124.

COMMUNITY MENTAL HEALTH—IN PERSPECTIVE

Paul Pantleo, Ph.D., and *Donald D. Megenity, Ed.D.**

The philosophical beginnings of the community mental health approach parallel changes in the attitude toward treatment of the mentally ill. Prior to the late 18th century, the mentally ill were either jailed or the responsibility for treatment at a local level was ignored (Zilboorg and Henry, 1941). In 1789 there was a cry within society for reform with more humane treatment of the mentally ill (Dain, 1965). Dain's work examined the various forces operating to produce these treatment reforms. As the moral treatment movement came into existence, a struggle for the responsibility of the care for the mentally ill developed. Lack of training, pressure to find somatic causes of insanity, emergence of state-supported institutions (brought on by Dorothea Dix and Clifford Beers' actions), and antagonism toward the indigent mentally ill aided in replacing the moral treatment philosophy of

*Dr. Paul Pantleo is Director of the Department of Mental Health, Southern Colorado State College, Pueblo, Colorado. Dr. Megenity is Head of the Psychology Department, Southern Colorado State College, Pueblo, Colorado.

organic pathology and incurability. As will be noted in the following pages, a revival of the basic notion of moral treatment can be seen in today's therapeutic efforts.

Recently, another revolutionary change in the treatment of the mentally ill has developed in relation to the concept of the mental hospital. The early conception of the hospital as a place to *keep* mentally disturbed patients created monolithic structures characterized by overcrowding and custodial care. Freedman (1967) details the manner in which these structures were developed because of economic and pragmatic considerations. The responsibility for care of the mentally ill fell upon the state, and large state mental hospitals were founded and placed away from large population centers. This removed the patient from his familiar environment and whatever treatment resources may have been available to him in his home community. The many problems that developed from this action and basic change in philosophy resulted in a swing away from the custodial mental hospital to smaller and more active treatment centers utilizing a therapeutic milieu approach (Bobbitt, 1963; Silverman, 1974).

National studies of mental health treatment resources were undertaken (Joint Commission on Mental Illness and Health) and more funds were made available at all levels (federal, state, local) to provide additional services for the mentally ill. As various pressures created a need for a community treatment approach, the community mental health center legislation came into being, again placing most of the responsibility at the community level (Freedman, 1967).

Bloom (1966), Felix (1966), and Yolles (1966) discuss various important issues and events that give one a greater perspective of the community mental health movement; whereas Foley and Sanders (1966), Bolman (1967), and Blackman and Goldstein (1968), concerned themselves with the theoretical basis of the development of the community mental health approach. Arising out of the belief that geographical dislocation results in non-therapeutic severance of family and community ties, supported by ego psychology, crisis theory, and past public health experience, the community mental health approach appears to be on a sound foundation.

The Community Mental Health Centers Act (Public Law 88–164, Public Law 89–105, and associated regulations) makes available appropriations for the construction of public and other non-profit community mental health centers and provides grants to cover a portion of the cost of hiring professional and technical staff at such centers. A center must offer at least five "essential" services to qualify for federal funds under the Community Mental Health Centers Act: (1) *inpatient care* for those individuals who need intensive care or treatment 24 hours each day; (2) *outpatient care* for adults, children, and families; (3) *partial hospitalization*, that is, day care and night care for those individuals who are able to work but need limited support or who are looking for suitable home arrangements; (4) *emergency care* on a 24-hour basis; and (5) *professional consultation and education* with community agencies. The regulations also include five additional services which, when present with the five "essential" ones, make up the comprehensive community mental health program: (6) *diagnostic service*; (7) *rehabilitative service*, comprised of both social and vocational rehabilitation; (8) *pre-care and after care*; (9) *training* for all levels of mental health personnel; and (10) *research and evaluation* concerning the effectiveness of the programs and the problems of mental illness and their treatment (Public Law 88-164).

Upon reviewing a number of articles related to the community mental health movement, several recurrent themes were noticed (e.g., Goldston, 1965; Bloom, 1966; Smith and Hobbs, 1966; Baker and Schulberg, 1967, 1969). To provide the reader with an understanding of the major theories and areas of emphasis characteristic of the community approach, a brief review of these themes follow.

Community involvement and community control is of major importance. The community accepts the responsibility of offering aid to its citizens who have mental health problems. To perform this function, local control over the goals and basic policies of the program is seen as being essential. An additional theme concerns the population upon which the program is focused. The entire constituency of a community is viewed as the target population rather than those few individuals who actively seek out treatment. The mental health services are provided to the members of the community in such a manner as to maintain continuity of care. As the recipients pass from one agency to the next, attention is given to the consistency of care. Lastly, there is an emphasis upon primary prevention. By neutralizing the injurious forces in a community before they have a chance to create mental illness, the old adage of "an ounce of prevention is worth a pound of cure" is put into practice.

Community mental health can be conceptualized as an approach in which emphasis is placed upon the interrelations between the individual and the community in which he lives. Consequently, the mental health professions have had to modify traditional theoretical approaches and develop a broad-gauged community orientation.

The community mental health approach not only demands new roles for the mental health professions but also requires new categories of personnel. The traditional model of the clinical psychologist is being modified to fit this growing need. Ira Iscoe (1974) states that "Conceptually, community differs from clinical. It deals with social systems, programs of interventions, and planning of environments. It basically aims at enhancing human competency and adheres to an ecological rather than a psychoanalytical model." As there is a major shortage of manpower in the mental health professions, new categories of personnel have been established to meet the rising needs. This movement in mental health has been described by Lobey (1970) as "the nonprofessional revolution." As early as 1964, undergraduate college students have been employed as child-care workers, helping professional teams with the problems of emotionally disturbed children (Megenity *et al.*, 1972). Gruver (1971) describes programs where college students work with professionals as aides to treatment programs in mental hospitals. Their role now includes such functions as play therapists and companion counselors for delinquents or school dropouts. Other college programs provide telephone crisis services for students in need of people to relate to over the telephone or to provide information about specialists they might contact for help (Tucker *et al.*, 1970).

High school students have been used with much success as "help agents" with hospital patients of the same age groups (Walker *et al.*, 1967). Housewives are finding ways to help in this nonprofessional revolution. They serve as therapeutic aides to mental health counselors. They have been trained in behavior modification techniques to carry on therapeutic programs with their own children. Behavior modification techniques can be learned with relative ease and, under professional supervision, the nonprofessional can be of great value in a mental health setting, be it in a hospital or community-based (Goldenberg, 1971).

Most nonprofessional training programs are based in metropolitan settings. There are scattered attempts, such as one reported by Megenity *et al.* (1974), to prepare Masters-degree level mental health workers to help non-metropolitan communities prepare nonprofessionals for service in their communities. Programs such as these show promise and should serve a real need if state and federal support continues to be provided. One final point about paraprofessional training is that it must be based on a career-ladder concept (Highlights of the Vail Conference, 1974) so that any formal training can be coordinated to allow the person to pursue higher levels of competency at a later date if he so chooses.

Another reason for the addition of a new staff category has been the theory that if mental health centers located in urban slums are to be able to understand and fulfill the needs of their recipient population, "indigenous" personnel will have to be recruited to serve as interpreters or resource bridges between the professionals and the clients. This indigenous non-professional has been conceptualized as a peer of the client who shares a common background, life style, language, and ethnic origin, the maintenance of which, for most professionals, would be both impossible and perhaps undesirable (Reiff and Riessman, 1965; Cowen, 1973).

One of the most exciting trends in the field of community mental health is the concern being generated for the non-institutionalized senior citizen (Mensh, 1973). Barrett (1972) describes this group and recommends ways in which to help them accept this phase of life. Several subsidized programs such as the Older American Act under Title III monies have enabled communities to establish resource development agencies for our senior citizens (Karlowski, 1973; Tyree, 1973). Kashner (1973) describes a seminar held for persons needing help in preparing for retirement. Programs such as these enable communities to combine resources in ways that have never been possible in the past (Vickery, 1974).

This new era in treatment of the mentally ill has begun—but not without its critics. It is the concept of comprehensive treatment, provided in the community for all those in need, that becomes a new idea and an extremely difficult challenge. Rather than providing an extensive discussion of the various critical issues, let it suffice to briefly mention the concerns of several writers.

1. More empirical evidence is needed to determine whether the basic hypotheses of community mental health are tenable. There exists some supporting evidence such as is reported by Goldenberg (1971), Thurman (1971), and Cowen (1973); but more is needed to show that geographic location of inpatient treatment bears a significant relationship to the outcome of treatment. Also, there is some indication that short-term treatment programs are more effective in one location than another (Silverman, 1974), but more studies are needed. Jones (1963) questions if the family in certain instances must remain intact to insure the most therapeutic gains on the part of the patient. The stresses and strains in low-income families are problem-creating and time away from these environments may be therapeutic for the patient. Jones also questions if community agencies can provide more economical service than a hospital. Moreover, the community mental health model is based on the assumption that if mental illness is treated early and intensively, improvement will occur (Glass, 1965). However, if the mental illness remains untreated, deterioration of a severe degree will transpire. Therefore, it is possible that this approach might be inadequate for many diagnostic categories—that is,

the neuroses and character disorders that are self-limiting in and of themselves (Cumming and Cumming, 1965; Albee, 1968).

2. The mental health field might not be able to do everything for everybody and do it well. The community mental health philosophy implies total mental health care for all those individuals in need of such. The point is made that if existing services were to be spread out over the entire catchment of population it would result in inadequate services for everyone (Albee, 1968). Moreover, there are not enough trained people in the area of mental health to carry out the charge of the "movement." Even if money were available, any expansion of the health services would depend largely on the availability of workers. The number of individuals desiring psychiatric treatment has grown as rapidly, if not more so, as the number of individuals able to supply this treatment (Jones, 1963; Glass, 1965; Whittington, 1965; Cravens, 1967; Albee, 1968).

3. The expansion of community-based centers might not stop the rising rate of admissions to public mental hospitals, since the new resources now may serve as casefinders of mental disorders that had been previously ignored or untreated. Also, the majority of public mental hospital patients come from lower socioeconomic groups or cultures that do not understand the need for professional help in mental illness. Increased community services seem to have little effect on admission rates to public mental hospitals from this category (Glass, 1965). There is some indication in this decade, however, that certain mental health centers are turning the tide (Shealey and Wright, 1972).

4. Community mental health centers have some major drawbacks. Confidentiality of the patient's medical record might be in jeopardy in facilities utilizing the community approach. Providers of care are ethically bound to protect the recipients of their services from embarrassment that may result from public knowledge of their problems. This is difficult within one agency or institution, and even more so in a treatment program where services are scattered throughout a complete community (Cravens, 1967).

5. Contrary to the theme of community involvement, a large number of semi-professional bachelor-degree level health workers probably will not be trained to work in the area. Although more manpower is desperately needed, the "first-class" centers may resist efforts to cut down their commitments to the core disciplines by training the lower levels. Also, since bachelor-level workers would be far down the status hierarchy, they would tolerate this inferior status position only for a short period (Albee, 1968). This is why it is important to provide a "ladder" model of education

and training so that paraprofessionals may advance if they so desire (Vail Conference, 1974; Megenity *et al.*, 1974).

6. Although the community mental health program proposes to provide comprehensive care to the total community, this does not always occur. Many community programs neglect the poor, the children, the aged, the disadvantaged, the alcoholic, and the drug addict (Albee, 1968).

7. Mental health workers do not have enough knowledge to rehabilitate patients on a one-to-one model, much less collectively. The point is adequately made that for the mental health worker there still exists an uncertainty concerning the treatment and care of the individual case (Dunham, 1965; Whittington, 1965). In shifting the emphasis from the institution to the community for the care of the mentally ill, some professionals in the field feel that the mental health profession may be transferring the care from trained staff to an untrained or ill-equipped staff or no staff at all (Titmuss, 1965).

These are critical issues; not all aspects of each have been resolved. Various programs are attempting to meet them head-on and much progress has been made. The best solution seems to be a compromise between traditional attempts and new innovations (Azoulay, 1970; Orden and Stoking, 1971; Beigel *et al.*, 1973). Theodore H. Blau (1974) sees the role of community psychology as involving "a wide variety of assessment procedures, interventions, evaluation, feedback and then the building of primary prevention systems which, in turn, should be subjective to formative and summative evaluation."

SUMMARY

Traditional approaches to the mental health problem are being challenged today by the community mental health movement. The enthusiasm for community treatment of mental illness can be traced to various historical origins. The community mental health movement is the *Zeitgeist* of today. It is being implemented by the mental health field. However, many mental health workers are cautious and sometimes critical of the community mental health philosophy. In general, however, progress is being made and there is more support. The public is becoming more aware of the problems concerning mental health and the community. There is much broader communication between established treatment centers and the new community agencies. Prevention is becoming as important as treatment. Mental hospitals are viewed now as "therapeutic communities" rather than as last-resort dumping grounds for people incapable of functioning normally. New developments include work being done to help the older American adjust to his new role (Karlowski, 1973). New modes are being tried to prevent crime and to treat offenders of the law as well as drug users and addicts (Lukoff *et al.*, 1973). Finally, broad theoretical models are being advanced to cope with the problems of overpopulation (Esser, 1971) and environmental modification to do away with variables causing deviant behavior (Skinner, 1971).

BIBLIOGRAPHY

Albee, G. W. Give us a place to stand and we will move the earth. Reprinted from President's Messages, 1966–1967, 20, *The Clinical Psychologist*, Nos. 1–4, 1968.

Azoulay J. Sur une tentative de psychanalyse appliquee (An attempt of applied psychoanalysis). *Interpretation*, Jan. 1970, **4**(1–2), 41–65.

Bailey, D. E. *Cluster analysis and the B C Try system*. Boulder, Colo.: Tryon-Bailey Associates, 1971.

Baker, F., and Schulberg, H. C. The development of a community mental health ideology scale. *Community Mental Health Journal*, 1967, **3**, 216–225.

Baker, F., and Schulberg, H. C. The community mental health ideology patterns of staff members at a changing mental hospital. Unpublished manuscript, Harvard Medical School, 1968.

Baker, F., and Schulberg, H. C. Community mental health ideology, dogmatism, and political-economic conservatism. *Community Mental Health Journal*, 1969, **5**, 433–436.

Barrett, J. H. *Gerontological psychology*. Springfield, Ill.: Charles C. Thomas, 1972.

Beigel, A., Bower, W. H., and Levenson, A. I. A unified system of care: Blueprint for the future. *American Journal of Psychiatry*, May 1973, **130**(5), 554–558.

Blackman, S., and Goldstein, K. M. Some aspects of a theory of community mental health. *Community Mental Health Journal*, 1968, **4**, 85–90.

Blake, R., and Dennis, W. The development of stereotypes concerning the Negro. *Journal of Abnormal and Social Psychology*, 1943, **38**, 525–531.

Blau, T. H. In reply to Ira Iscoe. *The Clinical Psychologist*, 1974, **27**, 3.

Bloom, B. L. The community mental health movement and the American social revolution. Unpublished manuscript, University of Colorado, 1966.

Bloom, B. L., Lang, E. M., and Goldberg, H. Factors associated with accuracy of prediction of posthospitalization adjustment. *Journal of Abnormal Psychology*, 1970, **76**, 243–249.

Bobbitt, J. M. *Mental health programs today and in the future*. Presented at Issues Conference of Mental Health, Minneapolis, May 1963.

Bolman, W. M. Theoretical and empirical bases of community mental health. *American Journal of Psychiatry*, 1967, **124** (Supp.), 8–13.

Carstairs, M., and Heron, A. The social environment of mental hospital patients: A measure of staff attitude. In M. G. Greenblatt, D. J. Levinson, R. H. Williams (Eds.), *The patient and the mental hospital*. Glencoe, Ill.: Free Press, 1957.

Cowen, E. L. Social and community intervention. In P. H. Mussen and M. R. Rosenweig (Eds.), *Annual review of psychology*. Palo Alto, Calif.: Annual Reviews, 1973.

Cravens, R. B. Impact of recent federal legislation: Community mental health services. *American Journal of Public Health*, 1967, **57**, 1201–1207.

Cumming, E., and Cumming, J. Some questions on community care. *Canada's Mental Health*, 1965, **13**(6), 7–12.

Dain, N. Concepts of insanity in the United States, 1789–1865. New Brunswick, N.J.: Rutgers U. Press, 1965.

Duhl, L. J. The psychiatric evolution. In S. E. Goldston (Ed.), *Concepts of community psychiatry—a framework for training.* Washington, D.C.: NIMH, 1965.

Dunham, H. W. Community psychiatry—the newest therapeutic bandwagon. *Archives of General Psychiatry*, 1965, **12**, 303–313.

Elms, A. C. (Ed.) *Role playing, reward and attitude change.* Cincinnati: Van Nostrand and Reinhold, 1969.

English, H. B., and English, A. C. *A comprehensive dictionary of psychological and psychoanalytical terms.* New York: David McKay, 1958.

Esser, A. H. (Ed.) *Behavior and environment: Use of space by animals and men.* New York: Plenum Press, 1971.

Felix, R. H. Community mental health: A great and significant movement. *American Journal of Psychiatry*, 1966, **122**, 1056–1057.

Foley, A. R., and Sanders, D. S. Theoretical considerations for the development of the community mental health center concept. *American Journal of Psychiatry*, 1966, **122**, 985–990.

Freedman, A. M. Historical and political roots of the community mental health centers act. *American Journal of Orthopsychiatry*, 1967, **37**, 487–494.

Gilbert, D. C., and Levinson, D. J. Ideology, personality, and institutional policy in the mental hospital. *Journal of Abnormal and Social Psychology*, 1956, **53**, 263–271.

Gilbert, D. C., and Levinson, D. J. "Custodialism" and "Humanism" in staff ideology. In M. G. Greenblatt, D. J. Levinson, and R. H. Williams (Eds.), *The patient and the mental hospital.* Glencoe, Ill.: Free Press, 1957.

Gilbert, D. C., and Levinson, D. J. Role performance, ideology, and personality in mental hospital aides. In M. G. Greenblatt, D. J. Levinson, and R. H. Williams (Eds.), *The patient and the mental hospital.* Glencoe, Ill.: Free Press, 1957.

Glass, A. J. The future of large public mental hospitals. *Mental Hospitals*, 1965, **16**, 9–22.

Goldenberg, I. I. The residential youth center: Problems of theory and research in the creation of a community based rehabilitative setting. In M. J. Feldman (Ed.), *Studies in psychotherapy and behavior change.* Vol. 2, *Theory and research in community mental health.* Buffalo: State University of New York Press, 1971.

Goldston, S. E. Selected definitions. In S. E. Goldston (Ed.), *Concepts of community psychiatry—A framework for training.* Washington, D.C.: NIMH, 1965.

Greenblatt, M. G., Levinson, D. J., and Williams, R. H. (Eds.) *The patient and the mental hospital.* Glencoe, Ill.: Free Press, 1957.

Gruver, G. G. College students as therapeutic agents. *Psychological Bulletin*, 1971, **76**, 111–127.

Highlights of the Vail Conference—Preliminary Report Recommendations. *The Clinical Psychologist*, 1974, **27**, 5–10.

Hollander, E. P. *Principles and methods of social psychiatry.* New York: Oxford University Press, 1967.

Hollingshead, A. B., and Redlich, F. C. *Social class and mental illness.* New York: Wiley, 1958.

Iscoe, I. Community psychology is different from clinical. *The Clinical Psychologist*, 1974, **27**, 3.

Janis, I. L. Attitude change via role playing. In E. F. Borgatta (Ed.), *Psychology: Readings and perspective.* Chicago: Rand McNally, 1969.

Jones, K. Revolution and reform in the mental health services. *Medical Care,* 1963, **1,** 155–160.

Karlowski, V. *Comprehensive service project description.* Senior Resource Development Center and Coordinator Agency, funded under Title III, Older Americans Act, 1965; City and County of Pueblo, United Fund of Pueblo County, 1973.

Kashner, J. *Annual report of the Southern Colorado Gerontological Institute.* Southern Colorado State College, Pueblo, Colorado, 1973.

Langston, R. D. Community mental health centers and community mental health ideology. *Community Mental Health Journal,* 1970, **6,** 387–392.

Lieberman, S. The effects of changes in roles on the attitudes of role occupants. *Human Relations,* 1956, **9,** 385–402.

Lobey, F. *The nonprofessional revolution in mental health.* New York: Columbia University Press, 1970.

Lukoff, I. F., Quatrone, D., and Hayim, G. J. Heroin use and crime in a methadone maintenance program: Interim Report. Washington, D.C.: U.S. Department of Justice, 1973.

Megenity, D., Russell, K., and Kerkoski, J. Undergraduate college students as child care workers in a state hospital. *Hospital and Community psychiatry,* 1972, **23,** 223–225.

Megenity, D., Snowden, R., and Pantleo, P. *Masters of science in non-metropolitan community psychology.* Unpublished proposal. Pueblo, Colo.: Southern Colorado State College, 1974.

Mensh, I. N. Community mental health and other services for the aged. In C. Ersdorfer and M. B. Lawton (Eds.), *The psychology of adult development and aging.* Washington, D.C.: American Psychological Association, 1973.

Moreland, J. K. Racial acceptance and preference of nursery school children in a southern city. *Merrill Palmer Quarterly,* 1962, **8,** 271–280.

Newcomb, T. M. *Social psychology.* New York: Holt, Rinehart & Winston, 1950.

Nunnally, J. *Psychometric theory.* New York: McGraw-Hill, 1967.

Orden, S. R., and Stoking, C. B. *Relationships between community mental health centers and other caregiving agencies.* Chicago: National Opinion Research Center, University of Chicago, 1971.

Parsons, T. *The social system.* New York: Free Press of Glencoe, 1951.

Pine, F., and Levinson, D. J. Two patterns of ideology, role conception, and personality among mental hospital aides. In M. G. Greenblatt, D. J. Levinson, and R. H. Williams (Eds.), *The patient and the mental hospital.* Glencoe, Ill.: Free Press, 1957.

Proshansky, H., and Seidenberg, B. (Eds.) *Basic studies in social psychology.* Chicago: Holt, Rinehart & Winston, 1966.

Public Law 88-164. Title II. Community mental health centers act of 1963. Regulations. *Federal Registration,* May 6, 1964, 5951–5956.

Public Law 89-105. Mental retardation facilities and community mental health centers construction act. Amendments of 1965. Regulations. *Federal Registration,* March 1, 1966, 3246–3248.

Reiff, R., and Riessman, F. The indigenous nonprofessional: A strategy of change in community action and community mental health programs. *Community Mental Health Journal,* 1965, Monograph No. 1.

Rokeach, M. Definition of attitude. In E. F. Borgatta (Ed.), *Social psychology: Readings and perspective.* Chicago: Rand McNally, 1969.

Schulberg, H. C., and Baker, F. Varied attitudes in community mental health. *Archives of General Psychiatry,* 1967, **17**, 658–663.

Scott, W. A., and Wertheimer, M. *Introduction to psychological research.* New York: Wiley, 1962.

Sharaf, M., and Levinson, D. J. Patterns of ideology and role differentiation among psychiatric residents. In M. G. Greenblatt, D. J. Levinson, and R. H. Williams (Eds.), *The patient and the mental hospital.* Glencoe, Ill.: Free Press, 1957.

Shealy, A. E., and Wright, P. A state wide epidemiological assessment of the effectiveness of community mental health services. *Journal of Clinical Psychology,* Jan. 1972, **28**(1), 109–111.

Silverman, R. E. *Psychology.* New York: Appleton-Century-Crofts, 1974.

Skinner, B. F. *Beyond freedom and dignity.* New York: Knopf, 1971.

Smith, M. B., and Hobbs, N. The community and the community mental health center. *American Psychologist,* 1966, **21**, 299–309.

Stotsky, B. A., Sachs, J. M., and Daston, P. G. Predicting the work performance of psychiatric aides by psychological tests. *Journal of Consulting Psychology,* 1956, **3**, 193–199.

Strauss, A., Schatzman, L., Bucher, R., Ehrlich, D., and Labshin, M. *Psychiatric ideologies and institutions.* London: Collier-Macmillan, 1965.

Thurman, D. G. The development of a community alcohol rehabilitation unit. *Rehabilitation Research and Practice Review,* 1971, **2**(1), 41–60.

Titmuss, R. M. Community care of the mentally ill: Some British observations. *Canada's Mental Health,* 1965, Supp. No. 49, 1–8.

Tryon, B. C., and Bailey, D. E. The B C Try computer system of cluster and factor analysis. *Multivariate Behavior Research,* 1966, **1**, 95–111.

Tucker, B., Megenity, D., and Vigil, L. Anatomy of a campus crisis center. *The Personnel and Guidance Journal,* 1970, **48**, 343–348.

Tyree, A. *Pueblo Senior Citizens Study Report,* funded under Title III, Older Americans Act, 1965, Division of the Colorado State Department of Social Services in cooperation with the Colorado Commission on Aging, Pueblo Community Council, Pueblo, Colorado, 1973.

Vickery, F. A. *Creative programming for older adults: A leadership training guide.* New York: Association Press, 1974.

Walker, C. E., Walpin, M., and Fellows, L. The use of high school students as therapists and researchers in a state mental hospital. *Psychotherapy: Theory, Research and Practice,* 1967, **4**, 186–188.

Wessen, A. F. Hospital ideology and communication between ward personnel. In E. G. Jaco (Ed.), *Patients, physicians and illness.* Glencoe, Ill.: Free Press, 1958.

Whittington, H. G. The third psychiatric revolution—really? *Community Mental Health Journal,* 1965, **1**, 73–80.

Yolles, S. F. Community mental health: Issues and policies. *American Journal of Psychiatry,* 1966, **122**, 979–985.

Zilboorg, G., and Henry, G. W. *A history of medical psychology.* New York: Norton, 1941.

HOMINOLOGY*

Theodore C. Kahn, Ph.D., Sc.D.

Hominology represents an innovative system of apperceiving what being human consists of. The term is derived from *hominidae*, the family of man developing throughout time.

This approach was developed in 1965 as an essential aspect of a new psychiatric residence program at Wilford Hall Hospital in San Antonio. Its aim was to change the physician's habitual focus on the client's disease to one on the client as a total human being who, in addition to all other kinds of problems, has a disease.

Many behavioral scientists before and after the early 19th century joined Kurt Goldstein, William James, and Adolph Meyer in lamenting "the fragmentation of the study of man" but no one actually did anything about it. And for good reason: it seemed to be a gigantic, complicated task fraught with the inevitable controversy of methodology and disciplinary proprietorship. Julian Huxley stated that we should "coin a new term" to describe the "comprehensive process" inherent in evolution when focused on man. But he, himself, failed to coin such a term. Until recently not much was done about the problem of dealing with man holistically.

Within the last five years, the consequences of fragmentation were finally recognized and, with a compensatory surge, the various behavioral science and social disciplines began to initiate whole-man concepts within the framework of their individual disciplinary orientations. A proliferation of separate and distinct "whole-man" studies emerged that often had little in common. Concepts in these studies were heavily weighted with ideas and historical perspectives drawn from the disciplines in which the studies evolved.

INTERDISCIPLINARY APPROACHES

Interdisciplinary and multidisciplinary approaches failed to offer the required solution. It was found that such methods seemed to reflect several biases instead of one, and that the parts simply did not fit together. Interdisciplinary studies lacked synthesis and integration of facts, and after exposure to them, students were sometimes more bewildered than

*Reprinted with permission from *Journal of Contemporary Psychotherapy*, Spring 1972, **4**(2), 67–73.

before. Clearly something different was required. A new multidimensional approach to the study of man was necessary, one having a nondisciplinary base so that it could be integrated and neutral from a disciplinary point of view. Hominology was designed to meet this need.

Growing away from its original setting, hominology was introduced as a college course in 1966 at Southern Colorado State College within the Department of Behavioral Science. The course started with 18 students and now, six years later, with two new teachers, approximately 500 students are enrolled in "hominology." Students' feedback confirms that the study of hominology not only offers them new theoretical perspective but has a wide range of applications, many of them therapeutic in nature..

It was unforeseen originally in the design of hominology that it could be utilized as an adjunct to psychotherapy. Psychiatrists, psychologists, student counselors, and teachers have reported success when they used the concepts of hominology in helping clients develop a new sense of self-awareness and a clearer realization of goals and values. When applied therapeutically, it has helped clients get out of the double bind that is inherent in the conflict between purpose in life and environmental limitations. It reportedly has filled a psychotherapeutic vacuum by helping therapists reduce their clients' value-conflicts—so common a phenomenon in our present-day civilization.

CHARACTERISTICS OF HOMINOLOGY

Hominology has five distinguishing characteristics: (1) it is nondisciplinary and nonspecialized; (2) it explores abstractions such as man's ethics, his moral values, his philosophical commitments; (3) it concerns itself with the emerging quality of humanization, which includes considerations of the past, present, and future; (4) it facilitates a philosophical self-examination by means of "hominolograms"—charts used by students or clients to identify their personal apperception of truth, reality, and ethical commitment; (5) it provides a nondisciplinary setting within which the student (or client) can prescribe his own course of future actions consistent with his self-concept and his new understanding of mankind's directional evolvement.

The textbook, *An Introduction to Hominology—The Study of the Whole Man*, was printed in 1969[201]. It went through a second printing in 1970 and was revised in 1972. During these years, special forms helpful in constructing hominolograms were also made available. These are used in some mental health clinics independent of hominology teaching, as a series of exercises in "Exploring the Self-Image"[201]. A number of clinicians report that these forms are a helpful adjunct to psychotherapy and psychodiagnosis. They elicit philosophical as well as psychological variables.

There are many hundreds of tests and devices that purport to measure the self-image based upon personality profiles, which by one way or another attempt to reveal basic emotional components. By utilizing philosophical commitments instead of personality variables a deeper understanding of a given problem is obtained since personality variables are primarily symptomatic manifestations of philosophical apperceptions.

Every client (and every person) adopts in his lifetime a particular philosophy of life that explains his behavior in a more fundamental manner than clinical descriptions can. In psychotherapy we have often ignored philosophy-of-action concepts which hominological techniques spotlight. Our tendency to neglect philosophical considerations that underlie clinical behavior stems from the fact that we are apparently capable of being able to cure a patient without having to take philosophical orientations into account. The consequence of this neglect is that often the therapeutic process represents an "immunization" rather than a genuine "cure." "Cure" implies that not only behavior has changed but also that the concept underlying the nonadaptive behavior has been modified. In psychotherapy today we are prone to restore the mask of sanity, which disguises the client's maladjusted inner core. This, however, does not add up to "cure" in the sense of an inner reorientation in depth.

Orthodox psychoanalysis originally aimed at a cure. The less complex therapies that are now popular appear to be satisfied with psychiatric "reform." There is a vast difference between these two. Hominological therapies again aim for cure, but in a completely different manner than Freudian methods do.

AN ANALOGY

Hominological therapy offers a concept of maladjustment that includes three contingencies. An analogy will help to clarify them: A person traveling by automobile may fail to reach his destination because of one (or more) of three reasons:

He has taken the wrong road.
He has taken the right road but is stalled by motor trouble.
He thinks, in error, that he has already arrived at his destination.

We realize that the "traveler" is the client; the "road" is the path of his life throughout time; and the "destination" is his life's goals and aspirations. Let us examine the causes of possible failure one by one. If we use the idea of the wrong road, we are implying that there exists a "right" road. Within current concepts, the "right" road is usually considered to consist of a satisfactory adjustment to social norms. Such an assumption ignores the client's personal philosophy of life. Regardless of what form normative behavior in any given social setting assumes, it is always extrinsic to an individual's personal inner self. Our concept of "cure" ignores what the client intrinsically believes in. As long as he goosesteps with the rest of society, a client has (by definition) been restored to normalcy.

THE FIRST FACTOR

Within the concept of hominology, however, there is a different conception of normalcy. Perhaps we can borrow from Shakespeare by describing this kind of normalcy as "to thine own self be true." Instead of utilizing norms that may differ widely from one kind of society to another, *consistency* with one's own philosophical commitments is required. Through the use of the hominolograms, personal commitments can be graphically identified, and it is postulated that when a human being is out of kilter with himself—when his actions and his philosophy conflict—he is hominologically "sick."

What happens if a client's behavior is antisocial or socially unacceptable even though it is self-consistent? Such an impasse rarely occurs; when it does, it is also subject to philosophical mediation. Adjustment is possible especially since the client using hominology knows exactly where his philosophical commitments (called Criteria of Reality) come from. By knowing what they are and how they were derived, it is usually within his power to make the adjustment required to line them up with the contemporary social norms of his society. He may deliberately decide not to line them up and suffer the consequences. Such people are "different" by deliberate choice and are not ill. No amount of psychotherapy will ever "cure" them.

ORIGINS OF THE PHILOSOPHICAL OUTLOOK

The Criteria of Reality that form the philosophical social underpinnings from which a given philosophical outlook is derived consist of the following elements:

1. Membership in the human species.
2. Membership in a specific culture (including membership in both a national and community group).
3. Membership in a social or economic class.
4. Membership in an ethnic or racial group.
5. Educational level and vocational achievement.
6. Membership in a group having a particular political orientation.
7. Membership in a group having a specific religious faith.
8. Living in a given time era; each time era has its unique socio-historical-technological identity.
9. Membership in a given family group, the vicissitudes of which we are likely to share.
10. Possession of a unique constitutional make-up that includes our total inherited characteristics, our natural endowments and defects, and our genetic biological predispositions.
11. Our individual life experiences, which consist of an interrelated composite of all the foregoing factors within the environment to which we are exposed.

THE SECOND FACTOR

The second factor of our analogy is: He has taken the right road but is stalled by motor trouble. In this case, a problem of philosophical-behavioral consistency does not exist. Instead, extrinsic events in the environment are primarily responsible for the maladjustment. Under these circumstances, current psychotherapeutic methods are appropriately used. Behavioral therapy, reconditioning, immunization, short-term psychoanalytical personality restructuring, all these may accomplish the desired goal. Traumatic and unexpected events in the environment (such as death of a near relative, loss of a job, a romance gone haywire) are typical of the "motor-trouble" that can stall progress on the road of life, and all of these are amenable to the types of psychotherapy now extant. After the motor is fixed, the client can proceed upon his journey.

THE THIRD FACTOR

Much is implied in the concept: He thinks, in error, that he has already arrived at his destination. What is the destination or goal of life? Most people would insist that this is quite a debatable point and that different people legitimately have different goals and life purposes.

Controversial as such a conclusion may be, hominology therapists feel that the human species emerging throughout time has a directional focus that offers similar generalized goals to all of the members of the species. If this concept is accepted, it offers psychotherapy a new dimension.

The theoretical generalized goal for mankind to which I refer has been described by a variety of writers and is not essentially a new idea. It has been put this way: Man's purpose within nature is to discover his potentiality. Such theorizings are consistent with hominology's attempt to derive meaning from mankind's evolutionary past.

The concept of goals within hominological therapy is akin to viewing the becoming of an adult as the "goal" of a child. A sequence of developmental levels that have a directional focus akin to growing up is postulated. We see a similar concept within biology, where clarification about the development of life is facilitated by hypothesizing progressive developmental stages. We are all familiar with the evolutionary concepts of the age of marine invertebrates, the age of fishes, the age of amphibians, the age of reptiles, the age of mammals, the age of man. Biology and paleontology would be hard pressed to develop meaningful ideas, and even to communicate effectively, if the use of evolutionary stages did not exist. Geological eras serve the same purpose. Each yields a concept of emergence through time and implies a directional thrust of nature.

Hominological therapy offers us a similar concept of phylogenetic developmental levels geared specifically to man. The growth of the individual from infancy to old age—the ontogenetic human development—has been made abundantly clear to all of us. In contrast, the idea of human phylogenetic equivalent to infant-adult developmental patterns has not previously been utilized in psychotherapy. Eight developmental stages are postulated, ranging from the potentiality of becoming (Level 1) to an age where the individual ego merges with the universe and is no longer identifiable (Level 8). By an evolutionary analysis akin to the one utilized in biology and geology, hominology places our present human situation between an emphasis on fulfillment (Level 6) and an emphasis on dedication to others (Level 7).

Adopting this theoretical framework even temporarily enables us to cope with the question of the "destination" to which we referred in the analogy. Thus, believing that fulfillment of our own personal desires—the self-actualization of Maslow—is the end of our journey leads to maladjustment. It places us in the position of thinking erroneously that we have already arrived at our destination when, in fact, we have a much longer way to go. It denies mankind's future. It is with this kind of maladjustment that psychotherapists often cannot cope by using conventional methods alone. Individuals who become acquainted with the concept of hominological levels learn to utilize specific techniques with which goals and purposes in life may be identified in order to gain phylogenetic maturity. This is another way of saying that a sense of "destination" can be imparted that gives life meaning. It is clear to anyone who has worked in the field of psychotherapy that giving a client a rational basis from which he can derive meaning and purpose in life can spell the difference between success and failure of the therapeutic effort.

The purpose of this paper has been to describe a multidimensional method of apperceiving man that, in a nondisciplinary manner, offers a new dimension in psychotherapy. Three different maladjusted situations were described, and these were discussed in terms of how hominology can be utilized as an adjunct to current clinical methods. Two of the three situations described required a philosophical appraisal in addition to the use of psychological assessment alone.

For further information in the use of hominological therapy see:

1. Hominology as an Aspect of Humanistic Psychology by Theodore C. Kahn, in *Sightings: Essays in Humanistic Psychology* by F. Richards and I. D. Welch (Eds.). Boulder, Colo.: Shields, 1973.
2. Hominology—The Approach to the Whole Man by Theodore C. Kahn, in *New Frontiers in Psychiatric Technology*. Sacramento, Calif.: National Association of Psychiatric Technology and the Colorado Psychiatric Technicians Association, 1969.
3. *Hominology—Psychiatry's Newest Frontier* by C. D. Jones. Springfield, Ill.: Charles C. Thomas, 1974.

APPENDIX B

Major Publishers of Psychological Tests

The following is a list of the names and addresses of publishers of psychological tests reviewed in this book. A complete list of test publishers can be found in *Seventh Mental Measurements Yearbook* by O. K. Buros[63].

American College Testing Program (ACT)
P.O. Box 168
Iowa City, Iowa 52240

American Guidance Services, Inc.
Publishers Building
Circle Pines, Minnesota 55014

Bureau of Educational Research and Service
C-6 East Hall
State University of Iowa
Iowa City, Iowa 52240

Bureau of Publication
Teachers College
Columbia University
New York, New York 10017

C P S Inc.
P.O. Box 83
Larchmont, New York 10538

College Entrance Examination Board
Educational Testing Service
Princeton, New Jersey 08540

Consulting Psychologist Press, Inc.
577 College Avenue
Palo Alto, California 94306

Educational Testing Service
Princeton, New Jersey 08540

Grune and Stratton, Inc.
381 Park Avenue South
New York, New York 10016

Harcourt Brace Jovanovich
757 Third Avenue
New York, New York 10017

Harvard University Press
79 Garden Street
Cambridge, Massachusetts 02138

Houghton Mifflin Company
110 Tremont Street
Boston, Massachusetts 02107

Institute for Personality and Ability Testing (IPAT)
1602 Coronado Drive
Champaign, Illinois 61820

Newman, Neame, Ltd.
London, England

The Psychological Corporation
304 East 45th Street
New York, New York 10017

Psychological Test Specialists
Box 1441
Missoula, Montana 59801

Science Research Associates, Inc.
259 East Erie Street
Chicago, Illinois 60611

Southern Universities Press
Now merged with Psychological
Test Specialists

Stanford University Press
Stanford, California 94305

C. H. Stoelting Company
424 North Homan Avenue
Chicago, Illinois 60624

United States Employment Service
Washington, D.C. 20210

University of Minnesota Press
Minneapolis, Minnesota 55455

Western Psychological Services
12031 Wilshire Boulevard
Los Angeles, California 90025

APPENDIX C

Selected Tests

Title	Author	Publisher
American College Testing Program Examination (ACT)	American College Testing Program	American College Testing Program
Arthur Point Scale of Performance Tests	G. Arthur	
Form I		Stoelting Company
Form II		Psychological Corp.
Bender Motor Gestalt Test	L. Bender	Western Psychological Services
Benton Visual Retention Test Revised Edition	A. L. Benton	Psychological Corp.
California Psychological Inventory (CPI)	H. G. Gough	Consulting Psychologist Press
Children's Apperception Test (CAT)	L. Bellak S. Bellak	C.P.S. Inc.
Columbia Mental Maturity Scale	B. Burgemeister L. H. Blum I. Lorge	Psychological Corp.
Crawford Small Parts Dexterity Test	J. Crawford	Psychological Corp.
Culture Fair Intelligence Test	P. Cattell	Institute for Personality and Ability Testing
Differential Aptitude Tests	G. K. Bennett H. G. Seashore A. G. Wesman	Psychological Corp.

Title	Author	Publisher
Draw-A-Person Test (DAP)	K. Machover	Charles C. Thomas
Edwards Personal Preference Schedule (EPPS)	A. L. Edwards	Psychological Corp.
Full Range Picture Vocabulary Test	R. B. Ammons H. Ammons	Psychological Test Specialists
General Aptitude Test Battery	U.S. Employment Service	U.S. Employment Service
Goldstein-Scheerer Tests of Abstract and Concrete Thinking	K. Goldstein M. Scheerer	Psychological Corp.
Goodenough-Harris Drawing Test	F. L. Goodenough D. B. Harris	Harcourt Brace Jovanovich
Graduate Record Examinations (GRE)	Educational Testing Service	Educational Testing Service
Grassi Block Substitution Test for Measuring Brain Pathology	J. R. Grassi	Western Psychological Services
Group Personality Projective Test (GPPT)	R. N. Cassel T. C. Kahn	Psychological Test Specialists
Harris Tests of Lateral Dominance	A. J. Harris	Psychological Corp.
House-Tree-Person Projective Technique	J. N. Buck	Western Psychological Services
Hunt-Minnesota Test for Organic Brain Damage	H. F. Hunt	University of Minnesota Press
Kahn Aphasia Test, Experimental	T. C. Kahn	Unpublished
Kahn Intelligence Test (KIT)	T. C. Kahn	Psychological Test Specialists
Kahn Test of Symbol Arrangement (KTSA)	T. C. Kahn	Psychological Test Specialists
Kuder Occupational Interest Survey	G. F. Kuder	Science Research Associates
Kuder Preference Record: Vocational–Form C	G. F. Kuder	Science Research Associates
Leiter International Performance Scale	R. G. Leiter G. Arthur	Stoelting Company
Lorge-Thorndike Intelligence Tests	I. Lorge R. L. Thorndike E. Hagen	Houghton Mifflin
Lowenfeld Mosaic Test	M. Lowenfeld	Newman, Neame, Ltd.
Make-A-Picture Story Test (MAPS)	E. S. Shneidman	Psychological Corp.

Title	Author	Publisher
Meir Art Judgment Test	N. C. Meir	Bureau of Educational Research and Service, University of Iowa
Miller Analogies Test	W. S. Miller	Psychological Corp.
Michigan Picture Test	S. Hartwell R. E. Walton G. Andrew M. Hutt	Science Research Associates
Minnesota Multiphasic Personality Inventory (MMPI)	S. R. Hathaway J. C. McKinley	Psychological Corp.
Otis-Lennon Mental Ability Test	A. S. Otis R. J. Lennon	Harcourt Brace Jovanovich
Peabody Picture Vocabulary Test	L. M. Dunn	American Guidance Service
Purdue Pegboard	Purdue Research Foundation	Science Research Associates
Quick Test	R. B. Ammons H. Ammons	Psychological Test Specialists
Raven Progressive Matrices	J. C. Raven	Psychological Corp.
Rorschach Test	H. Rorschach	Hans Huber, Grune and Stratton (United States distributor)
Scholastic Aptitude Test (SAT)	College Entrance Examination Board	College Entrance Examination Board
Seashore Measures of Musical Talents (rev. ed.)	C. E. Seashore *et al.*	Psychological Corp.
School and College Ability Test (SCAT)	Educational Testing Service	Educational Testing Service
Shipley Institute of Living Scale for Measuring Intellectual Impairment	W. C. Shipley	Mrs. J. H. Boyle (distributor)
Sixteen Personality Factor Questionnaire	R. B. Cattell	Institute for Personality and Ability Testing
Stanford-Binet Intelligence Scale	L. M. Terman M. A. Merrill	Houghton Mifflin
Strong Vocational Interest Blank (SVIB)	E. K. Strong	Stanford University Press
Symonds Picture-Story Test	P. M. Symonds	Bureau of Publication, Teachers College, Columbia University

Title	Author	Publisher
Thematic Apperception Test (TAT)	H. A. Murray	Harvard University Press
Vocational Apperception Test	R. B. Ammons M. Butler S. A. Herzig	Southern Universities Press
Wechsler Adult Intelligence Scale (WAIS)	D. Wechsler	Psychological Corp.
Wechsler Intelligence Scales for Children (WISC) (WISC-R)	D. Wechsler	Psychological Corp.
Wechsler Preschool and Primary Scale of Intelligence (WPPSI)	D. Wechsler	Psychological Corp.
World Test	C. Buhler G. Kelly	Psychological Corp.

APPENDIX D

Ground Rules for Group Sessions

1. *Commitment.* You have volunteered to be a participant in this group. It is an old cliché, but you will get out of the group experience only and to remain in the group for the duration of the experience. Try to involve yourself to the fullest possible extent in all of the activities of the group. It is an old cliché, but you will get out of the group experience only what you put into it.

If at any time you become disproportionately uncomfortable with any of the activities of the group, it is your responsibility to temporarily discontinue your involvement and inform one of the facilitators of your feelings. Please do not leave the room. Some anxiety and apprehension is quite typical and appropriate during an experience of this kind. Try to face your feelings and work them through rather than fleeing from them.

2. *Alcohol and drugs.* The use of alcohol or drugs immediately before or during a group session is prohibited and there will be no smoking while a session is in progress.

3. *Confidentiality.* What we say here is confidential. No one will repeat anything said here to persons outside the group, unless it concerns only himself.

4. *Facilitator.* The group facilitator is responsible for three things only: he protects the integrity of every member, their being heard, and is responsible for creating a proper environment.

5. *Group members must accept full responsibility for all of the behavior they display in the group.* In addition, they must assume responsibility for the things that happen to them as a result of their behavior. They cannot blame their family, society, personal feelings, or bad luck for the things that have happened to them in the past or that will happen to them in the future.

6. *Communication.* Our first purpose here is to make contact with one another. We do this through exploring, listening, and responding. Listen carefully to yourself as well as others. Try to develop your capacity for empathy and understanding.

The focus and content for group interation is the "here-and-now." This includes your present feelings, your feelings toward other members of the group, and discussion of the processes that are occurring within the group. Topics should relate directly to the present dynamics of the group.

Try to be as honest and open as possible and to express yourself as you *really* are and *really* feel. Try to say what you *really* mean, not necessarily what you think will be most acceptable to the other members or the group as a whole.

Assume your share of the responsibility for the nature and direction of the group interaction. If you are bored, unhappy, or cannot see the relevance of what is happening within the group, *do something about it.* It is *your* group, too.

Talk directly to the person with whom you are trying to communicate. Look at the other person; maintain eye contact with him. When referring to yourself, use the pronoun "I." When talking to another member of the group, use his name or the pronoun "you." Do not use second- and third-person pronouns ("he," "she," "they") when addressing someone in the group.

Talk so that you can be heard clearly by the entire group. Do not form splinter groups, "cheerlead," or "kibitz."

7. *Conflict resolution.* Do not allow interpersonal conflicts between yourself and another member(s) to go unresolved. *Follow through* when conflicts arise; do your utmost to work them out to the satisfaction of both (all) parties involved. (This necessitates operating from the premise that *change* in personalities and behavior can occur, that you can become a different person than you are right now.) Resolution of conflicts is seldom easy, but your facilitators will try to help you bring it about.

8. Keep your goals in mind and make an honest effort to meet these goals.

I will attend the group session meeting each ______ from ______ to ______. At this time I will participate in the evaluation of the related experience. I accept the ground rules and will abide by them.

Signed____________

Date____________

APPENDIX E

*Methodology for Revising and Restandardizing the WISC**

Alan S. Kaufman†

A. THE STANDARDIZATION

The Wechsler Intelligence Scale for Children—Revised (WISC-R)‡ was standardized on 2200 children—200 at each of 11 age groups between $6\frac{1}{2}$ and $16\frac{1}{2}$. The sample was stratified in accordance with 1970 Census data on age, sex, race, geographic region, and occupation of head of household. In addition, white and nonwhite children were selected from urban and rural areas in approximate Census proportions. The WISC-R spans the ages 6–16 whereas the 1949 WISC spanned the 5–15 year age range.

B. SUPPLEMENTARY CORRELATIONAL STUDIES TO BE REPORTED IN THE MANUAL

1. Test vs. retest scores on WISC-R of children from six age groups.
2. WISC-R scores vs. scores on WPPSI for age 6–0 and WAIS for age 16–11.
3. WISC-R scores with Stanford-Binet scores for children from four age groups.
4. WISC-R scores with Stanford-Binet scores for a group of mentally retarded children.

*Presented at the symposium, "The Restandardization of the WISC" (Wechsler Intelligence Scale for Children). APA Convention, Montreal, August 1973.

†Affiliation: The Psychological Corporation.

C. CONTENT OF WISC-R

Test*	Total Number of Items in WISC-R Edition	Number of Items Retained from 1949 WISC	Number of 1949 WISC Items Modified	Number of New Items
Verbal				
Information (30)	30	19	2	9
Similarities (16)	17	9	2	6
Arithmetic (16)	18	8	5	5
Vocabulary (40)	32	21	0	11
Comprehension (14)	17	9	0	8
Digit span (14)	14	14	0	0
Performance				
Picture completion (20)	26	14	1	11
Picture arrangement (11)	12	3	4	5
Block design (10)	11	9	0	2
Object assembly (4)	4	3	1	0
Mazes (8)	9	8	0	1
Coding	The coding test is unchanged.			

*Number of items in current WISC test is in parentheses following the test name.

Of the 183 items in the 1949 WISC, 117 (64 percent) are included in the WISC-R and an additional 15 items (8 percent) are included with modifications. Thus, 72 percent of the current items have been retained in the WISC-R, either intact or with some modification. In addition, the Coding test (Coding A for children below 8; Coding B for ages 8 and above) has survived intact.

D. MISCELLANEOUS INFORMATION

1. Comments about the WISC were collected from psychologists throughout the country. Particular attention was paid to items that were criticized as being unfair to minority groups.
2. The Picture Completion and Picture Arrangement items include pictures of whites and blacks of both sexes.
3. The same five Verbal and five Performance tests that were mandatory for the 1949 WISC are mandatory for WISC-R.
4. Concerning administration, scoring, and test content:
   a. The Mazes scoring rules have been simplified and are now essentially the same as WPPSI rules.

b. For Comprehension items in which the child is required to give 2 answers to receive full credit, the examiner is now permitted to ask the child to "give another reason why. . ."

c. In the Similarities test, the analogies items have all been deleted (e.g., Lemons are sour but sugar is ____). All items are now in the format of, "In what way are a cat and a mouse alike?"

d. In the Picture Arrangement test, the preliminary items requiring the child to put pictures together to form an object (e.g., dog) or a scene (mother with train set) have been deleted. All items now require the child to arrange the pictures to make a story.

E. AVAILABILITY

Available early 1974.

*Glossary**

The following glossary has been prepared to assist the reader in understanding the psychological nomenclature used in this book. Only terms that have not been defined within each chapter have been included. Therefore, terms have been presented under appropriate chapter headings.

CHAPTER 1

Bio-feedback: A conditioning process in which the conscious control of normally unconscious or subliminal physiological functions and accompanying psychological states may be gained through the utilization of bio-electronic feedback instrumentation.

Graphology: The study of handwriting as a tool in the identification of personality characteristics.

Hedonistic: Characteristic of individuals oriented toward excessive need gratification and personal pleasure.

Hypnosis: A trance-like state characterized by a narrowing of attention and a heightening of suggestability.

Hysteria: A term including a variety of neurotic disorders such as hysterical conversion reactions characterized by neurotically produced physical symptoms of organic diseases.

Phrenology: Study of the relative shape and contours of the skull based on the hypothesis that certain shapes, contours, and cranial projections are indicative of personality characteristics.

"Test-wise": Knowledge of appropriate test responses prior to taking a test.

*Prepared by E. Ronald Franzen, University of Northern Colorado.

CHAPTER 2

Percentile rank: Also called centile, a statistical measure derived from an ordered list of scores indicating in percent the number of scores above or below which any score is located.

Prodromal signs: The characteristic signs or patterns that may occur in advance of the onset of a disease.

Psychograph: A pattern of responses through psychological testing that provides basic behavioral and character indices.

Temporal error: Environmental or behavioral changes that cannot be predicted or accounted for statistically.

CHAPTER 3

Basal age: The relative intellectual or difficulty level of intelligence testing at which an individual is capable of responding appropriately to all test items.

Correlation: A statistical treatment of paired sets of data, whereby the degree of relationship between the two sets may be determined.

Mean: Sometimes called "arithmetic mean" or "average," found by dividing the sum of any set of scores by the number of scores.

Mental age: A relative measure of the mental development of a person, determined by intelligence testing.

Raw score: The score obtained on a test before any statistical analysis is begun, usually the number right or the number wrong.

Reliability: A measure of the extent to which a test may be relied upon to produce the same consistent results.

Standard deviation: A statistical measure of the variability of a set of scores.

Standardized: A standardized test is one that has been administered to a representative sample of a population in an attempt to gather normative data and develop uniform administration and scoring procedures.

Validity: A term used to describe the extent that a test measures what it is intended to measure.

CHAPTER 4

Blind analysis: This method is more correctly referred to as the "laboratory method of test evaluation." The evaluator uses only the test performance results and case history to make an assessment of the client. It is considered appropriate if other specialists have evaluated the client by personal interview.

Gerontological: Refers to the science dealing with the study of persons who are in the older age groups.

Psychometrist: A technician trained to administer and score tests but not qualified to evaluate them. Also, sometimes used to describe a psychologist who specializes in the construction, scoring, and evaluation of tests.

Siblings: Sisters or brothers from the same parents.

Sociometric techniques: Therapeutic as well as diagnostic techniques that assess and facilitate the effectiveness of an individual's interactions in group and interpersonal relationships.

Subjective: Conclusions that are subjective are based on a person's experience, judgment, reasoning, and intuition rather than on statistical data. Subjective judgments represent the art rather than the science of therapy and evaluation. (Opposite of objective.)

Sublimation: Defense mechanism that redirects socially unacceptable behaviors.

CHAPTER 5

Aversive stimuli: Any disagreeable stimuli in operant conditioning, such as electric shocks, that negatively reinforce behavior.

Character disorders. Also called behavior disorders and sociopathic personality. Refers to individuals who lack a sense of social responsibility and are motivated only by personal gain.

Covert: An activity or process that is not directly observable.

Manic-depressive: Psychotic reactions characterized by periods of extreme excitement (manic) alternating with periods of deep depression.

Norms: Refers to statistically determined standards gathered from a representative group of people that permit the comparison of individual scores with these standards.

Operant conditioning: A method designed to obtain desired behavior changes by conditioning the learner to react in a specified manner to environmental stimuli.

Sadomasochistic: From "sadism"—meaning pleasure derived from inflicting pain—combined with "masochism"—which means pleasure in experiencing pain. This behavior usually has actual or symbolic sexual implication.

Significant others: Also called "important others." Persons such as fathers, mothers, and important leaders in an individual's environment that exert a powerful influence on the self-concept and behavior of the individual.

T scores: A type of standard score that is obtained by multiplying a Z score (a measure of the number and direction of standard deviation units) by 10 or 100 and adding 50 or 500 to the result. Individual T scores may be compared to standardized scores.

CHAPTER 6

Akinesia: (Also called akinesis.) The loss or impairment of generalized motor functions.

Amnesia: An acute loss of memory due to physical or emotional trauma. Similar to aphasia and fugue states in that there is an impairment of memory and understanding. However, aphasia results from brain damage, fugue states are dissociative reactions and amnesia is the result of definable stress.

Anaesthesia: The loss or impairment of tactile sensitivity and, sometimes, sensitivity to pain.

Anosmia: The loss or impairment of the sense of smell.

Ataxia: The loss or impairment of muscular coordination.

Dyskinesia: The loss or impairment of an individual's ability to perceive the relative location of his body parts.

Extinction: The process of withholding all reinforcement in an attempt to eliminate unwanted behaviors.

Fugue: Dissociative reaction wherein individuals develop a loss of memory in regard to their past lives, but otherwise appear to be normal.

Involutional melancholia: A psychosis associated with women (usually after menopause) characterized by depression, apprehension, and agitation stemming from feelings of loss of self-worth and status. Male equivalency is sometimes called "climacteric."

Paraesthesia: (Also called paresthesia.) Abnormal sensations such as tingling, creeping, or pricking, often associated with irritation or injury of a sensory nerve.

Somnambulism: Sleepwalking in which the patient may do many seemingly normal tasks while actually being asleep.

CHAPTER 7

Acting out: Antisocial behaviors in which normally repressed impulses and behaviors are expressed openly.

Autism: Behavior characterized by withdrawal patterns and self-centered thought processes that are understood only by the person himself. Complete self-immersion, usually associated with psychosis.

Catatonic: Type of schizophrenic reaction. Two types: (1) extreme stupor with muscular rigidity; (2) extreme and dangerous hyperactivity referred to as catatonic excitement. Sometimes there is an alternation of these two states.

Cyclothymic personality: Individuals who characteristically and frequently experience shifts in moods, from elation to depression, without apparent reason.

Dé jà vu: An abnormal feeling that what is being experienced now has somehow or somewhere been experienced before.

Delusions: Pathological thought processes, ideas, or beliefs not involving perceptual disturbances as in hallucinations. Associated with psychosis.

Folie à deux: A close interpersonal relationship usually involving two people who, because of their proximity, develop the same psychotic symptomatology.

Hallucinations: Pathological sensory perceptions (which may involve any of the senses) without a real external stimulus, such as seeing, hearing, feeling, smelling, or tasting things that are not really there. Associated with psychosis, drugs, or severe physical illness.

Hebephrenic: Type of schizophrenic reaction, characterized by inappropriate affect, somatic delusions, hallucinations, and child-like behavior. Often repetitive and senseless verbalization accompanied by a grin or laughter.

Hypomania: Mild excitement in certain types of neuroses. Hypo means *less than*; hyper means *more than.*

Ideas of reference: A pathological delusional thought process usually found in the paranoid type of schizophrenia, wherein individuals without any valid basis think that others are referring to them on the radio, television, in the newspaper, or in a conversation.

Incipient psychosis: Psychotic reactions that are in the process of developing. Symptoms may not yet be severe.

Malingering: The intentional falsification of test results and/or feigning of abnormal symptoms.

Omniscience: Having an infinite knowledge of all things.

Paranoid: Extreme and persistent suspiciousness often associated with abnormal mental states. There may be varying types. Examples: paranoid personality; paranoid schizophrenia, paranoia.

Psychasthenia: A neurotic condition consisting of an incapacity to resolve doubts or uncertainties, or to resist fears and obsessions that one knows are irrational.

Reactive Psychosis: Psychosis whose onset was precipitated by environmental stress.

Schizophrenic: The most common form of psychotic reactions, involving many and sometimes special symptoms. There are paranoid, simple, hebephrenic, affective, and catatonic types.

Simple schizophrenia: Psychotic syndrome, characterized by shallow affect and a gradual withdrawal from all other people. Patient usually acts in a feeble-minded manner and is sometimes mistakenly classified as mental defective.

CHAPTER 8

Agnosia: Loss or impairment of perceptual functions due to brain damage involving loss of ability to recognize familiar stimuli.

Aphasia: Disorders due to brain damage in which individuals may not be able to speak, read, write, or otherwise recognize and coordinate verbal behavior.

Apraxia: Cerebral condition characterized by an inability in the performance of psychomotor tasks.

Broca's area: Frontal area in the brain that controls symbolic functioning associated with speech.

Cognitive: Pertaining to higher thought processes, such as reasoning, thinking, and memory.

Congenital: Pertaining to conditions that are present at or as a result of birth.

EEG: Electroencephalogram, sometimes called "brain-wave test." A diagnostic procedure using electronic instrumentation in order to detect the presence of brain pathology.

Functional condition: Abnormal psychological reactions not caused by organic pathology.

Neurological signs: Indicators (often of the reflex type) of nervous system dysfunction and the presence of organic disease.

Perseverate: Pertaining to verbal or motor behavior that is repetitive and resistant to change. Usually associated with severe pathology.

Premorbid personality: The condition of the personality before the onset of illness.

Psychological homeostasis: Psychologic, cognitive, and emotional balance believed to be associated with good adjustment.

Psycho-motor-spatial: Perceptual characteristic involving eye-hand coordination and space perception.

Visual-psycho-motor performance: Measurable abilities involving the coordination of visual and muscular activity.

CHAPTER 9

Assertion training: Behavioral modification technique designed to increase assertiveness by reinforcing assertive behavior through relaxation in first imaginary and, finally, in real situations. Also called expressive training.

Aversive training: The conditioning or negative reinforcement of any response through the utilization of unpleasant stimuli, such as electric shock.

Counter conditioning: A technique in behavior modification that inhibits anxiety by repeatedly presenting a neutral or positively reinforcing stimulus in close proximity to a stimulus that previously produced anxiety.

Discrimination training: A subject learns to discriminate between similar stimuli when appropriate responses are reinforced and inappropriate responses are extinguished.

Ego: The part of the psyche in psychoanalytic theory that is essentially the conscious, observable self and mediates between the Id (Instinctual drives) and the Super-Ego (ideas of right and wrong, or conscience).

Free association: Technique used in psychoanalytic therapy to bring unconscious motives to the conscious level by expressing feelings in a free and uninhibited manner.

Galvanic skin response: Changes in the electrical resistance of the skin due to increases or decreases of exocrine (sweat gland) secretions, which accompany changing affective states.

Reciprocal inhibition: Concept found within behavior modification theory in which anxiety produced responses may be extinguished by the conditioning of antagonistic responses.

Successive approximations: In operant conditioning, the gradual shaping of behavior through the reinforcement of successively more difficult approximations toward a final desired behavior.

Systematic desensitization: A technique used by those employing learning theory therapies in which clients are first trained in deep muscle relaxation and then are taught to maintain relaxation while imagining a series of increasingly more anxiety producing situations.

Visceral: Pertains to the internal organs.

CHAPTER 10

Affective: Pertaining to the feelings and/or moods that accompany behavior.

Altruistic: Characteristic of individuals demonstrating a high regard for the rights and needs of others and motivated to act unselfishly.

Analytic therapy: Or psychoanalytic therapy, developed by Freud, wherein intense therapy sessions involving unconscious motives and their influences on conscious behaviors are explored.

Eclectic: The borrowing from many schools of thought in an attempt to develop the best set of philosophies and techniques.

Empathy: The ability of an individual to understand another person's feelings and affective states with depth and clarity derived from a successful identification with this person.

Hominology: The *Encyclopedia Britannica Yearbook* (1969) defines it: a generalized study of man without regard to traditional academic disciplines. The term is derived from *hominidae*. The approach offers new guidelines for self-understanding and for studying human behavior.

Hypothesis: A statement or proposition offered in advance of empirical evidence that attempts to explain certain phenomena under investigation.

Phenomenologists: Persons advocating the study and explanation of human behavioral phenomena without exclusive reliance on empirical science. Intuition and metaphysics may also be considered as important.

Psychotherapy: An all-inclusive term for the treatment of behavioral and adjustment disorders using psychological techniques, regardless of specific orientations.

Reinforcement: Any event that acts as an incentive in response to behavior or that increases the likelihood that the behavior will occur again.

Self-actualization: A human drive advocated by many psychotherapeutic approaches involving the discovery and full development of individual potential.

Transference: In psychoanalytic therapy, the client's transferring of feelings from earlier interpersonal relationships to the analyst.

CHAPTER 11

Criteria: Standards of measurements against which experimental evidence may be compared.

Empirical: The basis of objective judgment derived from experimental data or statistical evidence. Opposite of subjective. The scientific rather than the "art" emphasis in therapy and evaluation.

Factor analysis: Statistical procedure used in the identification and analysis of interrelated factors in test items or other types of evaluation procedures.

CHAPTER 12

Deviant behavior: Any behavior that deviates from an established norm.

Enzyme systems: Catalyst-substrate reaction that promotes metabolic processes.

Etiology: The study of the causes of disorders.

Lesion: Localized damage to an organ or body part usually as a result of injury or disease.

Psyche: Refers to the mind.

Psychopharmacology: The science that studies the effects of drugs on behavior.

Soma: Refers to the body.

CHAPTER 13

Acting out: Antisocial behaviors in which normally repressed impulses and behaviors are expressed openly.

Atonement: Counteracting behaviors about which a person feels guilty.

Compensation: An over-emphasis on personal strengths, or over-gratification in some areas as a defense against weaknesses and failures.

Displacement: The expression of aggressive behaviors upon targets less threatening than those that initiated a frustration. (Taking it out on something or someone else.)

Dysphoria: A disturbance characterized by anxiety, restlessness, dissatisfaction and general feeling of unhappiness.

Ego-defenses: Also called defense mechanisms. Unconscious processes manifested in many ways that guard against anxiety and tend to increase feelings of self-worth by distorting reality. The following may be considered representative of the various types:

Emotional insulation: (Also called "isolation.") Guarding against real or potentially anxiety-producing situations by emotionally withdrawing. (Such as "Not getting one's hope up too high.")

Escapism: Escaping anxiety-arousing stimuli by alternative behaviors such as perpetual optimism, preoccupations, "illness."

Fantasy: Also daydreaming. Bolstering self-worth by imaginary accomplishments or status.

Free-floating anxiety: Anxiety that cannot be referred to any specific cause or stress-producing situation.

Hysterical personality: Characteristic of individuals suffering from neurotic symptoms simulating organic illness without real organic pathology. Also, associated with many kinds of behavioral problems, often manifested by repression.

Identification: An attempt to increase feelings of self-worth by associating oneself with important figures or institutions.

Insomnia: A restlessness in or an inability to sleep, generally a function of nervousness and/or neurotic anxiety.

Intellectualization: An ego defense mechanism that shields an individual from anxiety-producing thoughts and situations by a rational intellectual, and isolated approach to daily and personal problems. Used as a defense against achieving insights.

Introjection: Incorporation of the values of another person into one's own ego structure.

Rationalization: Making "rational" and hence justifiable excuses for one's behavior.

Reaction formation: Defense mechanism typically used by individuals in an attempt to disguise socially unacceptable impulses by adopting mannerisms that are opposite.

Regression: Retreating psychologically to an earlier developmental level.

Repression: The conscious and/or unconscious exclusion of anxiety-arousing stimuli from the thought processes. (Putting it out of one's mind.)

Self-concept: An individual's perceptions of himself and his self-evaluation of his interaction with the social and physical environment.

Sublimation: Defense mechanism, that redirects socially unacceptable impulses into new and more socially acceptable behaviors.

Substitution: Using a different person, emotion, or object as a target for expressing hostility than the source of the frustration when the source is unavailable or considered to be too dangerous.

Sympathism: Actively seeking sympathy by relating one's troubles to another person in an attempt to increase feelings of being wanted or pitied.

APPENDIX A

Alpha brainwave rhythm: The electro-chemical activity of the brain between 8 and 13 cycles per second. Commonly associated with calm, relaxed states when eyes are closed.

Apperceptions: Refers to cognitive processes involved in the evaluation and appreciation of experiences.

Colitis: A bowel disorder that may have psychological causes characterized by abdominal cramps, and alternating periods of diarrhea and constipation.

Ego psychology: Refers to psychological schools of thought influenced heavily by classical psychoanalysis, but with less emphasis on the unconscious.

EMG feedback: Electromyographic feedback. A bio-feedback technique used in the reduction of muscular and psychological tension and migraine headaches. The process involves giving the subject an awareness of his reactions using perceptive feedback of electromuscular activity in the auditory or visual sensory modalities.

Facial tics: The sometimes neurotically caused twitching or jerking of one or more muscles.

Paleontology: The science of earlier forms of life through the study of fossils.

Phylogenetic: Refers to evolutionary development of a species.

Index

TITLES IN THE PERGAMON GENERAL PSYCHOLOGY SERIES

Vol. 1. J. WOLPE—*The Practice of Behavior Therapy, 2nd Edition*
Vol. 2. T. MAGOON *et al.*—*Mental Health Counselors at Work*
Vol. 3. J. MCDANIEL—*Physical Disability and Human Behavior, 2nd Edition*
Vol. 4. M. L. KAPLAN *et al.*—*The Structural Approach in Psychological Testing*
Vol. 5. H. M. LAFAUCI & P. E. RICHTER—*Team Teaching at the College Level*
Vol. 6. H. B. PEPINSKY *et al.*—*People and Information*
Vol. 7. A. W. SIEGMAN & B. POPE—*Studies in Dyadic Communication*
Vol. 8. R. E. JOHNSON—*Existential Man: The Challenge of Psychotherapy*
Vol. 9. C. W. TAYLOR—*Climate for Creativity*
Vol. 10. H. C. RICKARD *et al.*—*Behavioral Intervention in Human Problems*
Vol. 11. P. EKMAN, W. V. FRIESEN & P. ELLSWORTH—*Emotion in the Human Face: Guidelines for Research and an Integration of Findings*
Vol. 12. B. MAUSNER & E. S. PLATT—*Smoking: A Behavioral Analysis*
Vol. 14. A. GOLDSTEIN—*Psychotherapeutic Attraction*
Vol. 15. F. HALPERN—*Survival: Black/White*
Vol. 16. K. SALZINGER & R. S. FELDMAN—*Studies in Verbal Behavior: An Empirical Approach*
Vol. 17. H. E. ADAMS & W. K. BOARDMAN—*Advances in Experimental Clinical Psychology*
Vol. 18. R. C. ZILLER—*The Social Self*
Vol. 19. R. P. LIBERMAN—*A Guide to Behavioral Analysis & Therapy*
Vol. 22. H. B. PEPINSKY & M. J. PATTON—*The Psychological Experiment: A Practical Accomplishment*
Vol. 23. T. R. YOUNG—*New Sources of Self*
Vol. 24. L. S. WATSON, JR.—*Child Behavior Modification: A Manual for Teachers, Nurses, and Parents*
Vol. 25. H. L. NEWBOLD—*The Psychiatric Programming of People: Neo-Behavioral Orthomolecular Psychiatry*
Vol. 26. E. L. ROSSI—*Dreams and the Growth of Personality: Expanding Awareness in Psychotherapy*
Vol. 27. K. D. O'LEARY & S. G. O'LEARY—*Classroom Management: The Successful Use of Behavior Modification*
Vol. 28. K. A. FELDMAN—*College and Student: Selected Readings in the Social Psychology of Higher Education*
Vol. 29. B. A. ASHEM & E. G. POSER—*Adaptive Learning: Behavior Modification with Children*
Vol. 30. H. D. BURCK *et al.*—*Counseling and Accountability: Methods and Critique*
Vol. 31. N. FREDERIKSEN *et al.*—*Prediction of Organizational Behavior*
Vol. 32. R. B. CATTELL—*A New Morality from Science: Beyondism*
Vol. 33. M. L. WEINER—*Personality: The Human Potential*
Vol. 34. R. M. LIEBERT *et al.*—*The Early Window: Effects of Television on Children and Youth*
Vol. 35. R. COHEN *et al.*—*Psych City: A Simulated Community*
Vol. 36. A. M. GRAZIANO—*Child Without Tomorrow*
Vol. 37. R. J. MORRIS—*Perspectives in Abnormal Behavior*
Vol. 38. W. R. BALLER—*Bed Wetting: Origins and Treatment*

TITLES IN THE PERGAMON GENERAL PSYCHOLOGY SERIES

Vol. 1. J. WOLPE—*The Practice of Behavior Therapy, 2nd Edition*
Vol. 2. T. MAGOON *et al.*—*Mental Health Counselors at Work*
Vol. 3. J. MCDANIEL—*Physical Disability and Human Behavior, 2nd Edition*
Vol. 4. M. L. KAPLAN *et al.*—*The Structural Approach in Psychological Testing*
Vol. 5. H. M. LAFAUCI & P. E. RICHTER—*Team Teaching at the College Level*
Vol. 6. H. B. PEPINSKY *et al.*—*People and Information*
Vol. 7. A. W. SIEGMAN & B. POPE—*Studies in Dyadic Communication*
Vol. 8. R. E. JOHNSON—*Existential Man: The Challenge of Psychotherapy*
Vol. 9. C. W. TAYLOR—*Climate for Creativity*
Vol. 10. H. C. RICKARD *et al.*—*Behavioral Intervention in Human Problems*
Vol. 11. P. EKMAN, W. V. FRIESEN & P. ELLSWORTH—*Emotion in the Human Face: Guidelines for Research and an Integration of Findings*
Vol. 12. B. MAUSNER & E. S. PLATT—*Smoking: A Behavioral Analysis*
Vol. 14. A. GOLDSTEIN—*Psychotherapeutic Attraction*
Vol. 15. F. HALPERN—*Survival: Black/White*
Vol. 16. K. SALZINGER & R. S. FELDMAN—*Studies in Verbal Behavior: An Empirical Approach*
Vol. 17. H. E. ADAMS & W. K. BOARDMAN—*Advances in Experimental Clinical Psychology*
Vol. 18. R. C. ZILLER—*The Social Self*
Vol. 19. R. P. LIBERMAN—*A Guide to Behavioral Analysis & Therapy*
Vol. 22. H. B. PEPINSKY & M. J. PATTON—*The Psychological Experiment: A Practical Accomplishment*
Vol. 23. T. R. YOUNG—*New Sources of Self*
Vol. 24. L. S. WATSON, JR.—*Child Behavior Modification: A Manual for Teachers, Nurses, and Parents*
Vol. 25. H. L. NEWBOLD—*The Psychiatric Programming of People: Neo-Behavioral Orthomolecular Psychiatry*
Vol. 26. E. L. ROSSI—*Dreams and the Growth of Personality: Expanding Awareness in Psychotherapy*
Vol. 27. K. D. O'LEARY & S. G. O'LEARY—*Classroom Management: The Successful Use of Behavior Modification*
Vol. 28. K. A. FELDMAN—*College and Student: Selected Readings in the Social Psychology of Higher Education*
Vol. 29. B. A. ASHEM & E. G. POSER—*Adaptive Learning: Behavior Modification with Children*
Vol. 30. H. D. BURCK *et al.*—*Counseling and Accountability: Methods and Critique*
Vol. 31. N. FREDERIKSEN *et al.*—*Prediction of Organizational Behavior*
Vol. 32. R. B. CATTELL—*A New Morality from Science: Beyondism*
Vol. 33. M. L. WEINER—*Personality: The Human Potential*
Vol. 34. R. M. LIEBERT *et al.*—*The Early Window: Effects of Television on Children and Youth*
Vol. 35. R. COHEN *et al.*—*Psych City: A Simulated Community*
Vol. 36. A. M. GRAZIANO—*Child Without Tomorrow*
Vol. 37. R. J. MORRIS—*Perspectives in Abnormal Behavior*
Vol. 38. W. R. BALLER—*Bed Wetting: Origins and Treatment*